Quality Software Management:

Volume 1
Systems Thinking

Quality Software Management:

Volume 1
Systems Thinking

by Gerald M. Weinberg

Dorset House Publishing
353 West 12th Street
New York, New York 10014

Library of Congress Cataloging in Publication Data

Weinberg, Gerald M.
    Quality software management / by Gerald M. Weinberg.
        p. cm.
    Contents: v. 1. Systems thinking.
    Includes bibliographical references and index.
    ISBN 0-932633-22-6 (v. 1) :
    1. Computer software – Development – Management. 2. Computer
software–Quality control. I. Title.
QA76.76.D47W45 1991
005.1'068–dc20   91-18061
                                                  CIP

CREDITS

Thanks to Infobooks for excerpts in Chapters 2 and 3: Geoffrey James, *The Tao of Programming.* Copyright © 1987; and *The Zen of Programming.* Copyright © 1988. Reprinted with permission of Infobooks, Santa Monica, Calif.

Thanks to McGraw-Hill for material in Chapter 2: from Philip B. Crosby, *Quality Is Free,* pp. 15, 16, 34, and 43. Copyright © 1979. Reprinted with permission of McGraw-Hill, New York, N.Y.

Thanks to Addison-Wesley for material in Chapters 1, 2, 3, 5, and 8: from T. Gilb, *Principles of Software Engineering Management,* p. 88. Copyright © 1988 Tom Gilb and Susannah Finzi, used by permission of Addison-Wesley Publishing Co.; Frederick P. Brooks, Jr., *The Mythical Man-Month,* p. 14. Copyright © 1975; Watts S. Humphrey, *Managing the Software Process,* p. 257. Copyright © 1989. Reprinted with permission of Addison-Wesley, Reading, Mass.

Thanks to Prentice-Hall for the diagram in Chapter 7: Robert B. Grady and Deborah L. Caswell, *Software Metrics: Establishing a Company-Wide Program,* Copyright © 1987, p. 9. Reprinted with permission of Prentice-Hall, Englewood Cliffs, N.J.

Cover Design: Dennis Stillwell

Distributed in the United Kingdom, Ireland, Europe, and Africa by John Wiley & Sons Ltd., Chichester, Sussex, England.

Distributed in the English language in Singapore, the Philippines, and southeast Asia by Toppan Co., Ltd., Singapore; and in the English language in Japan by Toppan Co., Ltd., Tokyo, Japan.

Printed in the United States of America

Library of Congress Catalog Number 91-18061
ISBN: 0-932633-22-6   12 11 10 9 8 7 6 5 4

To Les Belady, Fred Brooks, Tom DeMarco,
Tom Gilb, Ken Iverson, Jean-Dominique Warnier,
and the thousands of others
who taught me about software engineering

Contents

Acknowledgments

I'd like to acknowledge the contributions of the following people to the improvement of this book:

Bill Curtis
Tom DeMarco
Ed Ely
Peter Morse
Eileen Cline Strider
Wayne Strider
Linda Swirczek
Dani Weinberg
Janice Wormington

In this book, I'll disguise all people and clients from whom I've obtained confidential information.

Preface

Poor management can increase software costs more rapidly than any other factor.
—Barry W. Boehm[1]

This book is a kind of anniversary present, commemorating my forty-year love affair with computers. Early in 1950, I read a *Time* magazine cover story[2] about computers, or "Thinking Machines." The cover itself was by *Time's* favorite cover artist, Artzybashef. It depicted an anthropomorphic electronic box. One eye looked at a paper tape held in the right hand while the left hand typed some output on a teletype. The box was topped with a Navy cap with lots of "scrambled eggs," and the caption read, "Mark III. Can man build a superman?"

A bit sensational, yes, but it made a profound impression on a sixteen-year-old about to graduate from high school. I may not recall many details of the article, but I clearly recall I decided on the spot that computers would be my life.

One of the facts that impressed me in the article was how big a factor IBM was in the business of building computing machines. In 1956, when I was unable to find a university that taught about computers, I went to work for IBM.

For thirteen years, I took IBM seriously, especially its THINK motto. IBM was right. Thinking was essential. But after a while, I noticed that IBM and its customers often honored thinking, but didn't practice it—especially in the software side of the business, which always seemed to take last place in the hearts of IBM's executives.

As far as I could tell, little THINK signs on each desk never helped us get software out the door. Yet IBM managers never seemed to do much else to help the process. Later, after I left IBM for an independent consulting career, I learned that IBM's managers were no different from the rest.

All over the world, software managers gave lip service to thinking, but didn't do much about it. For one thing, they never understood the reasons that people didn't think when they ought to. Of course, I didn't understand either.

Looking back, I realize why the *Time* article had so impressed me. In school, everyone told me how smart I was. True, I did outstanding work on all sorts of tests, but I never seemed to be able to think effectively about my own life. I was a miserable kid, and I thought that thinking machines might help me solve my problems.

Well, thinking machines didn't solve my problems; they made them worse. When I tried to build software, the computer unfailingly accentuated all my mistakes. When I didn't think right about a program, the program bombed. The computer, I learned, was a *mirror* of my intelligence, and I wasn't too impressed by my reflection.

Later, when I wrote larger programs in concert with other people, I learned that the computer was not just a mirror, but a *magnifying* mirror. Any time we didn't think straight about our software project, we made a colossal monster. I began to learn that if we were ever to make good use of thinking machines, we would have to start by improving our own thinking.

I began to study thinking as a subject in itself, particularly thinking as applied to software problems. Through the generosity of IBM, I went back to school and wrote a thesis on using computers as tools to mirror our minds. I traveled all over the world, visiting software organizations and studying how they think about software. I shared ideas with people, and tried to put those ideas into practice on software projects. I observed what worked and what didn't, and I revised my ideas. I published some of them and then used feedback from hundreds of readers to refine them. This book summarizes what I have learned up to now about managing software projects effectively.

Why is managing software projects so important? One of the predictions in that ancient *Time* article was the following:

> Around each working computer hover young mathematicians with dreamy eyes. On desks flecked with frothy figures, they translate real-life problems into figure-language. It usually takes them much longer to prepare a problem than it takes the machine to solve it.
>
> These human question-askers are sure to lag farther and farther behind the question-answering machines.[3]

Not all of the predictions in the article came true (up until now), but this one certainly did. Since that day when I became one of those dreamy-eyed young "question-answerers" (the word "programmer" hadn't yet been coined), I have learned that there are three fundamental abilities you need if you're not to lag farther and farther behind the question-answering machines:

1. the ability to observe what's happening and to understand the significance of your observations

2. the ability to act congruently in difficult interpersonal situations, even

though you may be confused, or angry, or so afraid you want to run away and hide

3.   the ability to understand complex situations (This ability allows you to plan a project and then observe and act so as to keep the project going according to plan, or modify the plan.)

All three abilities are essential for quality software management, but I don't want to write a large, imposing book. Therefore, like any good software manager, I've decomposed the project into three smaller projects, each one addressing one of these fundamental abilities. For reasons that will become clearer in the book, I am starting with the third ability: *the ability to understand complex situations.*

In other words, this is a *think* book. Its motto is the same as IBM's, because it's my way of paying back IBM and others for the wonderful things I've received from forty years in the software business. I can imagine no finer gift than helping people, as others have helped me, to think more effectively about a subject that is so important to them personally, as well as to the world.

Part I
Patterns of Quality

In the midst of the struggle over software quality, it sometimes seems that producing and maintaining software is a random series of events. In a situation of chaotic overload, that's a comforting idea. If the events are truly random, then you need not waste time thinking about what you should do. Just keep struggling as hard and as long as you can, so nobody can blame you for failure.

But if you sit back and reflect for a moment, you'll notice that producing and maintaining software is *not* a random series of events. There are patterns, and these patterns offer an opportunity to take control of our products, our organizations, and our lives.

In case your own life in the software industry has been too frantic for you to notice, I'll use the first few chapters to explore the concept of cultural patterns, introduce the major cultural patterns in software, and examine what's necessary to move from one pattern to another.

1
What Is Quality?
Why Is It Important?

*You may fool all the people some of the time;
you can even fool some of the people all the
time, but you can't fool all of the people
all the time.*
—Abraham Lincoln

People in the software business put great stress on removing ambiguity, and so do writers. But sometimes writers are intentionally ambiguous, as in the title of this book. "Quality software management" means both "the management of quality software" and "quality management in the software business," because I believe that the two are inseparable. Both meanings turn on the word "quality," so if we are to keep the ambiguity within reasonable bounds, we first need to address the meaning of that often misunderstood term.

1.1 A Tale of Software Quality

My sister's daughter, Terra, is the only one in the family who has followed Uncle Jerry in the writer's trade. She writes fascinating books on the history of medicine, and I follow each one's progress as if it were my own. For that reason,

3

I was terribly distressed when her first book, *Disease in the Popular American Press*,[1] came out with a number of gross typographical errors in which whole segments of text disappeared (see Figure 1-1). I was even more distressed to discover that those errors were caused by an error in the word processing software she used—CozyWrite, published by one of my clients, the MiniCozy Software Company.

   The next day, too, the *Times* printed a letter from "Medicus," objecting to the misleading implication in the microbe story that diphtheria could ever be inoculated against; the writer flatly asserted that there would never be a vaccine for this disease because, unlike smallpox, diphtheria re-
   Because *Times* articles never included proof—never told *how* people knew what they claimed—the uninformed reader had no way to distinguish one claim from another.

Figure 1–1.   Part of a sample page from Terra Ziporyn's book showing how the CozyWrite word processor lost text after "re-" in Terra's book.

Terra asked me to discuss the matter with MiniCozy on my next visit. I located the project manager for CozyWrite, and he acknowledged the existence of the error.
   "It's a rare bug," he said.
   "I wouldn't say so," I countered. "I found over twenty-five instances in her book."
   "But it would only happen in a book-sized project. Out of more than a hundred thousand customers, we probably didn't have ten who undertook a project of that size as a single file."
   "But my niece noticed. It was her first book, and she was devastated."
   "Naturally I'm sorry for her, but it wouldn't have made any sense for us to try to fix the bug for ten customers."
   "Why not? You advertise that CozyWrite handles book-sized projects."
   "We tried to do that, but the features didn't work. Eventually we'll probably fix them, but for now, chances are we would introduce a worse bug—one that would affect hundreds or thousands of customers. I believe we did the right thing."
   As I listened to this project manager, I found myself caught in an emotional trap. As software consultant to MiniCozy, I had to agree, but as uncle to an author, I was violently opposed to his line of reasoning. If someone at that moment had asked me, Is CozyWrite a quality product? I would have been tongue-tied.
   How would you have answered?

1.2   The Relativity of Quality

The reason for my dilemma lies in the *relativity of quality*. As the MiniCozy story crisply illustrates, what is adequate quality to one person may be inadequate quality to another.

1.2.1   Finding the relativity

If you examine various definitions of quality, you will always find this relativity. You may have to examine them with care, though, for the relativity is often hidden or, at best, implicit. Take, for example, Crosby's definition:

Quality is "conformance to requirements."[2]

Unless your requirements come directly from heaven (as some developers seem to think), a more precise statement would be

Quality is conforming to some person's requirements.

For each person, the same product will generally have different "quality," as in the case of my niece's word processor. My MiniCozy dilemma is resolved once I recognize that to Terra, the people involved were her readers; and to MiniCozy's project manager, the people involved were the majority of his customers.

1.2.2   Who was that masked man?

In short, quality does not exist in a nonhuman vacuum.

Every statement about quality is a statement about some person(s).

That statement may be explicit or implicit. Most often, the "who" is implicit, and statements about quality sound like something Moses brought down from Mount Sinai on a stone tablet. That's why so many discussions of software quality are unproductive: It's my stone tablet versus your Golden Calf.

When we encompass the relativity of quality, we have a tool to make those discussions more fruitful. Each time somebody asserts a definition of software quality, we simply ask

Who is the person behind that statement about quality?

Using this heuristic, let's consider a few familiar but often conflicting ideas about what constitutes software quality.

Zero defects is high quality
- a.   to users whose work is disturbed by those defects
- b.   to managers who are criticized for those defects

Having lots of features is high quality
- a.   to users whose work can profit from those features—if they know about them
- b.   to marketers who believe that features sell products

Elegant coding is high quality
- a.   to developers who place a high value on the opinions of their peers
- b.   to professors of computer science who enjoy elegance

High performance is high quality
- a.   to users whose work taxes the capacity of their machines
- b.   to salespeople who have to submit their products to benchmarks

Low development cost is high quality
- a.   to customers who wish to buy thousands of copies of the software
- b.   to project managers who are on tight budgets

Rapid development is high quality
- a.   to users whose work is waiting for the software
- b.   to marketers who want to colonize a market before the competitors can get in

User friendliness is high quality
- a.   to users who spend eight hours a day in front of a screen using the software
- b.   to users who can't remember interface details from one use to the next

1.2.3   The political dilemma

Recognizing the relativity of quality often resolves the *semantic* dilemma. At the start of a book on quality, this is a monumental contribution, but it still does not resolve the *political* dilemma:

More quality for one person may mean less quality for another.

For instance, if our goal were "total quality," we'd have to do a summation over *all* relevant people. Thus, this total quality effort would have to *start* with a comprehensive requirements process that identifies and involves all relevant people.[3] Then, for each design, for each software engineering approach, we would have to assign a quality measure for each person. Summing these measures would then yield the total quality for each different approach.

In practice, of course, no software development project ever uses such an elaborate process. Instead, most people are eliminated by a prior process that decides

Whose opinion of quality is to count when making decisions?

For instance, the project manager at MiniCozy decided, without hearing arguments from Terra, that her opinion carried minuscule weight in his software engineering decision. From this case, we see that software engineering is *not* a democratic business. Nor, unfortunately, is it a *rational* business, for these decisions about who counts are generally made on an emotional basis.

1.3 Quality Is Value to Some Person

The political/emotional dimension of quality is made evident by a somewhat different definition of quality. The idea of requirements is a bit too innocent to be useful in this early stage, because it says nothing about *whose* requirements count the most. A more workable definition would be this:

Quality is value to some person.

By "value," I mean, What are people willing to pay (or do) to have their requirements met? Suppose, for instance, that Terra is not *my* niece, but the niece of the president of the MiniCozy Software Company. Knowing the reputation of MiniCozy's president for impulsive emotional action, the project manager might have defined quality of the word processor differently. In that case, Terra's opinion would have been given great weight in the decision about which faults to repair.

In short, the definition of quality is always *political* and *emotional,* because it always involves a series of decisions about whose opinions count, and how much they count relative to one another. Of course, much of the time these political/emotional decisions—like all important political/emotional decisions—are hidden from public view, which suits software people who like to appear rational. That's why very few people appreciate the power of this definition of quality.

What makes our task even more difficult is that most of the time, these decisions are hidden even from the conscious minds of the persons who make them. That's why one of the most important actions of a quality manager is to bring such decisions into consciousness, if not always into public awareness. That will be one of our major tasks.

1.4 Precision Cribbage

To test our understanding of this definition as well as its applicability, let's consider another story: One of the favorite pastimes of my youth was playing cribbage with my father. Invented by the poet Sir John Suckling, cribbage is a card game that is very popular in some regions of the world, but essentially unknown in others. After my father died, I missed playing cribbage with him and was hard pressed to find a regular partner. Consequently, I was delighted to discover a shareware cribbage program for the Macintosh, Precision Cribbage™ by Doug Brent, of San Jose, California.

Precision Cribbage was a rather nicely engineered piece of software, I thought, especially when compared with the great majority of shareware. I was especially pleased to find that it gave me a good game, but wasn't good enough to beat me more than one or two games out of ten. Therefore, I sent Doug the requested postcard from my hometown as a shareware fee and played many happy games.

After a while, though, I discovered two clear errors in the scoring algorithm of Precision Cribbage. One was an intermittent failure to count correctly hands with three cards of one denomination and two of another (a full house in poker terminology). This was clearly an unintentional flaw because sometimes such hands were counted correctly.

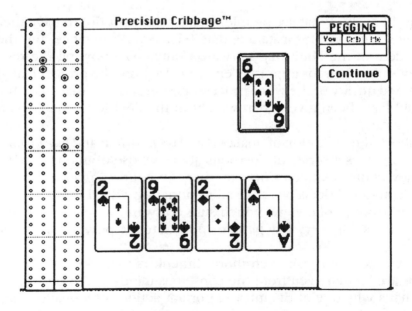

Figure 1-2.   An example of a miscounted cribbage hand. The correct score is 4, not 8.

The second error, however, may have been a misunderstanding of the scoring rules (which were certainly part of the requirements for a program that purported to play a card game). It had to do with counting hands that had three cards of the same suit when a fourth card of that suit was cut. In this case, I could actually *prove* mathematically that the algorithm was incorrect.[4] What makes this story relevant is that even with two scoring errors in the game, I was sufficiently satisfied with the quality of Precision Cribbage to keep on playing it for at least several of my valuable hours each week and pay the voluntary shareware fee, even though I could have omitted payment with no fear of retribution of any kind.

In short, Precision Cribbage had great value to me, value that I was willing and able to demonstrate by spending my own time and (if requested) money. Moreover, Doug's correction of these errors would have added very little to the value of the software.

1.5   Why Improving Quality Is So Difficult

The tale of Precision Cribbage demonstrates that meeting requirements is not an adequate definition of quality unless you're willing to accept a most unconventional definition of requirements. It also demonstrates the inadequacy of definitions of quality based on errors, such as:

Quality is the absence of error.

Such definitions are easy to refute, yet they have dominated thinking about quality software for many years. This makes it easy for software developers and managers to ignore requests to improve software quality. But don't they want to improve quality, even if nobody else was asking for it, just to satisfy their own pride? Of course they do, but nothing happens. Why not?

1.5.1   It's-not-too-bad effect

The stories of CozyWrite and Precision Cribbage are typical of hundreds of cases I could cite, and you could undoubtedly supply many examples of your own. If you asked the developers, "Are you interested in a high-quality product?" I'm sure their professional pride would supply the answer, "Of course!"

But suppose you asked specifically about improving CozyWrite or Precision Cribbage. The developers would reply, "But it already *is* a good product. Of course it has bugs, but *all* software has bugs. Besides, it's better than the competition." And, of course, all three of these statements are provably correct:

1.   People are using their product, and are happy with it, so it is of good quality.

2.   All software has bugs (at least we can't prove otherwise).

3.   People buy it over the competition, so it must be better in their opinion.

Under the circumstances, there's very little motivation to improve the quality unless pushed from the outside. If people stop using their product or stop buying it, the developers may decide to improve quality, but by then it will probably be too late. Organizations that sell software simply fade away when faced with a competitor that operates in a more effective manner.

Organizations that produce software internally for larger organizations have little competition, so they simply stagnate. Whether or not their stagnation matters depends on what their parent organization defines as "quality." If the parent gets the value it needs, and doesn't know any better, the stagnation continues. Once the parent becomes dissatisfied, however, a crisis begins.

1.5.2   It's-not-possible effect

Did you know that if you were 8'6" tall, you could get a job as a starting center with a team in the NBA and earn $3,000,000 a year? Now that you know that, why aren't you starting on a growth program? It's a silly question, because you don't know *how* to grow several feet taller.

Did you know that by reducing the faults in your software to fewer than one in a million lines of code, you could increase your market by $3,000,000 a year? Now that you know that, why aren't you starting on a quality program? It's a silly question, because you don't know *how* to reduce software faults to fewer than one in a million lines of code.

Philip Crosby, in *Quality Is Free*,[5] says that the motivation for improving quality always starts with a study of the cost of quality. (I prefer the term "value of quality," but it's the same idea.) In my consulting, I frequently talk to managers who seem obsessed with cutting the cost of software, or reducing development time, but I seldom find a manager obsessed with improving quality. It's easy for them to tell me what it's worth to cut costs or expedite a schedule, but the value of improved quality seems to be something they've never thought of measuring.

Yet when I suggest measuring the value of quality, they often respond as if I told them to measure the value of growing to 8'6". Why bother measuring the value of something that you don't have the slightest idea how to achieve? And why try to achieve something whose value you don't appreciate? Figure 1-3 shows this vicious cycle in the form of a *diagram of effects*, a form of diagram that I will explain later and use throughout this volume. For now, let's just concentrate on what it says about why improving quality is so difficult.

The diagram of Figure 1-3 can be read optimistically or pessimistically. Optimistically, it says that once an organization begins to understand the true value of quality, its motivation to improve will rise, which will drive its understanding

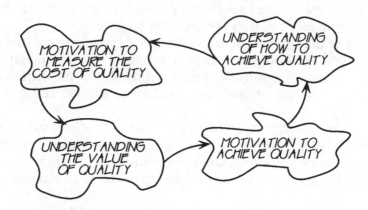

Figure 1–3.   A vicious cycle that prevents organizations from starting to improve quality.

of how to improve, which will in turn lead to a better understanding of the value of quality. That's why Crosby likes to start organizational change with a cost of quality study.

Pessimistically, though, the cycle can be seen as inhibiting a change to higher quality. If there is no understanding of the value of quality, there is no motivation to achieve quality, and thus no improvement in the understanding of how to achieve quality. And without knowing how to achieve quality, why would anyone try to measure its value?

1.5.3   Lock-on effect

Figure 1-3 happens to be a simple example of a *lock-on effect*. A locked-on system tends to hold itself to an existing pattern, even against logical reasons to change. An excellent example of a lock-on is the choice of a standard programming language. Once an organization is using a single programming language—for whatever historical reasons—the cost of changing increases, the motivation to study the value of other alternatives decreases, and the knowledge of how to obtain those alternatives disappears. As a result, the organization locks on to the language, just as a country locks on to the side of the road used for driving.

In this volume, we'll see many examples of lock-on situations, but for now we simply want to note that lock-ons occur in clusters. When you lock on to a particular programming language, you also tend to lock on to some or all of the following:

- a set of software tools supporting that language
- hardware systems that support a particular dialect of that language
- people trained in particular schools

- people hired from certain other organizations
- a set of consultants specializing in that language and tools
- a community of other users of that language
- a set of managers who rose through the ranks using this language
- professional books and training oriented to that language
- a philosophy of software engineering associated with that language
- a user interface philosophy associated with that language

Each of these characteristics, in turn, may lock the organization on to another set of characteristics. Attempting to change the standard programming language thus produces a ripple through the entire organization, and each furrow of this ripple is met by a variety of mechanisms that attempt to prevent a change.

It doesn't matter that changing the language would be good for the organization. As Virginia Satir, the family therapist, used to say,

"People will always choose the familiar over the comfortable."

1.6   Software Culture and Subcultures

All these interrelated lock-ons produce patterns. Every time Dani Weinberg (my anthropologist partner) and I arrive at a new organization to consult on managing software organizations, we quickly notice two essential facts:

1.   No two software organizations are exactly alike.

2.   No two software organizations are entirely different.

Because of (1), it's not possible to have off-the-rack solutions to really important problems of software management; but because of (2), we don't have to start from scratch with every new organization. There are commonalties from one software organization to another, even though they are different sizes, in different industries, working with different programming languages, in different countries, and even in different decades. This book is very much concerned with those commonalties.

An anthropological way of expressing this observation is that there is some sort of *software culture* that transcends boundaries of time, space, and circumstance. You can verify the existence of this software culture in a number of ways. For one thing, software books sell very well in English all over the world. The software culture is very much an English-language culture. The books also sell well in translation, and the same software jokes continue to be funny all over the world. Software meetings are international, and surveys of attendees show that they cross industries and age groups as well. We are fortunate that such a software culture exists, for it allows us to learn from one another. Thus, any truths that we have learned with our clients should have potential value for you and your organization.

One of the most valuable truths Dani and I have learned is that within the overall software culture there are a few different patterns—clusters of characteristics that organizations have in common. One way of distinguishing these patterns is to observe *the quality of the software they produce.* We have come to believe that software organizations lock on to a particular level of quality, and that change is prevented by the *conservative nature of culture.* This conservatism is manifested primarily in

- the satisfaction with their current level of quality
- the fear of losing that level in an attempt to do even better
- the lack of understanding of other cultures
- the invisibility of their own culture

Quality is important because quality is value. The ability to control quality is the ability to control the value of the software efforts. To reach a new culture of quality software, you as developers and managers must learn to deal effectively with these factors. That is the subject of this book.

1.7   Helpful Hints and Suggestions

1. Of course you can't do a perfect job of identifying all potential users of your software and determining what they value, but that doesn't mean you won't benefit from trying. In fact, you'll probably find it beneficial just to try doing it in your own mind. Once you've experienced those benefits, you may decide to interview at least a few major users to find out where their values lie.

2. Because of the conservative nature of culture, attempts to change are always met with resistance. You will be better able to cope with such resistance if you recognize it as attempts to preserve what is good about the old way of doing things. Even better will be to begin a change project by acknowledging the value of the old way, and determining which characteristics you wish to preserve, even while changing the cultural pattern.

1.8   Summary

√ Quality is relative. What is quality to one person may even be lack of quality to another.

√ Finding the relativity involves detecting the implicit person or persons in the statement about quality, by asking, Who is the person behind that statement about quality?

√   Quality is neither more nor less than value to some person or persons. This view allows us to reconcile such statements as

- Zero defects is high quality.
- Having lots of features is high quality.
- Elegant coding is high quality.
- High performance is high quality.
- Low development cost is high quality.
- Rapid development is high quality.
- User friendliness is high quality.

All of these statements can be true at the same time.

√   Quality is almost always a political/emotional issue, though we like to pretend it can be settled rationally.

√   Quality is not identical with freedom from errors. A software product that does not even conform to its formal requirements could be considered of high quality by some of its users.

√   Improving quality is so difficult because organizations tend to lock on to a specific pattern of doing things. They adapt to the present level of quality, they don't know what is needed to change to a new level, and they don't really try to find out.

√   The patterns adopted by software organizations tend to fall into a few clusters, or subcultures, each of which produces characteristic results.

√   Cultures are inherently conservative. In software organizations, this conservatism is manifested primarily in

- the satisfaction with a particular level of quality
- the fear of losing that level in an attempt to do even better
- the lack of understanding of other cultures
- the invisibility of their own culture

1.9   Practice

1.   I wrote to Doug Brent, telling him how grateful I was and showing him the two erroneous cases, but I haven't gotten a reply so far. I wouldn't mind if Precision Cribbage were corrected, but I wouldn't pay very much for the corrections, because their value was reduced once I had an approximate cribbage program with which to play. Discuss how the value, and thus the definition of quality, changes for a particular software product over time as early versions of the product, or competing products, come into use.

2. Produce a list of characteristics that an organization might lock on to when standardizing a given hardware architecture.

3. What evidence can you produce to indicate that people in your organization are indeed satisfied with the level of quality they produce? How does the organization deal with people who express dissatisfaction with that level?

2

Software Subcultures

I have had discussions with executives in hundreds of different businesses and industries. Regardless of the nation, product, service, or group, I am never disappointed. Someone always says: "You have to recognize that our business is different." Because they usually see only their business, they never realize how alike most businesses are. Certainly the technology and the methods of distribution can be very different. But the people involved—their motivations and reactions—are the same.
—Philip B. Crosby[1]

What Crosby says about business in general is certainly true for software businesses. In this chapter, I'll introduce the major groupings of software patterns, or subcultures, and relate them to Crosby's work summarized in his Quality Management Maturity Grid.

2.1 Applying Crosby's Ideas to Software

Those of you who have read *Quality Is Free* will notice how consonant my views of software quality are to Crosby's views of quality in general. In particular, you will notice that I share the view that the critical factor is always, as Crosby says, "the people involved–their motivations and reactions." Even so, few people have had much success in directly applying Crosby's approach to software engineering. That's because, as I've said,

1.   No two organizations are exactly alike.

2.   No two organizations are entirely different.

I have changed Crosby's approach to account for the differences, so I need to explain several areas in which my approach to software quality differs from Crosby's.

2.1.1   Conformance to requirements is not enough

Crosby is very clear in defining quality as "conformance to requirements."

> If a Cadillac conforms to all the requirements of a Cadillac, then it is a quality car. If a Pinto conforms to all the requirements of a Pinto, then it is a quality car.[2]

That's an excellent definition as long as the requirements are correct. I'm not an expert in manufacturing, so I can't say how frequently manufacturing requirements are clear and correct. I am an expert in software engineering, however, and I can definitely assert that software requirements are seldom even close to being correct. If the customer wants a Pinto and you build a car that conforms to all the requirements of a Cadillac, that is *not* a quality car.

Many writers on software quality have missed the point that software development is *not* a manufacturing operation. It does *contain* manufacturing operations, such as the duplication of software once developed. Indeed, some of my clients have successfully applied Crosby's definitions and his approach to making accurate copies of completed software. Software duplication, however, is generally not one of the most difficult parts of software development (Figure 2-1).

In software development, therefore, we've had to generalize the definition of quality to the one we developed in the previous chapter:

Quality is value to some person(s).

Requirements are not an end in themselves, but a means to an end—the end of providing value to some person(s). If requirements correctly identify the important people and capture their true values, this definition reduces precisely to Crosby's conformance to requirements. In software work, however, we cannot assume this ideal situation, so much of the development process is concerned with more closely approaching the "true" requirements.[3] Therefore, much of what we need to understand about quality software management concerns this parallel development of requirements and software.

Designing/ Creating	Pseudo- Manufacturing*	Manufacturing
Requirements	Low-Level Design	Duplication of Disks
High-Level Design	Coding	Printing of Manuals
Documentation	Code Conversion	

*Pseudo-Manufacturing operations have some properties of manufacturing mixed with some properties of designing and creating.

Figure 2–1.   Some of the processes in software development are manufacturing operations and some resemble manufacturing in a few of their aspects. These can definitely apply Crosby's approach to achieve high quality.

2.1.2   Zero Defects is not realistic in most projects

Because software development is only partly a manufacturing process, Crosby's goal of *Zero Defects* is not realistic. It is realistic for the manufacturing parts of the process, such as code duplication and probably coding itself (once the design is accepted as a true representation of the true requirements). And perhaps in ten or twenty years, it will be realistic for the design process itself, at least the low-level design (Figure 2-1).

However, in thirty-five years of software building and consulting, I've never seen anything approaching zero defects in requirements work. If you examine those software projects that claim to have zero defects, you will find that they always start with an accepted requirements document, as in

1.   conversion of a program from one language to another, in which duplicating the behavior of the original program is taken as the absolute requirement. There are now companies that can consistently do such conversions on fixed schedules with fixed prices—and zero defects guaranteed.

2.   creating a program for a new environment, using a standard requirement, as in the creation of a new COBOL compiler.[4]

Thus, for the foreseeable future, most of us will have to manage software development in a "dirty" environment, where requirements cannot be assumed to be correct. To ignore this reality would be to play the ostrich, not the quality software manager.

2.1.3   There is an economics of quality

Crosby writes,

> The third erroneous assumption is that there is an "economics" of quality. The most-offered excuse managers have for not doing anything is that "our business is different." The second is that the economics of quality won't allow them to do anything. What they mean is that they can't afford to make it that good. . . . If they want to make certain that they are using the least expensive process that will still do the job, they should get deep into process certification and product qualification.[5]

Again, this assumes that there is a correct set of requirements to start the process. If the requirements are correct, it is not the development manager's job to decide what is gold plating and what is essential. The requirements answer all such questions once and for all. If there is only one right way, there cannot be any question of the *economics of quality.* As Crosby correctly notes,

"It is always cheaper to do the job right the first time."

However, when the customers' values are not known and, even worse, when the customers are not known, then we don't know what the "things" are. We may produce things right, but discover they are not the right things. That's why the requirements process can produce or destroy value, and that's why there's an economics of quality in any software project that includes a requirements process.

This *economics of requirements quality* certainly argues for getting the requirements right in the first place. If you can do it, then by all means take that approach. If you cannot, however, the politics or emotions of negotiating value (quality) will permeate your project and make it much harder.

2.1.4   Any pattern can be a success

In the examples of the previous chapter, we saw that even errors in conformance to formal requirements don't necessarily destroy the value of a software product, and that trying to meet every last requirement can result in destroying value for a subset of the customers. That's why the battle cry of so many software development managers is,

Don't touch the program!

or, even more conservative,

> Don't touch the (software development) process!

Although this "don't touch" attitude is often ridiculed by software engineering theorists, it makes sense economically. If the way you now produce and maintain software is wholly satisfactory, don't work on changing it; work on maintaining it. If your customers are happy, it would be foolish to change.

As we'll see, collapse of either a program or a process is an ever-present possibility for most software managers. If your customers are mildly unhappy, then you're probably in the right pattern but not doing it as well as you could. Don't change your basic pattern, but improve it by small, safe changes that don't risk collapse.

If you're currently in the *wrong* pattern, trying to improve it by small changes is like creating ever more detailed maps for the wrong trip. If you're supposed to go from Miami to Cleveland, detailed maps of the Los Angeles metropolitan area are not only useless, they're distracting. If your customers are unhappy, it will be fatal *not* to change. If you're not in the appropriate pattern, choose the pattern that will give you the quality and cost you need and work within that pattern to do it well.

Quality is the ability to consistently get what people need. That means producing what people will value and not producing what people won't value. Don't use a sledgehammer to crack a peanut. Don't use a nutcracker to break up a wall. Choose the pattern that will give you the quality and cost you need and work within that pattern to do it consistently.

Working consistently is the essence of a pattern or subculture. Working consistently to give value to your customers is the essence of success. Therefore, any subculture can be a success.

2.1.5   *"Maturity" is not the right word*

It's very tempting when writing about cultures to slip into a judgmental mode. For instance, some people find it hard to believe that *any* software subculture can be a success. They are like the pigs in Orwell's *Animal Farm*[6] that accept the concept "All animals are created equal ... but some are more equal than others." Some people agree, "Any software culture can be successful ... but some are more successful than others."

Most often, this judgment slips in covertly. Crosby, for example, describes five different stages of quality management in his Quality Management Maturity Grid. The Grid is a strikingly useful tool, but a better name would have been simply Quality Management Grid. The word "maturity" is not a fact but a judgment—an *interpretation* of facts. At the very least, it doesn't fit the facts.

Maturing normally goes in one direction, but Crosby gives several examples of organizations falling back, as in this quote:

> We were Enlightened [one of the maturity stages] for a couple of years, then we got a new general manager who thinks quality is expensive. We'll have to drop back a stage or two until he gets educated.[7]

In everyday language, "mature" means "having attained the normal peak of natural growth and development." There's nothing particularly "natural" in the progression through Crosby's stages. Indeed, Crosby is at great pains to emphasize the vast amounts of work involved to change from one stage to another.

Moreover, I have observed many software organizations that have attained "the normal peak" in the sense that they are going to stay right where they are unless something abnormal happens. They are good enough, and investing in attaining another stage or pattern would serve no organizational purpose. As we've seen, cultural patterns are not more or less mature, they are just more or less *fitting*. Of course, some people have an emotional *need* for perfection, and they will impose this emotional need on everything they do. Their comparisons have nothing to do with the organization's problems, but with their own.

The quest for unjustified perfection is not mature, but infantile.

Hitler was quite clear on who was the "master race." His definition of Aryan race was supposed to represent the mature end product of all human history, and that allowed Hitler and the Nazis to justify atrocities on "less mature" cultures such as Gypsies, Catholics, Jews, Poles, Czechs, and anyone else who got in their way. Many would-be reformers of software engineering start their work by requiring their "targets" to confess to their previous inferiority. These little Hitlers have not been very successful.

Very few healthy people will make such a confession voluntarily, and even concentration camps didn't cause many people to change their minds. This is not "just a matter of words." Words are essential to any change project because they give us models of the world as it was and as we hope it to be. So if your goal is changing an organization, start by dropping the comparisons such as those implied in the loaded term "maturity."

2.2 Six Software Subcultural Patterns

To my knowledge, Crosby was the first to have the idea of stages of process maturity. He noticed that the mostly manufacturing organizations with which he worked could be studied *according to the quality of their production*. If he knew the quality of their product, Crosby could make predictions about what practices, attitudes, and understanding he would find inside the organization.

Crosby's observation was something we organization consultants use all the time, an application of Boulding's Backward Basis,[8] which says

Things are the way they are because they got that way.

In other words, you can study products to learn about the processes that produced them in much the same way that archaeologists study levels of technology from the remains they dig up from ruins. Like the archaeologists, Crosby discovered that the various processes that make up a technology don't merely occur in random combinations, but in coherent patterns. Crosby named his five patterns or stages based largely on the management *attitudes* to be found in each:

1.   Uncertainty

2.   Awakening

3.   Enlightenment

4.   Wisdom

5.   Certainty

In their article "A Programming Process Study,"[9] Radice et al. adapted Crosby's stratification by quality scheme to software development. Watts Humphrey[10] expanded on their work and identified five levels of *process maturity* through which a software development organization can grow. These levels are called

1.   Initial

2.   Repeatable

3.   Defined

4.   Managed

5.   Optimizing

These names are more related to the *types of processes* found in each pattern, rather than to the attitudes of management.

Other observers quickly noted the usefulness of Humphrey's maturity levels. For example, Bill Curtis of the Software Engineering Institute noticed that a parallel classification could be made simply on the basis of *the way people were treated* within the organization. He proposed a *software human resource maturity model*[11] with five levels:

1.   Herded

2.   Managed

3. Tailored

4. Institutionalized

5. Optimized

Our own consulting work with organizations is guided by the anthropological model of *participant observation,*[12] by which we observe what people are doing and saying at the bottom levels, not just what management is doing and saying. We particularly look for *the degree of congruence between what is said and what is done* in different parts of the organization. Classifying organizations by their degree of congruence, we add a pattern (Oblivious) and identify five other patterns that roughly match the other systems of patterns as follows:

√ Oblivious: "We don't even know that we're performing a process."

√ Variable: "We do whatever we feel like at the moment."

√ Routine: "We follow our routines (except when we panic)."

√ Steering: "We choose among our routines by the results they produce."

√ Anticipating: "We establish routines based on our past experience with them."

√ Congruent: "Everyone is involved in improving everything all the time."

This is the classification I'll use throughout the book to describe organizations.

2.3 Pattern 0: Oblivious

Pattern 0 is not a professional pattern, but we add it because it is the most frequent source of new programs, and it can be used as a baseline against which other patterns can be compared. In Pattern 0, there is no software development organization separate from the software user. An example of Pattern 0 would be my developing a special little database to keep track of my own pulse and blood pressure, a spreadsheet to keep track of my scores at Precision Cribbage, or a BASIC program to drive a simulation game in one of my seminars. I have no manager, no customer, no specified processes. Indeed, I probably have little or no awareness that I am doing something called software development, like Molière's gentleman who was unaware that he had been speaking prose all his life. If asked, I would probably say I was solving a problem. That's why we call Pattern 0 Oblivious.

Not only are the people using Pattern 0 oblivious to their doing software development, but so are most writers on software development. I asked one of my clients, the information systems manager of a large corporation, to survey the number of groups working in each of the various patterns. The estimates were

0.	Oblivious	25,000
1.	Variable	300
2.	Routine	2,600
3.	Steering	250
4.	Anticipating	0
5.	Congruent	0

The IS manager told me he had never really thought about the 25,000 people in the organization who had been given access to PCs or time-sharing. He worried about what would happen when they became aware that they were doing software development. If they came to his organization for help, was that his job?

They would become aware, of course, only when their quality became unacceptable. What saves information systems managers from the Oblivious pattern is a psychological phenomenon known as *cognitive dissonance*—the tendency to find confirming evidence for previously made decisions. How many people will admit that they don't value the product of their own hands and brain? Indeed, this might be called the pattern of the Superindividual.

If asked why they are using this pattern, the Pattern 0 people would probably say, "Nobody else can give me what I want, or can really understand me." The characteristic magic posture of this pattern is that of a god: omniscient and omnipotent. At times, playing god can be a lot of fun.

Whether because of fun, cognitive dissonance, or some other factor, Pattern 0 is highly successful at producing satisfied users. In this work, we are not particularly interested in Pattern 0 except as a standard against which other patterns are often weighed.

2.4   Pattern 1: Variable

Pattern 1, Variable, often follows Pattern 0 when problem solvers become aware, rightly or wrongly, that they are out of their depth. It is the first of the patterns to involve a distinction between the developer and user of software, so it's hard for the developer to remain oblivious to the process of software development. Because this is the first pattern to have this separation of responsibility for quality, it's the first pattern in which *blaming* appears as a substantial software development activity.

2.4.1   The superprogrammer image

Crosby says of this pattern, "Management has no knowledge of quality as a positive management tool," but I go a step further. A characteristic of Pattern 1 is

There is no knowledge of management as a development tool.

This pattern could well be called the pattern of the Individual Programmer. The ideal here is the Superprogrammer, and the slogan is "If we succeed, it's because of a superprogrammer." A variant of this pattern has the slogan "If we succeed, it's because of a superteam (led, of course, by a superprogrammer). This is the idealized pattern for Mills's "chief programmer concept"[13]—a compact "surgical team" headed by a superprogrammer. It is also the pattern in hardware development described by Tracy Kidder in *The Soul of a New Machine.*[14]

2.4.2   When Pattern 1 is successful

Like all the other patterns, Pattern 1 is often successful. I commonly find this pattern in young companies producing software products for microcomputers. At the slightest provocation, any member of the organization will relate an elaborate "creation myth" about the heroic feats of the founding team. Often, as the new company grows, it evolves to Pattern 2, but retains the myths of Pattern 1. These myths have great value in recruiting new programmers. Thus, one of my clients spoke about the "small team" that worked on a project—later, I discovered that more than 250 people took part at various times in its three-year duration.

Another place where Pattern 1 is found to be successful is in a large organization where a pool of programmers serves some important group of specialists. Information centers are often structured as programming pools, but are typically more specialized. In aircraft companies, I have seen the pool attached to the engineers; in an insurance company, to the actuaries; in a bank, to the foreign exchange specialists. These pools can be highly effective at satisfying the needs of the specialists, and can add much value to the company.

2.4.3   The ideal development structure

The ideal development structure in Pattern 1 is what I would call the Star in the Closet. If the project is patently too large for one star, the ideal is the skunkworks. Pattern 1 organizations may have some procedures, but they don't cover most parts of the actual process. Besides, they always abandon any procedures at the first sign of crisis.

In Pattern 1, Curtis says, the typical personnel practices may include

- Selection: Find out if the candidate saw yesterday's game.
- Appraising performance: Hold a quick review before leaving on a trip.
- Organization development: Build morale over a beer after work.

According to Curtis, "Software personnel are treated as a purchasable commodity," but I think the word "commodity" is imprecise. Personnel are "purchasable," but more in the sense that professional athletes are purchasable. The commodity model is more often seen in Pattern 2, as we shall see below.

In Pattern 1, purchasing a "star" is the only hope the organization has of improving quality. The belief system is very much like voodoo (send in a hair or the fingernail of the key player, leader, or programmer) or cannibalism (which gives you the power of the person whose brain you eat).

Humphrey says that the first step in statistical control is to achieve rudimentary predictability of schedules and costs. Since performance in Pattern 1 depends almost totally on individual efforts, the variability in schedules and costs depends almost totally on the variability in individuals. Studies of individuals have consistently shown variations of 20:1 or more in schedule, cost, and error performance among professional programmers,[15] so it makes sense that this is the level of variation we see in Pattern 1.

In Pattern 1, the best predictor of project schedule, cost, or quality is the specific programmer who does the job, thus reinforcing the belief system characteristic of this pattern. The programmer gets all the credit, as well as all the blame.

2.5   Pattern 2: Routine

Pattern 2 arises for several reasons. An organization may be dissatisfied with the tremendous variation in Pattern 1; it may never have experienced Pattern 1, but may simply need to build software that obviously requires more than a small team; or the projects may not be that big, but do require coordination with other organizations. In any case, managers decide they can no longer afford to leave the programmers alone.

2.5.1   The superleader image

Crosby characterizes the managers in this pattern as "beginning to recognize that quality management can help but is unwilling to devote time and money to make it happen." There are several reasons they don't provide the money or time:

- They don't appreciate the value of what can be accomplished.
- They don't know what is needed to accomplish changes.
- They believe that pushing the programmers is all they need to do the job.

A programmer in one Pattern 2 organization said of his managers, "They think they're managing a salami factory." This pronouncement characterizes both the management style and the view of programmers who would prefer to be working in Pattern 1. The prevailing myth in Pattern 2 is that of the superleader:

"If we succeed, it's because of a supermanager (but there aren't very many of those). If we fail, it's because our manager is a turkey." This attitude is expressed beautifully in the following excerpt from *The Tao of Programming:*

> Why are the programmers nonproductive?
> Because their time is wasted in meetings.
>
> Why are the programmers rebellious?
> Because the management interferes too much.
>
> Why are the programmers resigning one by one?
> Because they are burnt out.
>
> Having worked for poor management,
> They no longer value their jobs.[16]

Managers in this pattern do institute procedures because they've been told that procedures are important to keep programmers under control. For instance, Curtis observes that by Pattern 2, management practices may have changed to

- Selection: Managers are trained in personnel interviewing.
- Appraising performance: Managers are trained in specific rating techniques.
- Organization development: An OD plan is created, morale is surveyed.

Both managers and programmers generally follow most instituted procedures. More often than not, though, they follow them in name only *because they do not understand the reasoning behind them*. That's why we call this pattern Routine.

For instance, when Curtis observes that managers are trained in specific performance rating techniques, that simply means that managers have taken courses. There is ordinarily no way to check on what processes managers actually use in their appraisals. When we do check, we find little correspondence between what the appraisal class outline said to do and what is actually done in appraisals.

2.5.2   When Pattern 2 is successful

Humphrey says that the Pattern 2 organization has achieved a stable process with a repeatable level of statistical control by initiating rigorous project management of commitments, costs, schedules, and changes. The operational word here, however, is "repeatable," not "repeated." A telling characteristic of Pattern 2 organizations is that they don't always do what they know how to do. As soon as they seem to be doing well on a series of projects, along comes one disastrous project that bypasses the procedures just when they are needed most. Worse than that, management takes action that further undermines the situation. Here's a memo issued by the manager of a project with a staff of 59:

> To: All Staff Members
> From: Bob Smith
> Re: Project Gateway
>
> We are now in the final push to bring Gateway to market. In the ten weeks between now and turnover date, the following rules will be in effect:
>
> 1. Everyone will be on scheduled ten-hour days, six days a week. This is the minimum work week.
>
> 2. There will be no time off for any reason. All class attendance is canceled. All vacation days are canceled. Managers are not to grant sick leave days.
>
> 3. We must ship a quality product. It's everyone's responsibility to reduce the bug count. Testing, especially, must become more efficient. By ship date, today's bug count in every area will be cut in half.
>
> 4. We must ship an on-time product. Further schedule slips will not be allowed, and all previous slips must be made up by turnover. Starting today, any schedule problems will be reported to me on a daily basis.
>
> Any developer, tester, or manager who violates any of these rules will be accountable to me. Remember:
>
> WITH TEAMWORK, WE CAN FULFILL OUR COMMITMENTS.

You'll be interested to know that this product was shipped on time, and the manager was rewarded for his stunning feat of management. Some people did disobey orders, however, and got sick. Moreover, the number of bugs was not cut in half. Instead, they more than doubled, and four months after shipment, the product was suddenly withdrawn from the field.

Such disasters are inevitable in Pattern 2 organizations. (In later chapters, we'll use detailed models to demonstrate why.) The primary reason, of course, is that Pattern 2 managers don't understand *why* they do what their routine procedures tell them to do. Thus, when things start to go wrong, they start issuing counterproductive orders—such as ordering people not to be sick.

2.5.3   *The ideal development structure*

A characteristic of Pattern 2 organizations is their desperate search for a silver bullet[17] to make a radical change in their performance. For instance, they often

introduce refined measurements that make no sense in their unstable environment. Or, they purchase sophisticated tools that are either misused or lie on the
shelf unused. This approach is what the anthropologists call "name magic." To
work name magic, you just say the name of the thing—structured programming,
CASE tool, IBM—and you have its full power at your disposal.

The ideal development structure for Pattern 2 is a manager supported by
powerful tools and procedures. When the jobs are routine, all the manager has
to do is ensure that everyone does every step in the right order. To do this
requires "mana," the personal charismatic power that resides in an individual. If
we just "Put Jack in charge," everything will be all right. Unless it isn't.

2.6   Pattern 3: Steering

2.6.1   The competent manager

Pattern 3 managers never depend on magic, but on *understanding*. Although
there are many exceptions, the average Pattern 3 manager is more skilled or experienced than the average Pattern 2 manager. Pattern 2 managers have often
come from a successful programming career with no particular talent for managing, no training in management, no great desire to manage, no time to acquire
experience in the job of management, and no role models to show them how to
manage. That may be why Pattern 2 managers so often overestimate the power
of their position.

I took a friend of mine—an organization consultant unaccustomed to working with such programming managers—on a consulting visit to one of my clients.
After three days of jointly interviewing people to determine the state of the organization, I asked him what he thought of their management style. "Evidently,"
he said, "the only style they know is Management By Telling."

Pattern 3 managers are different. They have a variety of skills required
to steer an organization, so they don't have to fall back on telling when their
project gets in trouble.

2.6.2   When Pattern 3 is successful

Pattern 3 managers either have more desire, training, and experience, or else
they are stamped from a different mold than Pattern 2 managers. Their procedures are not always completely defined, but they are always *understood*.
Perhaps because of this understanding, Pattern 3 managers generally follow the
processes they have defined, even in a crisis. That's why they can successfully
manage larger, riskier projects with a greater degree of success.

If you examine the "typical" project, Pattern 3 may not look spectacularly
better than Patterns 1 and 2. In Pattern 3, however, more projects are "typical"
because there are much fewer outright failures. When a project starts, you can

bet it will finish successfully—with value to the customers delivered on time and within budget.

2.6.3   The ideal development structure

Of course, Pattern 3 processes are more flexible because managers choose them on the basis of their most recent information about what is actually happening. That's why we call this the Steering pattern.

Life in a Pattern 3 organization is much less routine than in a Pattern 2 organization, and the programmers are generally much happier with their work. They often display contempt for Pattern 1 programmers who don't appreciate the rewards of working in a well-managed operation.

Humphrey says that the Pattern 3 organization has defined the process as a basis for consistent implementation and better understanding. He adds the important observation that advanced technology can usefully be introduced into this Pattern, but no earlier. In Pattern 3, tools are actually used and they are used rather well.

2.7   Pattern 4: Anticipating

Speaking at a recent symposium, Humphrey presented data gathered from U.S. Department of Defense organizations and contractors[18] that participated in an assessment of their software processes. Humphrey and his colleagues at the Software Engineering Institute found that 85 percent of the projects were at the lowest level of software maturity; 14 percent at level 2; and 1 percent at level 3. They found no projects yet at levels 4 or 5.

My own experience is similar. I have seen projects, or parts of projects, that had elements said to belong in Humphrey's level 4, but certainly not an entire organization. Therefore, whatever I say about level 4 (or Pattern 4) is partial or based on indirect knowledge or theory.

According to Crosby, the Pattern 4 manager is similar to the Pattern 3 manager but sits at a higher level in the organization and has a higher level of understanding concerning quality management. Instead of merely *reacting* to instabilities, the Pattern 4 organization *anticipates* them, and acts in advance.

According to Humphrey's extrapolation of Crosby's ideas to software, Pattern 4 managers have procedures that they understand and follow uniformly. Moreover, the organization has initiated comprehensive process measurements and analysis. This is when the most significant quality improvements in individual projects begin.

2.8   Pattern 5: Congruent

Crosby says that at Pattern 5, quality management moves to the highest level or optimal performance. Managers consider high-quality management an essential part of the company system, such as in the American Express Company, where the CEO has named himself Chief Quality Officer as well.[19]

Humphrey predicts that level 5 organizations will understand and follow procedures, which everyone is involved in improving all the time. This provides the organization with a foundation for continuing improvement and optimization of its process.

2.9   Helpful Hints and Suggestions

1.   At times, it's easy to be misled about an organization's pattern. To take one example, Pattern 1 organizations rarely have much trouble with overruns, which might indicate they are Pattern 3 organizations. The reason they don't have overruns, however, is that overruns generally involve poor management, and in Pattern 1 there is essentially no management at all. Thus, there is nobody with the authority to make the boomerang-type actions that drive a project into overruns.

2.   When things are going well in a Pattern 2 organization, it's easy to mistake it for a Pattern 3. Only in reaction to adverse circumstances do the differences become clear. Both use planned procedures, but only Pattern 3 people know how to respond effectively to deviations from their plans.

2.10   Summary

√   Philip Crosby's ideas in *Quality Is Free* can be applied to software, though perhaps with several modifications.

√   In software, conformance to requirements is not enough to define quality, because requirements cannot be as certain as in a manufacturing operation.

√   Our experience with software tells us that zero defects is not realistic in most projects because there is diminishing value for the last few defects. Moreover, there are requirements defects that tend to dominate once the other defects are diminished.

√   Contrary to Crosby's claim, there is an economics of quality for software. We are not searching for perfection, but for value, unless we have a psychological need for perfection not justified by value.

√   Any software cultural pattern can be a success, given the right customer.

√   Maturity is not the right word for subcultural patterns because it implies superiority when none can be inferred.

√   We can identify at least six software subcultural patterns:

- Pattern 0: Oblivious
- Pattern 1: Variable
- Pattern 2: Routine
- Pattern 3: Steering
- Pattern 4: Anticipating
- Pattern 5: Congruent

√ Hardly any observations exist on Patterns 4 and 5, as almost all software organizations are found in other patterns.

√ In this book, we shall be concerned primarily with Patterns 1 through 3 and how to hold on to a satisfactory pattern or move to a more satisfactory one.

2.11 Practice

1. Recall this advice: If the way you now produce and maintain software is wholly satisfactory, don't work on changing it; work on maintaining it. If your customers are happy, it would be foolish to change.

   For this maxim to make sense, however, you need a way of knowing if the way you now produce and maintain software is wholly satisfactory. Describe how an organization can know this, consistently. Describe how *your* organization can do this consistently.

2. If you can't keep your product stable, how do you know if you'll be able to keep your process stable, and vice versa? (Develop this.)

3. The term "levels" is also used for what Crosby calls "maturity stages." Discuss the pros and cons of the term "levels" for subcultural patterns.

4. Quality is value to the user. Discuss the case in which managers and developers who are also users of a software system have higher or just different standards from the paying customer's, and they become displeased at having to work on what they think is a low-quality project, even if it's good enough for the customer.

3

What Is Needed to Change Patterns?

A group of programmers were presenting a report to the Emperor. "What was the greatest achievement of the year?" the Emperor asked. The programmers spoke among themselves and then replied, "We fixed 50% more bugs this year than we fixed last year." The Emperor looked on them in confusion. It was clear that he did not know what a "bug" was. After conferring in low undertones with his chief minister, he turned to the programmers, his face red with anger. "You are guilty of poor quality control. Next year there will be no bugs!" he demanded. And sure enough, when the programmers presented their report to the Emperor the next year, there was no mention of bugs.
—Geoffrey James[1]

For emperors who believe in name magic, it's easy enough to appear to change patterns. But if you want to make a real change in your software culture, you have only yourself to fool. Unfortunately, if you're caught up in a certain subculture, you're also caught up in its thought patterns—habits of thought that always tend to preserve the culture, not change it.

3.1 Changing Thought Patterns

As consultants, we've found that the quickest and surest way to classify organizations into similar patterns is by the way people think and communicate.

3.1.1 Thought and communication in various patterns

Oblivious (Pattern 0). Individualism is the key. People just program, don't know they are programming, and will rabidly deny they are programming.

Variable (Pattern 1). Emotion and mysticism drive everything. People don't use words in a consistent way, and they don't seem to know how to count. A typical quote from the repair log of a Pattern 1 organization is, "This works under the most current sources.... I've fixed several bugs and made a lot of changes in the application code since this release, so I believe that these fixed the bug." Translated into precise language, this means, "I did a lot of big magic, so I drove the devil away."

To see these thought patterns in action, watch how problems are handled. Everything is reactive and individual, with half-cocked solutions based on poor problem definitions. There's a lot of heat, but not much light.

Routine (Pattern 2). Most reasoning is informal through rather imprecise words, though some common and reasonably useful definitions are beginning to come into use. Statistics are used, but are almost always misused and misunderstood. One manager explained that the group couldn't start spending more time on requirements and design because "we spend sixty-five percent of our time debugging."

In Pattern 2, there is an unjustifiable *certainty* about what is known. For instance, managers don't know who the twenty-times better (20:1) programmers are, but they think they know.

Another key thought pattern is linear reasoning—A caused B. This single-cause, single-effect logic works fairly well as long as things stay routine. Such oversimplified reasoning, however, frequently produces conclusions that are actually contrary to fact. Usually, this happens when something extraordinary arises, such as a project running late (which is actually not that extraordinary in this pattern, but people erroneously believe it is).

Problem solving is not much better than in Pattern 1. More people may be ordered to tackle major problems, so statistics may provide a better chance of reasonable solutions. Only short-term solutions are attempted, however, and these often have reverse long-term effects.

Steering (Pattern 3). People use words with precision. They can also reason through use of graphics, and are not restricted to linear thinking. Because there is less blaming, people are less afraid to face problems directly. They usually consider the side effects of their solutions. Consequently, they handle emergencies better and try to become proactive to prevent emergencies.

Pattern 3 people may spend a lot of time debating measurements, but they really have not yet gotten much benefit for their big investment in measurement effort. At times, their measurements are meaningless or backward, and may get them into trouble. For one thing, their process may not yet be stable enough to make their measurements meaningful.

Anticipating (Pattern 4). Organizations now have stability of process and of measurement, and stability in their way of talking about things. Crises may shake them, but a persuasive manager or customer can no longer coax, force, or trick them out of doing things the proper way.

Pattern 4 people habitually think in terms of the future, asking, What effect will this action have? Therefore, what crises they do experience are not caused by their own management practices.

Congruent (Pattern 5). Presumably, members of this pattern of organization would talk and act with scientific precision. It would be hard to observe their problem solving style because the organization would prevent most problems before they happened.

3.1.2 Using models to change thinking patterns

I wrote this book to assist software managers in making transitions from one pattern to another, especially from Patterns 1 and 2 to Pattern 3. To make such transitions—or even to ensure that you can retain your present pattern—you must start with the quality of thinking. You can tell where your organization is by studying the quality of the thinking, and you can imagine where you want to go by imagining what thinking will be like. Remember:

When the thinking changes, the organization changes, and vice versa.

In this volume, I'll show how members of each subculture use models—implicit or explicit—to guide their thinking. At *all* levels, models support the need for clear, correct communication. Using explicit models is another way of talking to each other, supplementing the vehicle of words with a more pictorial, dynamic, and possibly nonlinear mode.

3.1.3 How precise should the models be?

At some advanced stage of development—corresponding to Humphrey's maturity levels 4 and 5—managers will be able to use such dynamic models to begin simulating their organization, so as to plan their future. These simulations can be used to predict project outcomes and play "what-if" games with different strategies in order to optimize the development process. Originally, I planned that this book would be filled with such precise simulations; but as the book developed, I realized that Pattern 1 and 2 organizations lacked the stable base on which to build such simulations. Therefore, I decided to leave this subject to others and concentrate on the practical problems of moving to Pattern 3.

In anticipation of the day when large numbers of Pattern 4 and 5 organizations begin to emerge, researchers have begun to explore more precise simulations. For instance, the day after I handed the original manuscript of this book to my publisher, I met Tarek Abdel-Hamid at the Monterey Software Conference and discovered that he and I have been working on parallel but complementary paths for a number of years.[2] He starts from the high end—how to model software projects to achieve Humphrey's higher maturity levels.[3]

I, on the other hand, start from the low end—how to get projects to be stable enough so that Abdel-Hamid's more precise modeling can be even more useful. None of my clients has a sufficiently stable process, let alone sufficiently precise data, to make it possible to simulate for precise prediction and control. That's why the models in this book simply explore gross dynamic effects that you must understand in order to stabilize your own development process.

3.1.4   What models do for you

There are many ways that models help you to communicate with one another in order to facilitate the move to a different pattern. First, you discover differences in your thinking early, before they show up as adverse consequences in your projects. Second, by working on ideas together in a public medium, and by understanding the reasons for various project practices, you facilitate team building, which is needed on any successful project.

Third, with models and a few sketches of project dynamics, new arrivals to the project can become productive sooner. Otherwise, as your project gets going, very little of the vast amount of communication gets recorded, so newcomers have a difficult time coming on board.

Fourth, your diagrams of effects give you a record that you can use to compare what you thought would happen with what actually happened. This gives you a starting point for improving your models, and then improving your processes for the next time. Finally, dynamic modeling gives you a powerful tool to become and stay creative. Although you keep improving your processes, controlling software projects will never become a routine job, and you'll always require lots of creative solutions.

3.2   Using Models to Choose a Better Pattern

In order to transform your organization from one pattern to another, you first must clearly identify what the two patterns are (where you are and where you're going). Then you need to develop the general models of the patterns themselves, for the models will give you a way to decide which pattern is better for you. For example, I took one client to visit another to observe how the host client coped with software. "Oh, if we could only do that well," said the visitor, to which the host replied, "But this is terrible. Our mission is to scrap this way of doing things for something that's *really* good."

3.2.1 Is your present pattern good enough?

The descriptions of the patterns in the previous chapter were intended to help you decide where you are now. You next must decide whether this pattern is bad or not. The following case study can help generate a model that will assist you in making that decision.

CASE STUDY A

Purple Mountain Software has sold 10,000 copies of its Purple Problem Predictor (3P) at $400 each. The original product is still being sold, but a major part of the company's current income is from selling new releases of 3P. Unfortunately, these releases are expensive to support and a large part of the company's expenses is handling customer services (phone calls and visits to large customers) for the new releases. The estimated cost of service per release is $10 per customer.

A new release is being planned. Purple Mountain believes it could cut errors and problems to $8 per customer by spending $50,000 to change the development pattern used for the release. Although Purple Mountain knows how to change its pattern, it won't because it only saves at most $20,000 ($2 × 10,000 customers if all choose to upgrade).

In short, Purple Mountain knows a better way to develop its releases, but under these economic conditions, it won't use it.

3.2.2 Organizational demands

Pure economic logic is not the only determinant of changes in development patterns. Managers don't make decisions based on pure economics, but on their *model of economics,* as shown by the following elaboration:

CASE STUDY A (CONTINUED)

Another impediment to Purple Mountain's pattern change is the internal cost accounting. The expense of changing the pattern will occur in the Development Manager's budget, but the savings will accrue to the Service Manager's budget. To make such a cross-department change would require high-level management's understanding and agreement, and nobody wants to disturb upper management.

Management's models of technology can also influence the choice of pattern in other ways. Consider the following case:

CASE STUDY B

Suppose Purple Mountain's technology reveals a technique that makes possible a change to the new pattern for only $10,000, instead of $50,000. Now, a $20,000 savings looks profitable, which shows how improving the technology of development changes the decision about what pattern to adopt.

Case Study B begins to explain why a pattern is a coherent set of attributes. At a given economic level, only techniques below a certain cost threshold will seem attractive. Organizations in similar economic circumstances will thus tend to arrive at the same pattern, but only if their information is adequate. Nobody will adopt a technique he or she doesn't know about.

3.2.3   Customer demands

What else might cause Purple Mountain's managers to change their mind? Consider these slightly different cases:

CASE STUDY C

Suppose Purple Mountain has 100,000 customers who will buy the upgrade. At $2 saved per customer, the total savings of $200,000 far exceeds the estimated cost of $50,000. In this case, changing patterns is worth the cost, though the cost accounting problem may still prevent the change.

CASE STUDY D

Service calls are not a cost to Purple Mountain alone. If its customers perceive fewer service calls as higher quality, they may increase their purchases of 3P, or recommend it to their friends. Suppose this extra value of the release increases 3P sales by 1,000 copies. The increase in revenue of $400,000 (1,000 × $400 per copy) also justifies spending $50,000 to change the pattern in order to improve the release. But does management calculate these numbers? Or doesn't it see the connection between quality and sales?

Clearly, Purple Mountain's customers can have a strong influence on the pattern chosen for 3P development, again assuming its managers are perceptive enough to understand the customers. If the managers are *not* perceptive enough, the realities of the organization will override the customer demands in influencing the development pattern they choose.

3.2.4   Problem demands

What else could cause Purple Mountain to change its decision? Consider these slightly different cases:

CASE STUDY E

Suppose Purple Mountain has another product, the Easy Everlasting Eliminator (3E). Purple Mountain estimates it can sell 10,000 copies of 3E for $4,000 each. Purple Mountain wants to earn this $40,000,000 revenue; but unfortunately, 3E is a much more complex product than 3P. Using its present development pattern, Purple Mountain estimates the development cost at $10,000,000, with only one chance in four that it will succeed in developing an acceptable product.

Clearly, if Purple Mountain wishes to get into the Eliminator market, it will either need to develop a larger market or adopt a new development pattern. To develop a larger market, it may have to add features to 3E, which can either increase its cost or reduce its chances of successful development unless a more effective pattern is adopted.

3.2.5   Choosing a point in pattern space

Figure 3-1 captures the essence of the lessons of these five case studies. Given informed, effective management, an organization chooses its software cultural pattern based on two factors:

1.   the demands of its customers or potential customers

2.   the demands of the problems it's trying to solve

An organization need not change in response to these demands. Sometimes, it can remain in the same pattern by trading customer demands for problem demands, in either direction.

CASE STUDY F

Suppose Purple Mountain tries to extend the functionality of 3P, but finds that it cannot deliver these extensions without increasing the number of service calls. It can, in effect, make the customers less demanding by such actions as

*   lowering the price of 3P, thus potentially widening the market
*   reducing the service level, such as by charging for calls

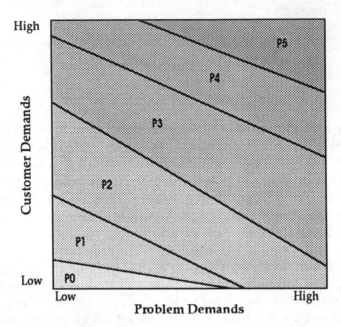

Figure 3–1.   An organization can be pressed to move to a different pattern by changing customer demands, changing problem demands, or both.

Figure 3-2 shows the effect of such moves in the pattern space. If they succeed, these decisions allow Purple Mountain to maintain its traditional development pattern. Of course, if it has strong competitors, lowering prices may not widen its market, and customers may swiftly depart if the service level is lowered.

Here's an example of a trade in the other direction:

CASE STUDY G

Suppose Purple Mountain tries to extend the market for 3P, but finds that it cannot produce a version of 3P at a cost that allows an attractive price. It can, in effect, make the problem less demanding by such actions as

- contracting with a third party to develop the new version
- eliminating difficult-to-implement functions from the require-ments

Again, these decisions, if successful, allow Purple Mountain to retain its development pattern (see Figure 3-3). Of course, its chosen third party may be no better at developing 3P than it is, and customers may not be forthcoming if functionality is less than a competitor provides.

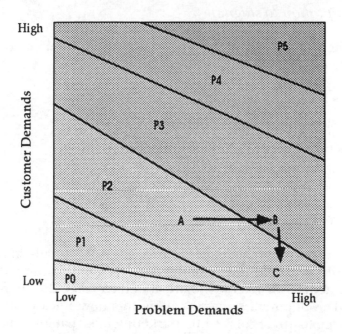

Figure 3–2.   An organization can retain its pattern (A in Pattern 2) in response to increased problem demands (B) by reducing customer demands (C).

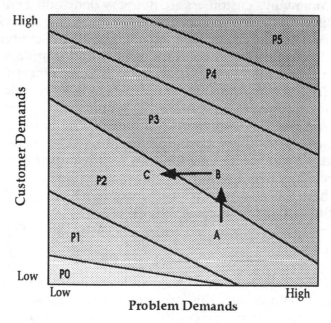

Figure 3–3.   An organization can retain its pattern (A in Pattern 2) in response to increased customer demands (B) by reducing problem demands (C).

3.2.6   The temptation to stagnate

In the end, then, a development organization may be able to remain in its present pattern for a long time if

1.   customers are not demanding

2.   problems are not growing in difficulty

3.   no competitor exists to offer customers alternatives

For example:

> CASE STUDY H
>
> Suppose Purple Mountain issues release 4.0 of 3P. It fails so often that a fix release is issued four months later. Several features that were behind schedule for release 4.0 are added to make the fix release attractive. Development suggests calling this new release 3P 4.01 and giving it free to buyers of 3P 4.0. Marketing kills that idea and relabels it 3P 5.0, with a price tag of $45. Purple Mountain sells 10,000 copies, grossing $450,000 as a reward for doing a lousy job of development.

Clearly, Purple Mountain's customers are not very demanding and the problems are not growing in difficulty, except for internally generated difficulties. Because 3P is the only product of its type, no competitor exists to offer customers alternatives, and consequently there is no incentive for Purple Mountain to improve its software development. Indeed, there is a clear incentive for it to get worse, so the customers will be grateful for each new fix release.

You may not approve morally of Purple Mountain's decision to become a less controlled software development organization. I certainly don't. But you'd better accept the fact that this sort of degeneration occurs all the time. Lacking outside demands, few software organizations improve their development practices out of purely moral motivation. Quality may be free in the long run, but in the short run, there will always be a cost barrier to making the transition.

Consider the case of another software product:

> CASE STUDY I
>
> Cloud City Software has a product with a dominant (ninety percent) market share. People buy this product because they recognize the name, and because they want compatibility with their colleagues who have already bought the product. In a meeting to discuss improvements to their software development process, the Vice President of

Marketing actually said, "We have the dominant product in the industry. Why would we want to change *anything*?" His argument carried the day.

Without clear business reasons to "jump the hump," Cloud City allowed its development practices to stagnate or in some ways even deteriorate. When a formidable competitor appeared on the scene, the Marketing Vice President suddenly demanded development process improvements. Given this motivation, Cloud City invested a lot of their surplus cash in the effort, but in the two and one-half years it took to shape up development, its competitor snatched away 47 percent of the market. In a competitive industry, short-term stagnation leads to long-term ruin.

3.3 Opening Patterns to Information

One of the reasons Cloud City Software couldn't revitalize its development process in a hurry was that a culture is a self-sustaining pattern that has remarkable powers of resistance to change. A great deal of that resistance derives from the thinking patterns themselves, which tend to be closed to ideas coming from outside the culture.

3.3.1 Circular argument

The principal device for closing a culture to information is the *circular argument*. For instance, consider these classics from American cultural history:

√   Women can't run a marathon without injuring themselves.
Therefore, don't allow women to run marathons for their own protection.
Therefore, never find out what women are capable of doing.

√   Members of an ethnic group aren't capable of learning much.
Therefore, don't waste money on schools for them.
Therefore, never find out what they are capable of learning.

Such circularities are repeated every day in the software business. They ensure that managers never find out what other patterns are capable of doing for their organizations. Some years ago, I helped a client make the transition from Pattern 2 to Pattern 3. The transition was necessary because they were producing telephone equipment that had to have down time of no more than one hour in forty years! They were so successful in achieving their goal that their development manager published an account of the process.[4] I was extremely pleased to have this written account because I hoped to use it as a guide for other organizations making a similar transition.

The very first time I showed the article to a Pattern 2 manager (in a beverage distributing company), he asserted, "That would never work here."

"Why not," I asked. "It should be quite straightforward. After all, their problems were *much* harder than yours."

"Their problems *couldn't* have been as hard as ours."

"Why not? You don't even have on-line systems, let alone systems that have to respond in real time."

"Even so, their problems couldn't have been as hard as ours because we could never get that kind of performance on *our* problems."

3.3.2   Classic software circle

In case you think that his reaction was an exception, I should tell you that I tried using the article the same way three more times. Each time, I got the same reaction. Not being a complete fool, I stopped using the article and tried finding another way to break this classic software circle:

√   We're doing the best possible job of software development.
Therefore, if other people are doing better, their problems must be easier.
Therefore, we never find out what other people are capable of doing in software development.

Such circles close the organization to information from the outside, and are found in examples such as this:

√   Consultants are carriers of bad software development practices.
Therefore, keep the consultants isolated from the other developers.
Therefore, never find out what other consultants know about software development.

They also render the organization impervious to information from inside:

√   Our superhero is infallible.
Therefore, if a project fails, it must be the fault of outsiders.
Therefore, never look for ways in which our superhero may be fallible.

The outsiders are typically users, maintainers, operators, or consultants. The superhero varies from pattern to pattern. In Pattern 0, it is the users themselves; in Pattern 1, the programmers; in Pattern 2, the managers.

√   Our superhero knows more about building software than anyone.
Therefore, if we have to investigate alternative ways of building software, assign the task to the superhero.

Therefore, never discover ways to develop software that our superhero doesn't understand.

3.3.3   The key to opening circular reasoning

None of these false cultural images is easily refuted except over a long period of time in which evidence accumulates in spite of the best efforts of the culture. The key question for opening these circular arguments is this:

Is your rate of success okay?

Unfortunately, organizations in those patterns that need it most (Patterns 0, 1, and 2) don't ordinarily keep records on their success rate. They also don't keep details on their failures and what they cost. As Boehm observes,

To date, there have been no studies establishing a well-defined productivity range for management quality. One reason for this is that poorly-managed projects rarely collect much data on their experiences.[5]

The closure of cultures to information means that the first step in breaking a cultural pattern is to open it to information. In our consulting, Dani and I use a variety of tactics to start the information flowing:

1.   Establish a system of technical reviews so that many people can see what's really happening inside their product.

2.   Send a few influential people to public seminars where they can hear about what other people do in face-to-face interaction, which is much harder to deny than ideas contained in articles.

3.   Ask upper management the scientific question, "How would you spot a failure (or poor quality)?" Once we have their own definition, we take cases, one by one, and apply it.

3.3.4   Developing trust

Of course, to be able to do any of these things, you have to have established some level of trust; otherwise any sign of failure is used to measure and punish people. Patterns 0 through 2 are *power* hierarchies, each based on lack of trust:

- Pattern 0. We don't trust anyone but ourselves.
- Pattern 1. We don't trust managers.
- Pattern 2. We don't trust programmers.

Patterns 3 through 5, however, are *trust* hierarchies, which is why they are able to improve themselves. Higher numbered patterns do not represent increased maturity, but do represent movement from more closed to more open systems:

- Pattern 0 is only as open as the individual is open.
- Pattern 1 is open to exchange of information between developer and user.
- Pattern 2 is open to information from the manager to developer and user.
- Pattern 3 is open in all directions for information about the *product.*
- Pattern 4 is open in all directions for information about the *process.*
- Pattern 5 is open in all directions for information about the *culture.*

Moving to more open patterns depends on *creating the subsystems that you can trust.* Why does trust work? The ability to trust subsystems reduces the amount of communication needed to get the job done because the amount of checking up is reduced.

Since trust reduces the need for data, increasing data flow is characteristic of a development system in trouble. Such a system lacks the information capacity to handle anything but the current crisis:

√   We're in deep trouble (because we don't know enough about building software).
Therefore, we don't have time to spend learning about how to develop software.
Therefore, we never learn how to stay out of deep trouble the next time.

If you have time to read this book, of course, you must not be caught in this, the most vicious cycle of all.

3.4   Helpful Hints and Suggestions

1. A great barrier to introducing change is *inertia from past success.* Inertia is like mass. The more success we carry over from the past, the more our past strength becomes our present weakness. For instance,

- Reusable code improves productivity, but may shut out improved solutions.
- Large volumes of code show that our services were valued, but may prove difficult to maintain.
- Practices that have evolved through much experience may be so firmly anchored that nothing new has a chance to be given a fair trial.

- People's attitudes toward specific ideas may be influenced by past experiences in somewhat different environments.

2. Regardless of what pattern we are trying to attain, there are three tasks we must accomplish. These tasks must be accomplished by any culture, as you can verify by studying the Bible or any religious guidebook to living.

- Present: Keep performing today; don't slip backward. ("Give us this day our daily bread.")
- Past: Maintain the foundation from yesterday; don't forget what you know. ("Honor thy father and thy mother.")
- Future: Build the next pattern to guide the change process. ("Where there is no vision, the people perish.")

Each of the six software subcultures works to maintain its past and present, but until you reach the higher patterns, this work is so difficult that the future gets left behind.

3. What is necessary to move from one pattern to another depends also on which move you are making. Here's a snapshot of what specific learnings are required for each move, and where they may come from:

- Pattern 0 to 1: Humility, produced by exposure to what others are doing
- Pattern 1 to 2: Ability, produced by technical training and experience
- Pattern 2 to 3: Stability, produced by quality software management
- Pattern 3 to 4: Agility, produced by tools and techniques
- Pattern 4 to 5: Adaptability, produced by human development

3.5 Summary

√ Each pattern has its characteristic way of thinking and communicating.

√ The first essential element in changing a pattern is changing thinking patterns that are characteristic of that pattern.

√ Thinking patterns consist of models, and new models can be used to change thinking patterns.

√ In the less stable patterns of 0 to 2, models need not be precise, but merely convincing. Indeed, precise models wouldn't make any sense without first establishing stability.

√   Models help to

- discover differences in thinking, before they have adverse consequences
- work on ideas as a group to facilitate team building
- understand the reasons for various project practices
- record communication so that newcomers can get productive much faster
- maintain a record that can be used to improve the processes for the next time
- be creative because projects are never routine

√   Before you set about choosing a better pattern, always ask, "Is our present pattern good enough?"

√   The pattern you choose depends on a trade-off between organizational demands, customer demands, and problem demands. These trade-offs can be represented by choosing a point in pattern space.

√   There is always a temptation for a software organization to stagnate by not choosing a new pattern, but instead by reducing customer demands or problem demands.

√   The process of recognizing that a new pattern is needed is hindered by circular arguments that close the organization to the information it needs.

√   The key to opening circular reasoning is asking, "Is your rate of success okay?" Such thinking, however, tends to prevent this question from even being asked.

√   Lack of trust tends to keep this key question from being answered truthfully, so that organizational change often begins with actions for developing trust.

3.6   Practice

1.   Recall an earlier question concerning this idea: "If the way you now produce and maintain software is wholly satisfactory, don't work on changing it; work on maintaining it. If your customers are happy, it would be foolish to change." Describe cycles your organization uses that prevent it from knowing "if the way you now produce and maintain software is wholly satisfactory."

2.   What are some ways your organization employs to reduce customer demands? What are some ways it reduces problem demands?

3.   Vicious circles are not confined to information. A lock-on occurs when a circular pattern of cause and effect reinforces the current state, which would otherwise be quite arbitrary. For instance, a country locks on to the "proper" driving side of the road. England locked on to the left side, while France locked on to the right side. If you drive on the right in England, the consequences quickly convince you to conform to the locked-on local practice. In other words, when you try to change, forces are triggered that tend to counteract the change.

There are many examples of lock-ons that tend to hold a software organization in its present pattern. We will explore many of them in this book after we develop some techniques for modeling and analyzing them. Before reading on, try to identify some lock-ons in your own organization's pattern, along with the forces that keep them in place.

Part II
Patterns of Managing

Patterns of software culture don't just happen. They arise from the nature of software itself interacting with the nature of human beings. In particular, they arise from the struggles of human beings to control the software process.

In the following chapters, we'll see how each pattern arises from a particular human model of how processes are controlled. We'll learn how to describe those models and analyze them for their consequences, particularly for the instabilities to which they are subject. Then we'll expose several of the most common types of instability found in software organizations—how they work and what their consequences are. Finally, we'll study the types of control actions managers use in their attempts to reduce that instability, including those actions that succeed and those that actually make the situation worse.

4

Control Patterns for Management

Without deviation, progress is not possible.
—Frank Zappa

It should be apparent by now that this is a self-help book. If you are not completely satisfied with the pattern you use to develop and maintain software, and if you can imagine that another pattern would be better, then this book is for you. For example, you may be at point A in Figure 4-1 and want to solve more difficult problems (point B); perhaps you are implementing a network for the first time. Or you may be at point D and need to reduce the number of failures (point E); perhaps your software is now going to be burned into ROM. Or you may be at point F and faced with creeping increases in problem difficulty and customer demands (point G).

Or, if you *are* satisfied with your present position (S), this book can show you how to stay satisfied in the face of disasters waiting to happen. In any case, you are concerned with control, and this chapter is about how each pattern has its characteristic pattern of control.

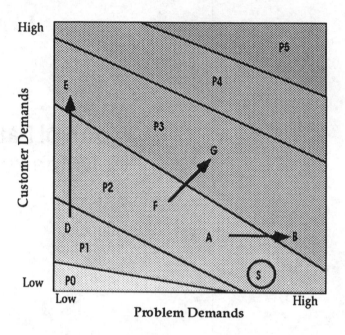

Figure 4–1.   This book is about moving from one pattern to another (A to B, D to E, F to G), or about ensuring that you remain where you are (S).

4.1   Shooting at Moving Targets

According to Humphrey, most organizations today are found in Pattern 1 or Pattern 2. They are there because their problem demands and customer demands do not require them to be elsewhere. When one set of these demands changes, however, these organizations begin to feel the pain. You can notice this happening because they tend to experience the classical cycle of grief.[1]

Their first response to control the pain is usually denial—controlling the information so they don't notice. When denial fails, they may blame others, because people generally prefer familiarity to comfort or efficiency. When blaming fails, they may try to remain where they are by trading off one set of demands against another. If trade-offs fail, however, they may reluctantly decide that they must accept a new pattern to retain control.

When do these demands change? The critical factor is how closely the success of software systems is tied to the success of the organization. An insurance company, for instance, may survive for decades with a Pattern 1 or 2 software organization—until one of its competitors manages to offer an on-line service to independent agents. A software company, on the other hand, may have to meet new customer demands almost daily, as competitors bombard the market with irresistible enhancements.

Aside from these outside influences, there is always the slow but steady growth of customer sophistication. Just think of the word processor you bought five years ago, versus what you can buy today. To see this slow increase in demand, compare the way you developed software five years ago with the way you do it today. For one reason or another, software quality and productivity are *moving targets*.

When teaching someone to shoot at a moving target, you cannot give instructions about which direction to shoot, because the direction is constantly changing. Instead, you must give general instructions about aiming guns, instructions that can then be applied to a wide variety of moving targets. That's why the study of patterns of software control starts with the question, What is needed to control *anything?*

4.2 Aggregate Control Model

One general approach to shooting at moving targets is the technique of *aggregation*.[2] Aggregate control is like shooting with a shotgun or, more precisely, with shrapnel. If you simply send more bullets flying through the sky in sufficiently random directions, you will increase your chances of hitting a target, no matter how it is moving.

4.2.1   Aggregation in the software industry as a whole

The aggregate approach to software engineering says roughly to be sure of getting a good product, start a large number of projects and choose the one that produces the best product. Indeed, if we look at the United States software industry, this is not a bad description of some of our successes. For example, there are now three Macintosh word processors that I think are reasonably good. But how many Macintosh word processor *projects* have been initiated in order to produce these three good *products*? I personally know of 14, and there are probably 140 that died before they got to my attention.

Is this a reasonable strategy? Perhaps not for the small, efficient Swiss, but from the point of view of the software *industry* in a large, rich country like the United States, aggregation is not as dumb a strategy as it first sounds.

4.2.2   Aggregation in a single organization

From the viewpoint of an individual software company, aggregation may be a useful way to ensure success in special circumstances. For instance, companies building life-critical systems have developed two or three independent programs, each of whose output is compared with the others. This redundancy ensures a higher level of reliability than they could be assured with one project alone, and is worth the extra cost.

Aggregation is most commonly used when purchasing software. Out of several products considered, you choose the best for your purposes. If your selection procedure is at all sensible, you should wind up with a better product than if you only considered one. Software salespeople, of course, are working hard to see that your selection procedure is not sensible.

Sometimes the use of aggregation is not fully intentional. Pattern 2 organizations frequently employ unintentional *serial* aggregation. When the first attempt to build a system doesn't turn out well, a second project is started. If the second doesn't turn out well, either, the organization may actually return to the first, now accepting its poor quality as the best of a bad lot. Other times, the unintentional aggregation is *parallel.*

For instance, one of my clients started three linkage editor projects in an attempt to get one editor that was fast (X), one that was compact (Y), and one that was full-featured (Z). As it turned out, editor Y was faster, more compact, and had all the features of X and Z, so it was kept and the others were discarded.

In general, however, this type of direct aggregation is probably too costly for all software work. A Pattern 1 organization may get a better sales analysis report by assigning the task to ten independent programmers and choosing the best program, but it's unlikely that any consultant could sell that technique to company management.

4.2.3   Natural selection in a Pattern 1 organization

Pattern 1 organizations do make great use of redundancy, but not in this obvious way. For example, one of the ways a Pattern 1 organization improves its productivity is through the random diffusion of useful software tools. In this pattern, we don't find an effective centralized tool development group, nor do we find an integrated effort at tool evaluation or distribution. Tools simply diffuse from one programmer or team to another more or less by accidental personal interaction.

In an aircraft engine company, for example, a pool of 61 programmers supported the engineers, one on one. I surveyed the use of tools and found that each of these programmers had at least one special job control procedure for running test traces of FORTRAN programs. In all, there were 27 different trace procedures. The most popular procedure was used by 12 programmers.

My survey probably biased the diffusion process. One of the programmers decided to redo the survey 14 months later and found that the number of procedures was down to 17. Twelve old procedures had disappeared from use, to be replaced by others. Two new variants of old procedures had appeared. The most popular procedure (now different from the former leader) had 22 users.

This Pattern 1 use of the aggregate strategy is analogous to natural selection, the process whereby variant species arise and are tested in the give and take of the natural environment.[3] Natural selection guarantees improved fitness for any environment, but it is *very* expensive and slow. But, then, Pattern 1 organizations are often rich and laid back.

4.2.4   Why aggregation is popular in Pattern 2 organizations

Pattern 2 organizations are also heavy users of aggregation. Paradoxically, aggressive Pattern 2 managers often destroy some of the "natural" aggregate strategies with their enthusiastic, but ill-informed, interventions to improve efficiency.

The Information Systems Department of a manufacturer of packaging materials represents a typical Pattern 2 organization. In discussions with its management, I found the following examples of aggregation as a management strategy:

- The managers were vaguely aware of the natural selection of tools, as in a Pattern 1 organization. They seemed a bit embarrassed to admit that this "uncontrolled" activity took place, and assured us that they planned to create a centralized tool group "as soon as the current crisis was over."
- When one project was not ready on time (that is, at its fourth rescheduled date), they determined "which component was to blame," and assigned two of their "best programmers" to bring this component "back into line."
- When one programmer quit "without warning" to return to college, they assigned another. They saw nothing unusual about this, because "programmers are always unpredictable." When we interviewed the newly matriculated student, she told us she had been accepted at the college in May. She left her job in September.
- One current project was to build software to analyze telephone patterns and billing on their centralized phone system. This project was more than two years late when a salesman from a software company visited. A week later, the salesman returned and walked out with an order for a telephone analysis package. The in-house project was killed and the people reassigned. Nobody complained.

As these examples show, aggregation is a frequent strategy in Pattern 2. Aggregation puts little burden on management, because it's a way to get satisfactory products without knowing much about what you're doing.

4.2.5   Aggregation in other patterns

Aggregation is a universal strategy, and no pattern is without its examples of the use of this technique. In the move to Pattern 3, however, we begin to see a more conscious use of aggregation and explicit manipulation of aggregation to aid in quality improvement. For instance, a medium-sized, full-service bank created a product evaluation group that purchased multiple candidates for various PC software functions. They subjected them to comprehensive field trials, then chose the one or two top candidates to be required or recommended.

In another case, a telemarketing company was having costly problems with intermittent and unpredictable system failures with its network. When rigorous analysis failed to reveal the source of the problem, the company's managers offered a reward for any programmer or operator who could catch an example while it was happening and manually institute a trapping procedure. In a few days, they captured more than twenty documented examples, from which their analysts were able to isolate the problem to one hardware component. When the vendor replaced that component, the problem disappeared, though they never did understand why.

This last example was pure hacking—trying anything at random until something worked—but it was harnessed by wise management for maximum effectiveness. Hacking is the ultimate aggregate strategy, and there's no way to do without it from time to time. It appears in all patterns (with different frequencies), though some patterns seem to view its use with shame. Somehow, they have a feeling that they could do better by improving their aim *before* they pull the trigger—and, in general, I'd have to agree.

4.3   Patterns and Their Cybernetic Control Models

Whereas aggregation is like shooting with a shotgun, *feedback control* is like shooting with a rifle. Although feedback control has existed for centuries as a practical engineering model,[4] cybernetics first studied feedback control explicitly in order to improve the firing of guns at moving targets in World War II.[5,6] Cybernetics, the science of aiming, is something that every software engineer needs to understand.

4.3.1   *The system to be controlled: The focus of Patterns 0 and 1*

The cybernetic model starts with the idea of a system to be controlled; it has inputs and outputs (Figure 4-2). For a system that produces software, the outputs are the software, plus "Other Outputs," which may include all sorts of things that are not the direct goal of the system, such as

- greater competence with a programming language
- software tools developed while doing the intended software
- stronger, or weaker, development teams
- stress, pregnancies, influenza, happiness
- anger toward management

- respect for management
- thousands of failure reports
- personnel appraisals

The inputs are of three principal types (the 3 R's):

- Requirements
- Resources
- Randomness

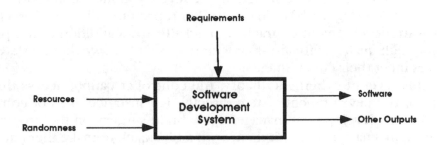

Figure 4–2.   The cybernetic model of a software development system to be controlled, which is also the Pattern 1 model of the entire process of software development.

A system's behavior is governed by the formula:

Behavior depends on both state and input.

Thus, control depends not only on what we put in (Requirements and Resources) and what gets in some other way (Randomness), but also on what's going on internally (the state).

Figure 4-2 represents the entire model of software development as understood by Pattern 1 organizations. In effect, it says, "Tell us what you want, give us some resources, and don't bother us." A bit more precisely, it says,

a.   "Tell us what you want (and don't change your mind)."
b.   "Give us some resources (and keep giving whenever we ask)."
c.   "Don't bother us (that is, eliminate all randomness)."

These are the abc's of Pattern 1 software development, and by listening for these statements, you can reliably identify a Pattern 1 organization.

If you drop the (a) statement above (the external requirements), you get the identifying phrases for Pattern 0, which already knows what it wants, without help, thank you. Figure 4-2 can thus be transformed to the Pattern 0 diagram by deleting the Requirements arrow, thus isolating the system from direct external control. Of course, random inputs, or cutting off resources, can disturb those individuals who are their own software development system.

4.3.2   The controller: The focus of Pattern 2

To get more quality (value) from your software development with this Pattern 1 model, you would have to use the aggregate approach—in effect pumping more resources into the development system. One way to do this would be to initiate several such development systems and let each do whatever it does best. If you want more control of *each* system, however, you must connect it to some sort of *controller* (Figure 4-3). The controller represents all your efforts to keep the software development on track, and is Pattern 2's addition to the problem of getting high-quality software. In effect, it says, "I'll *make* those #$!$&*# programmers meet their commitments!"

At this level of cybernetic theory, the controller cannot access the internal state of the development system directly. For instance, it's not considered kosher for the development manager to do brain surgery on the programmers to make them smarter, or to hit them with a blackjack to make them more motivated. So, in order to be able to control, the controller must be able to change the internal state indirectly through the inputs (the lines coming out of the controller and into the system). Examples of such change to the programming staff include

- offering training courses to make them smarter
- buying them tools to make them seem smarter
- hiring Harvard graduates to make them smarter (on the average)
- offering cash incentives to make them more motivated
- offering more interesting assignments to make them more motivated
- firing Berkeley graduates to make the others more motivated (on the average)

The control actions are added to the system's *uncontrolled* inputs (the Randomness), either by changing requirements or changing resources. Notice that no matter what the controller does to these inputs, there is still randomness coming in, which simply represents all those external things that the controller cannot totally control. An example of randomness is everyone on the project coming down with the flu. Although the controller has some control over the input of flu virus (such as paying for flu shots), it is inconceivable that anyone would ever be able to guarantee that no productive time will be lost to viral infections—regardless of memos to the contrary. Some Pattern 2 managers find this thought most frustrating.

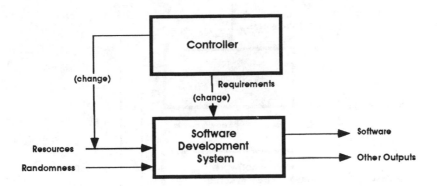

Figure 4–3.   A model of a software development system controller (Pattern 2).

4.3.3   Feedback control: The focus of Pattern 3

An effective method of limiting losses due to flu is to send people home at the first sign of symptoms. The Pattern 2 controller pictured in Figure 4-3 cannot do this, however, because it has no knowledge of what the system is actually doing. A more versatile and effective model of control is the *Feedback Control Model* shown in Figure 4-4. In this model, which represents the Pattern 3 concept of control, the controller can make measurements of performance (the lines coming out of the system and into the controller) and use them as an aid in determining its next control actions.

But feedback measurements and control actions are not enough for effective control. We know that *behavior depends on both state and input.* In order for the control actions to be effective, the Pattern 3 controller must possess *models* to *connect* the state and input with the behavior—models of what "depends" means for this system.

Overall, for feedback control to operate, the system of control must have

- an image of a *desired* (or D) state
- the ability to observe the *actual* (or A) state
- the ability to compare state A and state D for differences
- the ability to act on the system to bring A closer to D

4.4   Engineering Management

A characteristic Pattern 2 mistake is to equate "controller" with "manager." A dangerous tendency of Pattern 2 managers is to think, "If I'm not actively issuing

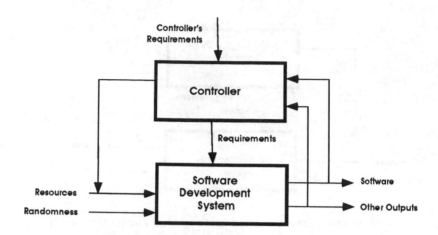

Figure 4–4.   The feedback model of a software development system requires feedback of information about the system's performance, plus requirements for the controller to compare with that information. This is the model that distinguishes Pattern 3 from Patterns 0, 1, and 2. It is also used by Patterns 4 and 5.

orders, things are not in control." That's why they're always exhibiting the First Law of Bad Management:

When something isn't working, do more of it.

Managers certainly are controllers, but they are not the *only* controllers. In any real development project, there are controllers at every level, and everyone is acting as a controller some of the time over some of the work. To the extent that non-managers—or small-m managers—are controlling their work, the (big-M) Managers' jobs are easier. They can *trust* the work to get done, so they have less need to communicate. And, when managers don't manage their work at all, the Managers can no longer trust the process, which makes their jobs impossible.

4.4.1   The job of management

In the Pattern 3 model, managing is essentially a controller's job. To manage an engineering project by feedback control, the manager needs to

- plan what should happen
- observe what significant things are really happening
- compare the observed with the planned
- take actions needed to bring the actual closer to the planned (see Figure 4-5)

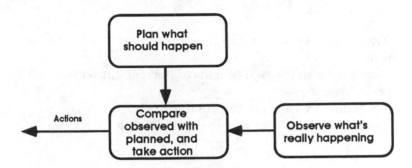

Figure 4–5.   In Pattern 3, management's job is to control a process that produces a desired product. Management plans what should happen, then observes what actually happens. Management's actions are designed on the basis of the difference between the planned and the actual results, then are fed back into the process being controlled.

A big part of the manager's job is ensuring that each of these parts is present, because if any is missing, the project doesn't have feedback control. Let's look at a common example of each one's being absent from a Pattern 2 software project, when the project's managers thought they were in control.

4.4.2   No plan for what should happen

The first phase of Project Alert was scheduled to be delivered to beta test sites on May 15; when May 15 arrived, the project manager ordered the existing development version shipped. When one of the team leaders objected that several key functions had not yet been implemented, the project manager replied, "Look, as long as we've not written down any requirements, they'll never know the difference."

This is a regression under pressure to Pattern 0 thinking: "We are the true customer, because we are omniscient." Although it's true that if there is no requirements document, anything you build matches the requirements document, it's not true that anything you build meets the customers' requirements. There is a world of difference between *requirements* and a requirements *document*.[7] In this case, it happens, the customers *did* notice.

4.4.3   Failure to observe what significant things are really happening

Project Est used sophisticated project management software to track every software component in the project. For a component to be marked complete in the database, it had to pass a review. So every time a team said their code was complete, the managers held a review.

Here were some typical comments from one of those reviews:

- "The team has put in 235 hours, compared with the scheduled 180 hours."
- "Four weeks of elapsed time have been spent, versus 3.5 weeks scheduled."
- "There are 437 lines of executable code."
- "There are 63 lines of non-executable code."

Notice that none of these observations are about the *quality* (the value) of the work, but only about its *quantity*—which is not surprising, as none of the managers had taken the time to inspect what the code actually did, nor were they qualified to do so. To their credit, the managers did interview the team leader, who was qualified to understand the code. She replied, "Yes, I think it's a good job. I know the programmers worked very hard on it."

This case is typical of a Pattern 2 organization that is trying to become a Pattern 3. These managers have learned that Pattern 3 managers depend heavily on observations of the true state of the project before taking actions, but they do not yet have a feeling for what makes an observation useful. Thus, although this review considered many observations, none of them had much to do with the *quality* of what they're trying to control.

For instance, if the managers are trying to control "total time spent," the 235 hours spent on the component *is* a significant observation. On the other hand, it tells little, if anything, about whether the work was completed or not.

It's easy to see, though, how the managers could make such a mistake. If 180 hours were scheduled and only 10 hours were worked, that might indicate the work was not completed. But it might also indicate the programmer had created a very clever design, for we know that 18:1 variations in programming time for the same component are not at all unusual.[8,9]

On the other hand, a *large* amount of time spent compared with an estimate may indicate that the work is completed, but in fact is more likely to indicate that the programmers experienced some unexpected difficulty—which, if anything, might make us suspect that the component was not finished correctly.

Or, if the managers were attempting to control project morale, then the team leader's remark about how hard the programmers worked might be a significant observation. Under the circumstances, however, it simply contributes to the false impression that this all too typical "review" had something to do with controlling software quality—a typical mistake in struggling to convert from Pattern 2 to Pattern 3.

4.4.4   Failure to compare the observed with the planned

When Project Gatsby—a comprehensive accounting package—was scheduled for delivery, the system test group announced to the managers that the system had successfully completed a volume test of 37,452 test cases, most of which had been generated by a test data generator. Unfortunately, the managers failed to ask the system testers how many of the 37,452 test outputs matched the planned outputs. Management was so impressed with the sheer volume of this effort that it not only ordered the system delivered, but told the Marketing Department to put the number "37,452 test cases" in its advertisements.

Pattern 3 managers would have been suspicious of the large number of test cases, because, for instance, at even one minute per test, it would take more than 15 weeks of full-time effort to examine 37,452 outputs. Pattern 3 managers know that control is not possible unless actual output is *compared* with planned output.

After the system had been angrily rejected by its first customers, I was called in to "help with the quality problem." I discovered that the outputs were sampled. A total of 136 samples had been carefully inspected, and of these, 43 were found to contain errors and were sent back to the programmers for fixing. After fixing, 19 were still wrong, so they were sent back for another attempt. This time, only 6 were still wrong, so the system testing was declared finished.

When I asked why they had run the other 37,316 tests, the test leader told me, "We wanted to see how the system held up under volume testing. It was really solid. We were able to run the entire test without a single system crash." Further questioning revealed that most of the 136 samples had been cases that originally crashed the system.

You can draw your own conclusion about how many of the other cases were correct. We'll never know unless the bankruptcy court releases the company's papers to the public.

4.4.5   Not taking action to bring the actual closer to the planned

Project MNQ was already running late when component C37—the system error handler—was put through a code review.[10] The proper functioning of C37 was essential to every other function in MNQ, but the review revealed that its code was full of serious errors. Moreover, its design was clumsy and prone to error when code was modified. The review's conclusion was that C37 should be scrapped, redesigned, and recoded.

The project manager, however, said, "We've got six months invested in C37, and we can't afford a six-month delay at this late date." As a result, the faulty C37 was used, which consistently caused trouble with the testing of every other component in the system. Ten months later, after the project manager had been fired, the new project manager scrapped C37 and assigned a crew to build a new one. They finished in less than two months, and there were essentially no more problems with error handling.

The first project manager thought the project was under feedback control because they were conducting technical reviews. But if a manager is not willing to take an action that will result in a six-month delay, what's the point of reviewing a piece of work that will take six months to rebuild? Without the possibility of controller action as a result of information from the code review, the review is a sham; it's a pseudo-review. If the project manager had no intention of acting when the information said to act, then the project would have been better off saving the time spent in doing the pseudo-review.

When top management has decreed that an organization will move from Pattern 2 to Pattern 3, the middle managers often conform in appearance only. Typically, they gather information, then don't use it. Upper managers (who are also stuck in Pattern 2 mentality) often label this behavior "malicious compliance." Usually, though, the middle managers simply don't understand, having been given no training in Pattern 3 thinking.

4.5   From Computer Science to Software Engineering

What would it take for you to do a better job than these failed Pattern 2 software managers? Of course, you have to have many personal qualifications, but before we get into those, let's simply look at the inputs you'll need. No matter how clever you may be, the feedback model says you can't successfully control anything for very long without information. Figure 4-6 shows what information has to be added to Figure 4-5 to make your job as the manager possible:

- What kind of product is wanted?
- By what processes can such a product be made?
- What's actually being made, by what process?

To answer the third question without speculating, you must have these two conditions:

- There must be *visible* evidence of how the process is going on.
- The process must be *stable* enough so that the evidence is meaningful.

These conditions are generally *not* met in Pattern 2 organizations, which is why they remain Pattern 2 organizations. Armed with these elements, you have the makings of a successful software engineer, consultant, or manager. All you have to do in out-of-control situations is look for which of them is missing. Ideally, you'll be able to see that they're missing *before* harmful actions are taken. Unfortunately, the Pattern 2 managers in the four cases just cited were unable to do that, resulting in typical Pattern 2 failures.

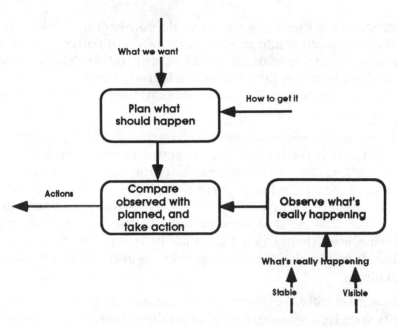

Figure 4–6.   In order to plan, management must know what is wanted and how to get it. In order to be observable, the product must be both stable and visible.

I'm not sure, in the four cases, why the managers were unable to do the right thing. In order to control software, you do need to understand software development processes, and some of them certainly did not understand the simple fundamentals of feedback control. But understanding is not enough. Quality software development does not simply require a science, such as computer science or cybernetics, but a *discipline*, an *engineering* discipline:

> *the application of scientific principles to practical ends as the design, construction, and operation of efficient and economical structures, equipment, and systems*

If you want to be a software *engineer*, rather than simply a software theoretician, you have to master yourself well enough to be able to apply your understanding in taking action. As Native Americans say, you must be able to "walk your talk." Although this volume will often emphasize the understanding needed, rather than the self-mastery, I'll remind you from time to time that it always should be there, as the foundation for everything else.[11]

4.6   Helpful Hints and Suggestions

1.   The essence of a pattern is what it can do consistently. Although an organization can turn out single products in a different pattern than the overall organization is capable of using, it will never produce one at a lower level. A Pattern 3 organization never turns out Pattern 2 products. If it tries to do so, the people are demoralized, the costs are higher, and the management is discredited.

2.   When trying to introduce change in software engineering practices (or any practices, for that matter), it's often better to work by addition, rather than subtraction. Instead of continually emphasizing what people are doing wrong, emphasize what they are doing right so that they will do more of it. Also, point out when or how things are missing, but not too many at one time. You may need to say something bad about their present state in order to motivate them to change at all, but don't overwhelm them with their sins. It only makes them feel powerless and unable to make any creative changes.

3.   Most writers on software quality equate errors with lack of quality, and lack of quality with lack of control. But errors don't mean you're out of control. You can set the level of errors that the customer can accept without loss of significant value, then control for that level. If you can't set and achieve your criteria, however, then you're out of control.

4.   Feedback control is often called "error control," because it is through the errors (deviations from requirements) that you get the information to control the system. Indeed, when there are no errors, the Pattern 3 control mechanisms remain dormant. (As Frank Zappa says, "Without deviation, progress is not possible.") In that case, an outside observer would have trouble distinguishing a Pattern 3 from a Pattern 2 organization. Moreover, the Pattern 3 managers would have difficulty telling if they were in control or if their sources of error control information had dried up.

5.   Figure 4-5 is a key to feedback control. The feeding back of action is, of course, the origin of the term "feedback," but Pattern 2 thinkers are often befuddled when they first encounter this diagram. They think the action arrow points in the wrong direction. When the direction of this arrow becomes intuitive, they are on their way to becoming Pattern 3 managers.

6.   Although feedback control is generally elegant and efficient, remember that you always have aggregate control available if you're willing to pay the price. Last week a client of mine found a project dead in the water because somehow their configuration control system had destroyed the latest version of a critical routine. Everyone had to wait until the routine was found or reconstructed, so the project manager told all nine people

to each do whatever they could to find, recover, reconstruct, or otherwise get back the critical routine. Within forty-five minutes, one of the programmers found an "erased" copy on an old disk. With the help of a recovery utility, the project was back at full speed in another fifteen minutes. Although it's true that the other eight programmers "wasted" an hour apiece trying some other method, they couldn't have done anything useful with the time anyway. Besides, there was no way to know in advance whose method was going to work the fastest.

7.   The purpose of this book is not to delve deeply into Patterns 4 and 5, but they are also intimately related to the Feedback Control Model. Roughly, Pattern 4 management applies feedback control not just to the product, but to the process itself. In other words, their "product" is the process. To make Figure 4-6 a picture of Pattern 4 management, we should add an arrow from "Observe" to "Plan."

8.   Pattern 5 management carries this feedback a step further, while preserving what is good about Pattern 4. Feedback control is applied to the entire organization's culture—the environment in which the Pattern 4 managers have to manage. In short, in Pattern 5 we see a recursive nesting of feedback control, at least to three levels of conscious management.

4.7   Summary

√   The Aggregate Control Model tells us that if we're willing to spend enough on redundant solutions, we'll eventually get the system we want. Sometimes this is the most practical way, or the only way we can think of.

√   The Feedback Control Model tries for a more *efficient* way of getting what we want. A controller controls a system based on information about what the system is currently doing. Comparing this information with what is planned for the system, the controller takes actions designed to bring the system's behavior closer to the plan.

√   The job of engineering management is to act as controller in engineering projects. Failures of engineering management can be understood in terms of the Feedback Control Model. Pattern 2 managers often lack this understanding, which often explains why they experience so many low-quality, or failed, projects.

√   Projects can fail when there is no plan for what should happen.

√   Projects can fail when the controller fails to observe what significant things are really happening.

√   Projects can fail when the controller fails to compare the observed with the planned.

√   Projects can fail when the controller cannot or will not take action to bring the actual closer to the planned.

4.8 Practice

1.   The aggregate approach is not always as expensive as it seems at first sight. For instance, developing three redundant systems can improve reliability in life-critical applications, but doesn't it cost three times as much? In practice, the cost of triple redundancy is usually less than double the cost of a single system. Develop at least three reasons for this cost-saving effect.

2.   A "good hack" is one that is done in full consciousness and opens possibilities for improvement. A "bad hack" is one that is done fuzzily and closes possibilities. Give an example from your experience of both a good hack and a bad hack.

3.   Give at least five examples of "Other Outputs" you have seen from a software development project. What information about the project did these "Other Outputs" carry?

4.   Give at least five examples of ways a Pattern 2 manager can make the programming staff "smarter." Give at least five examples of ways to make them more motivated. Discuss what effects these ways can have on the "Other Outputs" of the development process.

5.   Think of a project you know that did not perform satisfactorily. Analyze the management's control actions on that project from the viewpoint of the Feedback Control Model. Did the managers know about feedback control? Did they think they were using it? Were they really?

6.   Quality doesn't mean much if you can't *consistently* get what you need. One measure of a pattern is what size system it can complete successfully, say, ninety-five percent of the time. Plot a graph of this measure for the different patterns. What level would be acceptable in your organization?

7.   Suppose the managers in a Pattern 3 organization suspected that their feedback about the development process was not reliable. Suggest what they might do. (This is the kind of thinking that Pattern 4 managers must do in advance.)

8.   Can the aggregate strategy be applied to the Pattern 4 task of controlling the process itself? Can it be applied to controlling the culture, as in Pattern 5? Explain your answers.

5

Making Explicit Management Models

More software projects have gone awry
for lack of calendar time than for all other
causes combined. Why is this cause
of disaster so common?
—Frederick P. Brooks[1]

To keep software projects from going awry, the controller must have accurate and timely observations about what's currently happening. But that's not enough. The controller also must have an explicit understanding about the *meaning* of those observations. Has the system really gone awry? If so, why? Is it because of lack of calendar time, or something else? This understanding of meaning is what I call the controller's *system models*. To a great extent, this volume is about the role system models play in software engineering.

5.1 Why Things Go Awry

In Figure 4-6, we saw that three kinds of information are needed to make the manager's job possible:

71

- What kind of product is wanted?
- By what processes can such a product be made?
- What's actually being made, by what process?

System models are critical to the last two questions because they affect both what you observe, and what you think about what you observe.

5.1.1 Role of system models

To understand the role of system models, consider an analogous control situation—keeping your automobile running reliably. When there's a click from the engine compartment of your car, the information is accurate and timely, but what does it mean? Here are three possibilities:

1. You don't even hear the click, because you are occupied with more important things.

2. The click sounds ominous to you, but the mechanic knows that it simply means you need to tighten the bolt holding the washer fluid vessel.

3. The click sounds irrelevant to you, but the mechanic knows it means you're about to run out of oil and burn up the engine.

If you do hear the click, both you and the mechanic have the same information. Only the mechanic, however, understands how the engine works and thus can attach appropriate *meaning*. Without the meaning of the click, you don't know the right thing to do in response.

Any software engineering manager needs system models of the software engineering system for the same reason—to know what's important to observe, and what is the right response to new observations. If you overhear a programmer say she found ten faults in one hour, is that important? If it's important, what does it mean? In this chapter, we'll begin our exploration of system models, models that tell us which software clicks are critical, and which can be ignored.

5.1.2 Implicit models

All managers use models to govern their management decisions, but in Pattern 1 and 2 organizations, most of those models are *implicit*. Such managers may never enunciate these models; but by observing their behavior, you can see that they act *as if* the model were true. Here are some examples of common implicit models (beliefs about how the world works) held by Pattern 1 and 2 managers and technical people:

- They will do what I tell them to do.
- They won't do what I don't tell them to do.
- All will go well.
- All will go well unless I have bad luck.
- Most software projects go awry for lack of calendar time.
- If I'm behind schedule, I can add people to make things go faster.
- Bugs occur at random.
- If I tell them not to have bugs, then bugs will be reduced.
- The more pressure, the faster they'll work.
- The customer is trying to make me look bad.
- The customer is out to get something for nothing.
- The customer is a nice guy.
- The vice president is my only customer.
- Managers don't understand programming.
- Managers do understand programming.
- Managers should understand programming.
- Managers shouldn't understand programming.
- Programmers don't understand management.
- Programmers understand management better than most managers.
- Twice as big a system will take twice as long, unless we use twice the people.
- Software development is a sequential process.
- If we find ten faults in one day, we'll find a hundred faults in ten days.
- We'll never find all the faults, so we'll never be done.
- If I can measure it, I can control it.
- If I can't measure it, it's not important.
- Women make better programmers.
- Women are better at maintenance; men are better at design.
- There's no difference in ability between men and women.
- Programmers lose their ability after age thirty.
- Older programmers are more valuable.
- The best programmers do the best job, and I know who they are.
- I know what's going on.
- If things go wrong, there's always somebody to blame.
- If things go right, it's because of good management.
- If things go wrong, it's an act of God.

You may agree or disagree with each of these models, but when they are not explicit, it's difficult to discuss them. And if they can't be discussed, they can't be tested and improved. And if the system models can't be improved, you can't move to a different cultural pattern—or even be sure of staying in your present pattern. That's why in this chapter, we'll introduce a notation for making system models explicit.

5.1.3   Inability to face reality

Many researchers, consultants, and observant software workers have studied the dynamics of software failure, and each has offered at least one explicit model of the process. Perhaps the most influential of these people has been Frederick P. Brooks. Brooks's *The Mythical Man-Month* was one of the first books to make explicit models of why software development is so troublesome. His vivid metaphor of the tar pit has stood the test of time, and Brooks's Law has become one of the Ten Commandments of software development. Because of this familiarity, Brooks's thinking provides compelling examples for exploring how models can be described and interpreted.

Over the years, I have learned much from Fred Brooks. I hope he will not feel I am presuming on our friendship if I take issue with one of his basic models, one that is contained in the quotation heading this chapter. Although it certainly *seems* that way to the harried manager, lack of calendar time is *not* the reason software projects have gone awry, but rather it is merely the reason other failures have been *detected*.

Because Pattern 1 and 2 organizations have lacked meaningful measurements and system models to interpret them, any meaningful measurement they do have takes on exaggerated proportions. There is one benefit of calendar time: It has a meaning that most of us can understand. When the calendar says it's April 15, and the due date is April 15, and the software isn't done, even the dullest manager knows that we've missed our due date!

That's why I would rephrase Brooks's model by saying

Lack of calendar time has forced more failing software projects to face the reality of their failure than all other reasons combined.

And this could be rephrased as

Lack of calendar time has forced more failing software projects to face the incorrectness of their models than all other reasons combined.

5.1.4   Incorrect models

Brooks gives five failure dynamics to support why calendar time seems so important. Each of these failure dynamics is an important model of software engineering, and each failure is based on at least one faulty system model, as explained in brackets below:

1.   Estimating techniques are poorly developed, and are based on the assumption that all will go well.

[Estimating, of course, depends on a model of the process being estimated. "All will go well" is a deep model that underlies many estimating models, especially the implicit ones.]

2.   Estimating techniques confuse effort with progress.

[A common modeling mistake is not distinguishing between two variables that are closely correlated under some circumstances, but not under all circumstances, as are effort and progress. Sometimes more effort means less progress. Other examples of models expressing such a faulty correlation are lines of code written versus progress; orders issued versus effectiveness of management; machine capacity versus tool support.]

3.   Software managers lack the personal effectiveness to be "courteously stubborn" (in Brooks's words).

[This may indeed be a matter of personal effectiveness, but the inability to be courteously stubborn could also arise from a lack of models concerning what to be stubborn about. If you don't think it's important for programmers to be free from interruptions, you're not likely to be stubborn about a work environment that discourages frequent or random interruptions.]

4.   Schedule progress is poorly monitored, partly because we have learned little from other engineering disciplines.

[Brooks implies—and I wholeheartedly agree—that software development is a type of engineering process, so that something could be learned from studying other engineering disciplines. More specifically, what could be learned is that certain system models are general enough to apply to any engineering development process.]

5.   Managers tend to add labor when they recognize a schedule slippage.

[The faulty model believes that more people make things go faster. Brooks offers a different model—the famous Brooks's Law—which I'll discuss below.]

In the years since the publication of *The Mythical Man-Month*, many software organizations have made progress on each of these dynamics of failure. But even when they've mastered *all* of them, they may still be stuck in the tar pit. Five dynamics don't begin to tell the story of software development.

There are dozens of important software system models, each describing at least one dynamic, or combination of behaviors forced by the structure of the model. To take one example, Brooks's mixing of symptom and cause led him to miss a system dynamic that is much more frequently seen today. We could easily argue for this model:

> **More software projects have gone awry for *lack of quality,* which is part of many destructive dynamics, than for all other causes combined.**

In other words, when quality starts to slip, so many dynamic forces are set in motion that most Pattern 1 and 2 managers are overwhelmed. Brooks's title, *The Mythical Man-Month,* is taken from Brooks's Law, which describes how adding man-months late in a project "begins a regenerative cycle which ends in disaster." If we really want to know why "more software projects have gone awry," Brooks's Law points toward the true villain:

> **More software projects have gone awry from management's taking action based on *incorrect system models* than for all other causes combined.**

In other words, it's not any particular dynamic that causes the most problems, but *misunderstanding the model behind the dynamic.*

5.2   Linear Models and Their Fallacies

The big mistake committed most often by software managers is choosing a *linear* model when nonlinear forces are at work. By all accounts, management everywhere seems to make this modeling mistake. One of the most common examples of such linear modeling is the assumption that the same pattern that produced quality small systems will also produce quality large systems.

Software life would certainly be comfortable if this linear model were true. Unfortunately, the difficulty of producing quality systems is exponentially related to system size and complexity, so as software gets bigger and more complex, old patterns quickly become inadequate. In many cases, the old patterns actually exacerbate the problems they are attempting to solve.

The assumption that big is just the same as small, only bigger, is a model—a linear model. I've given this model a name, the *scaling fallacy*. This model is important in software dynamics because the fallacy is held by the great majority of Pattern 2 managers and usually leads managers into software crises.

5.2.1   Additivity fallacies

To understand the importance of nonlinear dynamics, we must start by understanding the difference between linear and nonlinear models. Most of the time, if we don't consciously reflect upon the way we are thinking, we tend to use linear models. In a linear model, $1 + 1 = 2$, rather than 2 + some correction factor. If we get \$1 from Denise and \$1 from Sid, we have \$2. Similarly, if we get a month's worth of code from Denise and a month's code from Sid, we have 2 months' worth of code.

It's easy to see from the second example how linear models might not accurately reflect the reality of the situation. Denise and Sid may work independently, in which case the linear model would be workable. On the other hand, they may interact and waste time communicating with one another, in which case we may get some nonlinearity:

1 + 1 = 2 – interference loss

Or they may stimulate one another to greater efforts:

1 + 1 = 2 + stimulation gain

Or there may be both losses and gains:

1 + 1 = 2 + stimulation gain – interference loss

In the case of Brooks's Law, adding people to a task late in a project increases the amount of work to be done because of coordination and communication problems, and decreases the available time of the experienced workers because of training time needed for the new workers (Figure 5-1). Project managers get into trouble, Brooks says, by believing in the myth of the man-month, which is a linear fallacy. It says that a month added to a month is two months, no matter whose month it is, and no matter when it is done.

5.2.2 Scaling fallacy

Linear models are easy to use because they have the property of *scaling up*, so that if 1 + 1 = 2, then 100 + 100 = 200. When Denise and Sid work together for one day, for example, the gains and losses may cancel out. So Arnette, their manager, may easily conclude that their work is additive. If she plans for Denise and Sid to spend 100 days working together, she may get a big surprise when their one day's work doesn't scale up to 100 days. She may discover that although 1 + 1 = 2, 100 + 100 does not = 200.

For instance, the interference loss may be only a start-up effect, and not cost much once Denise and Sid know how to work together. Or the interference loss may grow with time, say, if Denise and Sid learn to dislike each other and try to subvert each others' work. Managers who assume that these effects won't occur expose themselves to committing the *scaling fallacy:*

Large systems are like small systems, just bigger.

One form of this fallacy applied to labor is Brooks's Law. Perhaps the most interesting question is why, now that the law has been so well-documented, managers continue to ignore it and add people late in projects.

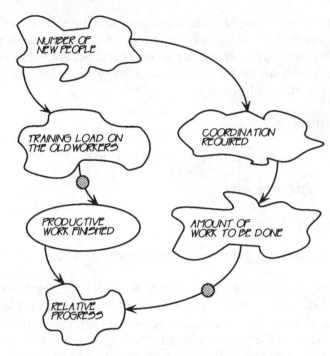

Figure 5–1.   The dynamics of Brooks's Law, in a diagram that shows why it is nonlinear. (See Section 5.3 for an explanation of the notation.)

Managers (and others) commit a scaling fallacy because linear models are often a useful first approximation for planning purposes. When presented with a new problem that seems twice as big as the previous one, we make a "guesstimate" that it will require twice as much effort. This might be a satisfactory point for *beginning* our estimating process, but we'll get in trouble if we stop there. The real world is seldom linear. That's why so many of our management illusions arise from assuming linearity when it doesn't apply. And that's why it's best to check for instances of the scaling fallacy and other common causes of nonlinearity before taking any action based on our linear models.

5.3   Diagram of Effects

One of the reasons we trap ourselves with linear models is that written and spoken language tend to be linear in the sense of saying one thing at a time. Therefore, when we think or talk about a model in words, it can be very difficult to express nonlinearities. That's why *diagrams* often help us to grasp how things *interact,* and why systems thinkers have a tool kit of diagrams ready to use.

   One of the favorite system description tools is the *diagram of effects,*[2] which consists primarily of nodes connected by arrows. Figure 5-1 of Brooks's Law, for example, is a diagram of effects. The rules for notation are as follows:

1. Each node stands for a measurable quantity, like work produced, hours worked, errors created, or errors located. I use the "cloud" symbol rather than a circle or rectangle to remind us that nodes indicate *measurements,* not *things* or *processes* as in flowcharts, data flow diagrams, and the like.

2. These cloud nodes may represent actual measurements, or they may represent conceptual measurements—things that could be measured, but are not measured at present. They may be too expensive to measure, or not worth the trouble, but the important thing is that they *could* be measured—perhaps only approximately—if we were willing to pay the price.

3. Sometimes when I wish to indicate an actual measurement currently being made, I use a very regular, elliptical cloud (see, for example, the cloud labeled "Productive Work Finished" in Figure 5-1). Most of the time, however, we'll use effects diagrams for *conceptual*—rather than mathematical—analysis, so most of the clouds will be appropriately rough.

4. An arrow from some node A to some node B indicates that quantity A has an *effect* on quantity B. We may actually know the mathematical dynamic of the effect, such as

$$\text{Relative Progress} = \frac{\text{Productive Work Finished}}{\text{Amount of Work to Be Done}}$$

    or it may be deduced from observations (as when new people are observed being trained by experienced people), or it may be inferred from past experience (as when new people are added, thus increasing the coordination required).

5. The general direction of the effect of A on B may be indicated by the presence or absence of the large gray dot on the arrow between them.

    a. No dot means that as A moves in one direction, B moves in the *same* direction. (*More* coordination means *more* work to be done; *less* coordination means *less* work to be done.)

    b. A dot on the arrow means that as A moves in one direction, B moves in the *opposite* direction. (*More* work to be done means *less* relative progress; *less* work to be done means *more* relative progress.)

6. Later, we will introduce other conventions for the diagram of effects; but for now, we can do useful work with this small set of symbols to give a recognizable graphic representation.

5.4   Developing a Diagram of Effects from the Output Backward

Let's work through a simple example to see how the diagram of effects helps us to create system models that in turn help us reason about system dynamics. For the moment, to avoid controversy, we'll confine ourselves to an example only remotely connected to software engineering.

Suppose you are a programmer working on a project that is slipping behind schedule. You notice you are suffering from back problems that are often severe enough to prevent you from working. Obviously, the more frequent these back problems, the less will be your programming productivity. In order to help get your project back on schedule, you decide to study the dynamics of your back problems by creating a model.

5.4.1   Starting with the output

The most common way to develop a diagram of effects is to start with the quantity whose behavior most interests you. In this case, the quantity may be something like

    a.   number of incidents of back pain
    b.   number of doctor visits for back pain
    c.   work time lost due to back problems

Each measure has advantages: (a) is a direct measure easily obtained from studying your calendar; (b) may be a closer measure of the *severity* of the back problems; (c) may be harder to measure, but is closer to our true interest—productivity.

5.4.2   Brainstorming backward effects

Suppose we choose to observe (c). The next step is to brainstorm all the possible measures that could affect work time lost due to back problems. This gives us the following list:

1.   Your weight may *increase* your back problems because of the greater leverage on your spine in all your activities, and the greater compression of disks between your vertebrae.

2.   The amount you exercise may *decrease* your back problems because you strengthen your back muscles (as long as the exercise is appropriate for this purpose).

3.   The kind of chair you use may affect your back problems, but "kind of chair" is not a measurable quantity. To use this effect, you have to imagine a scale of something like "orthopedic quality of chair." If you can't think

of how to measure it even conceptually, you can't use it in the diagram. This doesn't mean you can't experiment with different chairs to establish some sort of measure of "orthopedic quality." Indeed, this kind of effort to establish metrics often yields the greatest benefits from the modeling effort.

5.4.3   Charting the backward effects

Suppose these are all the effects we can think of, and suppose we decide to discard (3). In Figure 5-2, we see a simple diagram of effects showing how weight and exercise may affect the amount of work lost due to back problems. One arrow indicates that more weight *increases* the amount of work lost, while less weight *decreases* the work lost. The dot on the other arrow indicates that more exercise *decreases* the amount of work lost, and vice versa.

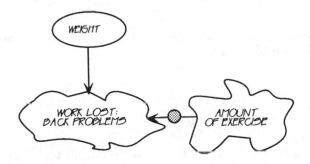

Figure 5–2.   The diagram of effects for a model of how weight and exercise affect the amount of work lost due to back problems.

This diagram of effects represents a very simple model. The point of the model, however, is not to be elaborate or even correct, but to stimulate thinking. Those of us who have suffered from back problems can look at this diagram and begin a discussion of what it omits and what it distorts, based on our own experience. As the discussion continues, we can create new diagrams that, we hope, reflect increasingly accurate and useful models. I will, in fact, elaborate upon this simple linear model as the chapter unfolds, showing how various nonlinear models could be diagrammed.

5.4.4   Charting secondary effects

Increased weight seems to increase the work lost from back problems. The most obvious reason is that more weight puts more of a load on the back, but there might be less direct effects as well. The next step is to brainstorm other connections among the nodes on the diagram. For example, more weight can lead to less exercise, because we feel more tired and less willing to get off the couch and go to the gym. Similarly, less weight could energize us to exercise more. If we believe this effect may be significant, we add the arrow from "Weight" to "Amount of Exercise," thus producing Figure 5-3, a slightly more elaborate model.

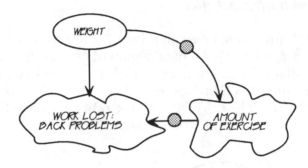

Figure 5–3.   A slightly more elaborate model of how weight and exercise affect the frequency of lower back crises.

5.4.5   Tracing the secondary effects

By tracing the paths in the diagram from "Weight" to "Work Lost," you'll see that weight has a *double* effect on back problems because there are two different paths from "Weight" to "Work Lost": one direct and one indirect (through "Amount of Exercise").

As you trace the indirect path, keep track of the dots. Two dots (or any even number) along a path represent two inverse effects and thus cancel each other. An additional increase in back problems is indirectly caused by increased weight or decreasing exercise. Thus, the diagram suggests that a ten percent increase in weight might lead to *more than ten percent* increase in work lost.

5.4.6   Explicitly indicating multiplicative effects

This increase in work lost may still be linear, though disproportionate to the weight increase. A ten percent increase in weight may produce a twenty percent increase in back pain, a twenty percent increase in weight may produce a forty percent increase in back pain, and so forth.

On the other hand, there may be medical reasons to expect that the effects of exercise and weight are not simply additive. In that case, we may want to indicate the multiplicative effect explicitly. Figure 5-4 shows how we could indicate an *interaction* between the two effects of weight on back problems by connecting the effects arrows before they enter the "Work Lost" node. Usually, however, we don't need this convention, because we are seeking other nonlinear effects that are even more powerful than simple multiplication.

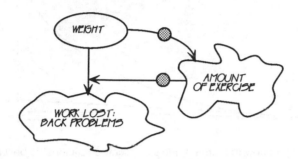

Figure 5–4.   A third model of how weight and exercise affect the frequency of lower back crises, with interaction effects, making the multiplication explicit.

5.5   Nonlinearity Is the Reason Things Go Awry

Figure 5-5 graphs the relationship between weight and back problems for different models:

√   The lower line is the prediction of the one-factor linear model of Figure 5-2.

√   The middle line is the prediction of the two-factor linear model in Figure 5-3.

√   The curved line is the prediction of the multiplicative model in Figure 5-4.

For a small increase in weight, symbolized by point W, the three models are very similar. Moreover, these are very smooth model curves, omitting numerous real-world factors that add noise to any observations. Using observations from a one percent weight increase, you can easily be fooled about which model best predicts the future of your back pain. As weight increases, however, the differences between the models become increasingly significant, even when masked by noise.

When you have a small weight gain, that's the time you can most easily do something to prevent back problems. Unfortunately that's also when you're least likely to be aware of impending difficulty. For this reason, you can't depend on observations alone to indicate that you may have a problem. By the time your observations tell you something's wrong, your back may have become exceedingly nonlinear, and the amount of exercise you'd need each day to be helpful would prove dangerous to your back.

This situation is similar to Brooks's managers who estimate project effort using a linear model. By the time they become aware their estimates have gone

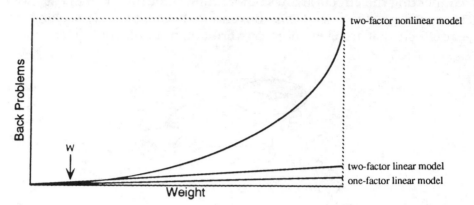

Figure 5–5.   A graph of how the three models predict the relationship between weight increase
                   and the frequency of lower back crises.

astray, they've gone so far astray that it's difficult to bring the project back on course. Indeed, the size of the intervention needed to close the gap may be so big that it's likely to cause more disturbances elsewhere—like adding a large number of people near the scheduled completion date.

That's why you need system models. Models expose and explain the nonlinear system dynamics so you can start doing something about your back problems before you actually start experiencing the pain—or about your project before you actually start experiencing the crisis.

5.6   Helpful Hints and Suggestions

1.   The most important thing about the diagram of effects is not the diagram, but the *diagramming*. When you are developing a diagram of effects to understand what is happening in a project, it's best to develop diagrams in a group and listen to the discussion that emerges. Listen, for instance, for hesitations, disagreements, and expressions of surprise. Hesitations may indicate lack of understanding of an effect. Disagreements may point to more than one effect, with some people noticing one and some noticing another. Surprise may indicate that some managers have been overlooking this effect.

2.   Don't get into arguments about what to include on the diagram. At first, include everything. Later, you can exclude factors that don't contribute to nonlinearities. For control purposes, nonlinearities will generally dominate linear effects, and so can often be ignored in real project planning after you've completed the diagram and identified all the nonlinear effects. But you'll want to retain any effect that's part of a feedback loop, as we'll see in the next chapter.

3. For many people, mathematical models of system dynamics are not easy to use or understand; but for others, they are a natural medium for communication. When making a mathematical model, start by translating a diagram of effects into a set of equations. First, replace the arrow with an "=" sign. Thus, for each node with at least one arrow entering, we get an equation with that node's measurement on the left-hand side, as in

Relative Progress $= f\,()$

This says that relative progress depends on some other measurements, which can be determined by the source of each arrow entering the relative progress node. Thus, we know that

Relative Progress $= f\,$(Productive Work Finished, Amount of Work to Be Done)

In this case, we know by the definition of relative progress that the function, f, is a simple division:

$$\text{Relative Progress} = \frac{\text{Productive Work Finished}}{\text{Amount of Work to Be Done}}$$

The gray dot indicates that the effects are in opposite directions; and sure enough, dividing by "Amount of Work to Be Done" means that the more work to be done, the less relative progress there is. Thus, the dot translates into some mathematical operation that reverses effects, such as division or subtraction.

In other cases, we may have to take measurements to determine the form of the equation. For instance, we might take measurements from several projects that added people and discover that a good estimate of the amount of coordination labor for the first four weeks is,

$$\text{Coordination Required} = \frac{(5.5\ \text{Hours})}{\text{Week}} \times (\text{New People Added})^2$$

If you are interested in this level of numerical description of many of the effects relationships in software development, see Boehm's *Software Engineering Economics*.[3]

When all the affected boxes have been thus translated, we have a set of equations describing the same system that is represented by the diagram.

The equations may all be linear equations (in which case, it is called a linear system); or some may be nonlinear. They may be algebraic, differential, or integral-differential equations; or they may be discrete or continuous equations (in which case, we have a discrete or a continuous system). Regardless of their final form, their development starts from the same diagram of effects. Only the solution methods will differ.

5.7 Summary

√ Every manager and programmer has models of how things work in their software pattern, though many models are implicit in their behavior, rather than stated explicitly. Things go awry in software projects because people are unable to face reality and because they use incorrect system models.

√ Linear models are attractive because of the principle of *additivity*. Linear systems are easier to model, easier to predict, and easier to control. Unfortunately, managers often commit the scaling fallacy because linear models are so attractive.

√ The diagram of effects is a tool for helping model system dynamics to reveal nonlinearities. Being a two-dimensional picture, it is more suited than verbal descriptions to the job of describing nonlinear systems.

√ One way of developing a diagram of effects is to start with the output—the variable whose behavior you wish to control. You then brainstorm and chart backward effects or other variables that could affect it. From these, you chart backward again, unveiling secondary effects, which you can trace through the primary effects to the variable of interest. You may want to explicitly indicate multiplicative effects because of their importance.

√ Nonlinearity is the reason things go awry, so searching for nonlinearity is a major task of system modeling.

5.8 Practice

1. The elliptical cloud indicates a clear measurement, but often measurements are not as clear as they seem (which will be one subject covered in Volume 2 of this three-volume series). For instance, "Weight" (in Figure 5-4) could mean several things, such as

    a.   the weight seen on a scale
    b.   an average of several scale weights over some period of time
    c.   perceived weight, according to tightness of clothing
    d.   fat weight versus muscle weight

Each of these measures may have a different dynamic in the weight-exercise-back pain system. Sketch at least one effects dynamic for each of the four alternatives.

2. Another choice for the "Weight" node is "Change in Weight." At the level of the diagram of effects, there's no difference between the two, but if you favor mathematical models, you'll see that the two views will produce different types of equations. Explain this difference. Then try to explain the difference to someone without mathematical training to the level of differential equations.

3. In the Brooks's Law dynamic (Figure 5-1), "Productive Work Finished" could be interpreted and measured in several ways. List at least three different interpretations. Sketch at least one effects dynamic for each of the alternative interpretations.

6

Feedback Effects

"Don't you think you'd be safer down on the ground?" Alice went on, not with any idea of making another riddle, but simply in her good-natured anxiety for the queer creature. "That wall is so very narrow!" "What tremendously easy riddles you ask!" Humpty Dumpty growled out. "Of course I don't think so! Why, if ever I did fall off—which there's no chance of—but if I did—" Here he pursed up his lips, and looked so solemn and grand that Alice could hardly help laughing. "If I did fall," he went on, "the King has promised me—ah, you may turn pale, if you like! You didn't think I was going to say that, did you? The King has promised me—with his very own mouth—to—to—" "To send all his horses and all his men," Alice interrupted, rather unwisely.
—Lewis Carroll[1]

If you don't pay attention to the system dynamics and wait instead until the curves of Figure 5-5 are clearly distinguishable, you will pay a lot greater price in pain and suffering before you finally solve the problem. Even with all this pain and suffering, however, the model of Figure 5-4 says you could still reverse the course of your back crisis, even though the price will be high. Sometimes, however, an action cannot easily be reversed, in spite of all the promises of help from upper management.

6.1   The Humpty Dumpty Syndrome

In the thirty years since I started using *Alice* as my guiding text for software engineering, I've witnessed the following sequence at least two hundred times:

1. A project manager (Humpty) becomes aware that he is sitting on a very narrow ledge of some sort.

2. Humpty tells his manager about his anxieties.

3. Humpty's manager says, "Don't worry, that's not going to happen. But, if it *does* happen, I'll bail you out with lots of resources. The only thing is you must not go around talking about this situation, or people will be alarmed (including *my* manager)."

4. Humpty goes back and keeps his mouth shut. He is able to keep quiet by convincing himself that nothing is really going to happen.

5. Sometimes, things do get better by themselves. More often, things go nonlinear and then Humpty has egg all over his face. Humpty's manager may initially support him with lots of resources, but he finally needs a scapegoat because things can't be put back together again. Guess who he chooses!

One variation of this *Humpty Dumpty Syndrome* is when a consultant (Alice) comes along in the middle of the process and tries to explain things to Humpty. Alice is powerless to make him understand why she's so worried, and Humpty is skilled at not facing reality (study the original to learn all the devices that Humpty uses to keep himself from listening to Alice).

The Humpty Dumpty Syndrome is probably what Brooks had in mind when he said, "Software managers lack the personal effectiveness to be 'courteously stubborn.'" In this chapter, we'll arm you and all software managers with a tool for courteous stubbornness. Armed with diagrams of effects, you'll be able to describe convincingly those system dynamics too strong to be reversed—no matter what the King promises.

6.2   Runaway, Explosion, and Collapse

The idea that you can always revoke previous actions to cure or prevent a runaway condition is based on two related fallacies: the *Reversible Fallacy* and the *Causation Fallacy*. Let's analyze each in terms of our back pain example.

6.2.1   Reversible Fallacy

The Reversible Fallacy says

What is done can always be undone.

If this were true, management would be a lot easier. If a control action didn't work out, you could just go back to where you were by reversing that action. For instance, if you get a back spasm from lifting a heavy rock, you could just stop lifting the rock and the spasm would go away. Similarly, if you lose your temper and fire half the staff, you could correct your mistake by hiring them back the next day. Neither backs nor employees are as reversible as that. What is done *cannot* always be undone. Figure 6-1 shows an analysis of the back pain crisis that does not allow you simply to reverse your troubles after reaching a given point.

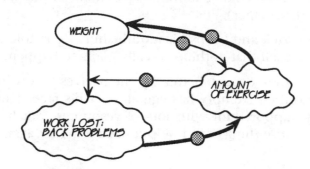

Figure 6–1.   A feedback model of the relationship between weight, exercise, and the frequency of lower back crises.

6.2.2   Causation Fallacy

The Causation Fallacy says

Every effect has a cause . . . **and we can tell which is which.**

That seems true enough in Figure 5-4, but the model of Figure 6-1 recognizes that causality is not always a one-way street. Not only does decreased exercise lead to greater frequency of back pain, but the more your back hurts, the less likely you are to exercise. Moreover, if you exercise less while eating the same amount, you will gain weight. Adding these two effects to the diagram leads to three *feedback cycles* in the model (Figure 6-2):

1.   back problems → less exercise → back problems

2.   less exercise → increased weight → less exercise

3.   back problems → less exercise → increased weight → back problems

Feedback cycles like these produce a strikingly different system dynamic than we have seen so far—a dynamic in which cause and effect cannot be separated. Cycles 1 and 2 are direct, and cycle 3 is less direct, but all three cycles are what we call *positive feedback loops*. We can determine that they are positive

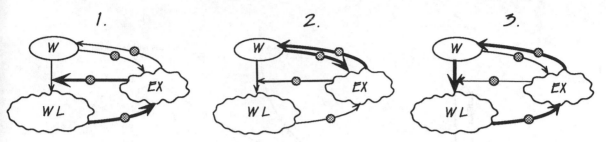

Figure 6–2.   Three different feedback cycles in the diagram of effects of Figure 6-1, shown by the paths traced in darker arrows.

feedback loops by tracing (multiplying) the dots along a path back to the beginning of the path. An even number of dots around the cycle means the loop is positive—or "self-reinforcing," or "deviation-amplifying," to use some other common terms.

For instance, gaining weight increases back problems, which decrease exercise, which increases weight, so that in the end, *weight increases weight*. Or *back problems increase back problems*. Or *less exercise leads to even less exercise*. Does gaining weight cause back problems, or do back problems cause gaining weight? So much for the Causation Fallacy.

6.2.3   Irreversibility: Explosion or collapse

Positive feedback—X increases X—is the recipe for explosion or collapse. Explosion and collapse are both runaway conditions. The difference between them *simply depends on the way you name the variables you are measuring*. In the system of Figure 6-1, weight will explode, exercise will collapse, work lost to back problems will explode, and your back itself will probably collapse. Figure 6-3 shows a graph of the explosion of back problems—or the collapse of your back—comparing two models. The simple multiplicative model may initially look more severe than the feedback model, but the nature of feedback is that its nonlinearities are ultimately much more powerful.[2] Eventually, the feedback curve shoots up and explodes off the scale of the graph.

Of course, work lost from back pain cannot actually grow infinitely (nothing can grow infinitely). When you reach one hundred percent lost work time, you will cross a threshold and the system of Figure 6-1 will "break." In other words, something so big will happen that the old model will no longer apply. When back pain causes you to miss one hundred percent of your work, you may lose your job or be forced to go on disability leave. Even worse, the collapse may lead you to the point where you must have back surgery. As anyone knows who has ever experienced back surgery, you're grateful for the relief (if the surgery was a success), but you're never quite the same as you were before you started on this runaway path.

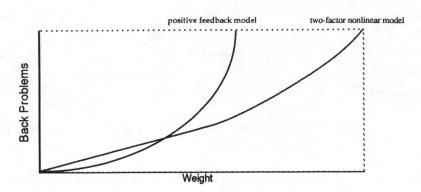

Figure 6–3.   A graph of the feedback model's prediction of the relationship between weight and the frequency of lower back crises.

Unlike the multiplicative nonlinearity of Figure 5-4, the nonlinearity of Figure 6-1 becomes *irreversible.* No matter how much you are willing to pay, it's never going to be the same old Humpty Dumpty.

6.3   Act Early, Act Small

Because of positive feedback cycles, back injuries are not reversible, and that's why doctors recommend a regime of weight reduction and curative exercise from the moment you experience the first symptoms of back problems. Patients are often foolishly optimistic—"it can't happen to me"—but doctors know from long experience with back system dynamics that a patient's back won't get better by itself.

6.3.1   Brooks's Law made worse by management action

The same is true in software engineering systems. As Brooks observed, managers are often foolishly optimistic about things going well. Moreover, when things do go poorly, managers imagine that they will get better by themselves. If Pattern 2 managers do realize there's a problem, they don't know how to reason about it or communicate about it, so they slip into the Humpty Dumpty Syndrome, which delays action even further. Then when they finally do realize that their nonlinear system doesn't fix itself, they may attempt too big a correction—landing on the project with both feet, starting an even worse nonlinear cycle.

Figure 6-4 shows a more complete Brooks's Law dynamic than in Figure 5-1, including a causal line from "Relative Progress" back to "Number of New People." (In comparing Figures 5-1 and 6-4, notice how I have collapsed several nodes to eliminate details that are not essential to understanding this dynamic.

This is similar to the collapse of detail in software design drawings or data flow diagrams, a technique that should be familiar to most readers.)

The new feedback line converts a mild multiplicative nonlinearity (like the two lines going into "Relative Progress" in Figure 6-4) into a full-blown positive feedback loop (involving the causal line in Figure 6-4). Instead of merely making the project late, a sufficiently foolish manager can make the project collapse.

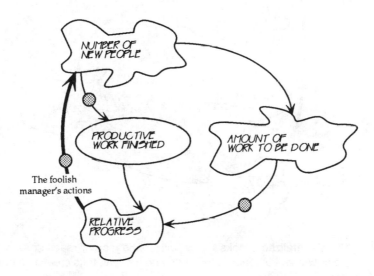

Figure 6–4.   The foolish manager's actions convert a mildly nonlinear dynamic into a full-blown positive feedback dynamic.

6.3.2   Generalized Brooks's Law

This effect of management actions to actually produce the collapse of a project is so common in Pattern 2 organizations that it is worthy of a name. I call it the *Generalized Brooks's Law* because it includes Brooks's original law as a special case. Figure 6-5 shows the generalized diagram of effects for Brooks's Law.

Notice that in the generalized law, the manager introduces nonlinearities in at least three different ways:

1.   by feeding back changes that contribute to the work load

2.   by feeding back changes that diminish the effective work force

3.   by waiting so long to make these changes that they have no chance of being effective unless they are big, and through this bigness, of creating other nonlinear effects within the project system

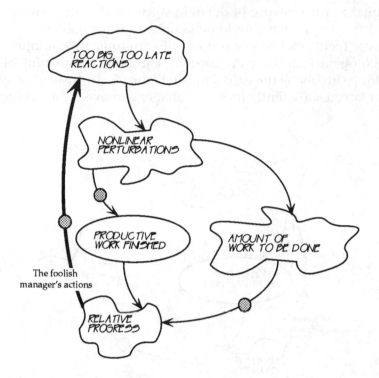

Figure 6–5.   The Generalized Brooks's Law, with management reacting as relative progress
grows worse, but reacting too large and too late, thus creating a nonlinear positive
feedback dynamic.

These actions will be all too familiar to anyone who has ever worked in a Pattern 2 organization.

6.4 Negative Feedback—Why Everything Doesn't Collapse

With all the positive feedback loops in the world, why doesn't everything collapse? Why don't some people ever have a back crisis? Isn't their system model
the same as ours? Although their model may be the same as the model of Figure
6-1, they probably run the feedback loops *in reverse*. For them, exercise keeps
their weight down, which keeps back problems down, which leaves them free
to exercise, which keeps their weight down. This leads not to a collapse of
the *back*, but to a collapse of back *problems*—a runaway to zero. This seems a
salubrious result, but because of the way the system is constructed, there are
hazards lurking in the shadows.

6.4.1   A system waiting for a disaster to happen

Because of these positive feedback loops, the model of Figure 6-1 is *unstable*. It may not be collapsing now, but it's just waiting for a runaway to happen in one direction or another—although a runaway to no back problems is a very desirable condition. The same cycle as the one producing gross overweight can produce problems like anorexia, all depending on how the cycle gets started. In reality, of course, other factors come into play before weight collapses to zero—total starvation and death.

When you analyze a software development organization, one of the first things to look for is positive feedback loops—disasters waiting to happen, like Humpty Dumpty sitting on a narrow ledge. Unless these unstable systems are stabilized in some way, all other management actions are merely cosmetic.

6.4.2   Negative feedback loops

There are many factors capable of stabilizing a dynamic system, and many cosmetic actions that can delay the inevitable. A back brace may allow you to keep on working for a week or so until a project is completed. At the same time, it weakens the muscles in your back so that if a disaster does come, it will be much worse. It also can give you a false sense of confidence, causing you to postpone actions that could prevent disaster in the long run.

In the same way, throwing lots of overtime hours into testing a bug-ridden system may delay the disaster for a short time, perhaps even long enough to get a shippable product. But, as we shall see later, it's likely to lead to a more complete and irreversible system collapse.

In the long run, only certain actions have the power to prevent collapse. In particular, only other feedback loops have the power to consistently offset the power of positive feedback loops. In living systems, there are often dozens or hundreds of such loops acting to regulate the essential variables of life, which is why life can be highly stable, even in a highly unstable environment. Each of these stabilizing loops is a *negative feedback loop*,[3] or a *deviation-reducing process.*

When listening to management proposals for correcting an unstable software project, I always check these proposals for negative feedback loops that will regulate the essential project variables. For instance, lots of overtime does add some feedback loops, but they are all positive and thus will worsen the situation. On the other hand, properly conducted technical reviews can participate in a number of negative feedback loops that may help get things under control.

6.4.3   How feedback loops regulate

Figure 6-6 shows one such feedback loop in the weight/back pain system. The amount you eat obviously has a positive effect on your weight. This model says that if your back hurts enough, you may lose your appetite and reduce your food intake. Tracing the loop of

more back problems → less eating → decreased weight → fewer back problems

shows that *more back problems tends to lead to fewer back problems.* Also, more weight tends to lead to less weight, and more work lost tends to lead to less work lost. Unlike the positive feedback loops, this negative feedback loop tends to have a stabilizing effect on all variables in the system.

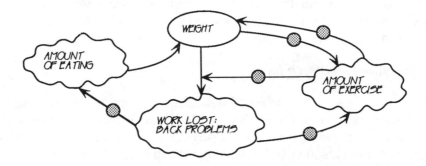

Figure 6–6.   A negative feedback loop added to the positive feedback model of the relationship between weight and the frequency of lower back crises. The amount of eating is reduced in the face of lost work due to back problems.

If you examine the original feedback model of controlling a software develop-ment system, redrawn as Figure 6-7, you'll now recognize that there are two main feedback loops connecting the controller and the software development system. This model of control is effective only if at least one of the feedback loops containing the controller and the system is negative. Deviations from the desired course of development events must lead to feedback of actions that di-minish those deviations, thus stabilizing the system. For instance,

- schedule slippage could lead to reduced requirements
- more errors could lead to more resources devoted to technical reviews
- people falling ill could lead to reduction of scheduled overtime
- poor customer acceptance could lead to additional design training
- any of the above could lead to additional management training

On the other hand, you'll recognize that this same diagram could also model *positive* feedback such as the Generalized Brooks's Law. If the controller does the wrong thing—like adding workers late in the project in an attempt to reduce schedule slippage—the situation will get worse. In fact, the controller's wrong actions could turn even a relatively benign linear system into a raging nonlinear one (as in Figure 6-4); and software development systems are decidedly not benign linear systems for reasons we shall soon discover.

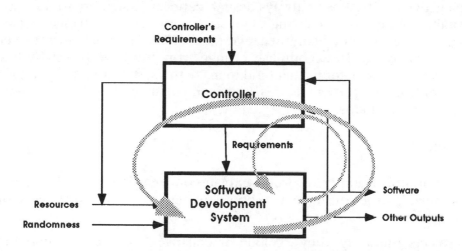

Figure 6–7.   The Pattern 3 model of controlling a software development system contains two feedback loops connecting "Controller" and "Software Development System"— one through "Resources" and one through "Requirements." In a Pattern 2 organization, either of these loops is often positive.

6.5   Helpful Hints and Suggestions

1.   In Figure 6-4, we removed some of the detail from the original Brooks's Law figure. This is an alternative way to develop diagrams of effects, the first way being output to input. You may wish to use this approach when you are dealing with general problems, such as the overall design of a new development or maintenance process. Start with the big variables and begin connecting them according to their effects. To determine what those effects are, explode each variable into a more detailed diagram of effects.

2.   A third way to develop diagrams of effects is to move from input to output. Use this approach when you are considering some action to improve one variable but first want to examine how the action may affect other variables, and thus avoid one of the traps of the Generalized Brooks's Law. Start with the variables you will change and work *forward* to other variables that they will affect (which might include feedback effects to themselves, perhaps counteracting what you are trying to do). Stop when moving forward yields no new variables.

3.   "Act early, act small" is a crucial maxim for Pattern 3 managers, and it can also be used to guide management training. To act early, you must sharpen

your powers of observation. To act small, sharpen your understanding of the subtleties of human behavior.

4.   Negative feedback isn't always desirable, because stability isn't always desirable. When you are trying to get an organization to change its pattern, you will encounter many negative feedback loops that work to keep it from changing. To accomplish change, you will have to establish some positive feedback loops that tend to make the system run away to the new pattern. Before you can do this, however, you'll need a solid understanding of stabilizing loops.

6.6   Summary

√   The Humpty Dumpty Syndrome explains one reason why project managers are unable to be courteously stubborn to their managers, and what happens as a result.

√   Projects run away—they explode or collapse—because managers believe one or both of these fallacies: the Reversible Fallacy (that actions can always be undone) and the Causation Fallacy (that every cause has one effect, and you can tell which is cause and which is effect).

√   The effect of Brooks's Law can be made worse by management action. Moreover, the same pattern of management action can lead to a Generalized Brooks's Law, which shows how management action is often the leading cause of project collapse.

√   One reason management action contrib ites to a runaway condition is the tendency to respond too late to deviativns, which then forces management to take big actions, which themselves have nonlinear consequences. That's why it's necessary to act early, act small.

√   Negative feedback is the only mechanism that has the speed and power to prevent runaway due to positive feedback loops in a system. The Pattern 3 controller has two major negative feedback loops with which to exercise control—one involving resources and one involving requirements.

6.7   Practice

1.   For the mathematically inclined, show why the equations derived from positive feedback loops lead to runaway conditions, using the method of translating diagrams of effects into equations given in the previous chapter. Explain your reasoning to people without your mathematical background. Did you resort to diagrams? Did they understand?

2.   Give three other examples of negative feedback actions a controller can

exercise through the requirements loop of Figure 6-7. Give three examples that can be exercised through the resources loop.

3. What other negative feedback loops could you construct to stabilize the system of Figure 6-1?

4. What other negative feedback loops could you construct to stabilize the system of Figure 6-5, the Generalized Brooks's Law?

5. What positive feedback loops could you construct to destabilize your own organization and drive it toward a new pattern?

7

Steering Software

In 1989, Watts Humphrey of the Software Engineering Institute was interviewed by the IEEE about SEI's five-level process maturity model. He said, "Although the SEI has found several projects at level 3, no company surpassed the second level."[1] In this chapter, we'll examine one of the major barriers to the transition to level 3 (or Pattern 3, as we prefer to call it). That barrier is the characteristic belief that binds managers to Pattern 2 (Routine): It's possible to make a project plan and follow it exactly.

We'll also look at what you need to free yourself from Pattern 2 thinking and move on to the characteristic belief of Pattern 3 (Steering): "Plans are rough guides. We need steering to stay on course."

7.1   Methodologies and Feedback Control

Even with the most accurate models, you won't always be successful at controlling every aspect of software projects, if only because of the randomness of the project's input. Nevertheless, meaningful measurements based on accurate diagrams of effects or models will lead you to make successful predictions more frequently than simple extrapolation would allow. But in order to *steer,* you need more than predictions of how the system will behave by itself. You also need *models of how your intervention will affect the system* you're trying to control. If you believe that plans can be followed exactly, you'll also believe that you're wasting your time modeling interventions–because in your mind, they will never be required.

7.1.1   Plans: The great contribution of Pattern 2

Plans for orderly software development are the great achievement of organizations arriving at Pattern 2. Individual organizations, as well as consulting organizations that serve hundreds of organizations, have undertaken major efforts to prescribe and document sequences of actions needed to control software. Integrated sets of these actions are often packaged and sold as methodologics.

A typical methodology prescribes an ideal series of steps that will take your project from beginning to end. A simple methodology might start with a feasibility study, followed by requirements, then high-level design, then detailed design, then code, then unit test, then system test, then beta test, then product release. Figure 7-1 shows the *Waterfall Process Model,* an early model still followed by many organizations that are either Pattern 2 or, more likely, Pattern 1 trying to become Pattern 2.

The original Waterfall Process Model is strictly a sequential plan, with the arrows between nodes translating into the words "followed by." After a few years, modified Waterfall Process Models began to appear (see Figure 7-2). The backward arrows in this model are sometimes referred to as "feedback" arrows, but this use of the term doesn't correspond to the conventional use in control theory. A better reading of these arrows is "sometimes followed by a return to." In programming terms, these arrows are backward GOTOs. Such backward arrows are in recognition that a purely linear process is not an adequate description for what really goes on in a software development process.

7.1.2   Why purely sequential methods don't always work

Here's a riddle: Many projects follow these sequential methodologies with great success, but other organizations can't seem to make them work. Why?

Before answering this riddle, consider the following parable: The first time my colleague Don Gause was to visit my house in the country, I gave him the following set of instructions over the phone:

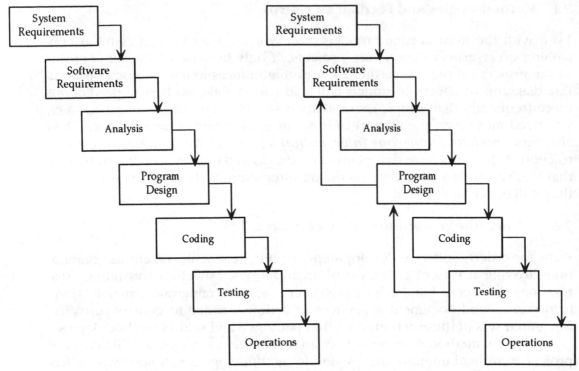

Figure 7–1. The Waterfall Process Model is essentially a sequence of steps, a program for human and machine activities. Note that this is not a diagram of effects, but a process model. The nodes don't represent measurements, but activities to be done. The arrows can be translated into the words "followed by."

Figure 7–2. Modified Waterfall Process Models were early attempts to indicate non-linear possibilities through (ideally, negative) feedback loops.

1. At Greenwood exit, leave Interstate 80 and go south 11 miles.

2. At the T, take Highway US 34 West.

3. When you reach Eagle, continue west 4 miles to 162nd Street.

4. Turn north on 162nd Street (a dirt road) and go .6 miles.

5. You will see a white house on the right, which is my house.

These seem simple enough, but Don left out the decimal point in step 4. After driving 6 miles (and an extra 2 miles for good measure) north, he couldn't find any white house on either side of 162nd Street. He searched in various ways for more than an hour (after all, he had a reputation as a problem solver to uphold), before he finally gave up and called me for further instructions.

Think of this as a metaphor for developing software under the direction of a sequential methodology. My instructions to Don were indeed an ideal set of instructions from an unknown spot on the Interstate to my house. This method is completely linear *unless Don makes a mistake*. Once the mistake is made, there is no provision for correction, no method describing what to do next.

My assumption was much like the assumptions underlying sequential methodologies for software development:

1.   There will be no mistakes.

2.   If there happen to be mistakes, they will be little ones.

3.   The responsible parties will certainly know how to correct such little mistakes.

This, then, is the answer to my riddle: Sequential methodologies are essentially linear processes, supplemented by *implicit* feedback. If nothing goes too far wrong, reasonable people can feed back small linear corrections, and that's the ideal way for a project to work. But things don't always happen that way, and sometimes a project gets thwacked by something decidedly nonlinear.

At the point when even one measurement in an effects diagram becomes nonlinear, the project's controller needs to know how to make appropriate nonlinear corrections—or at least not unknowingly contribute to the nonlinearity. Some managers make appropriate corrections instinctively, but as projects grow more complex, instinct falters. That's why we need *explicit* models of controller interventions; we need guides to steering.

7.1.3   Methodologies can discourage innovation

There's a more subtle reason why sequential methodologies fail, as suggested by yet another metaphor—the Triptik®, a trip guide issued by the American Automobile Association (AAA) to its members (see Figure 7-3 for an example).

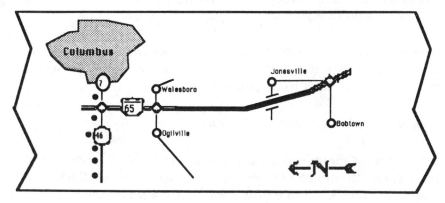

Figure 7–3.   A small segment of the AAA Triptik that Dani and Jerry were using to find their way to the AAA meeting.

Some years ago, Dani and I were driving to a meeting of the American Anthropological Association (also AAA), using the plan provided in the Triptik guide by the other AAA. We had stopped to visit our friend Jim Fleming in Columbus, Indiana. As we started out of Columbus on State Highway 7 to Interstate 65, we saw a sign pointing down County Road 46 to the town of Gnaw Bone.

Now, I had always been fascinated that there was a place called Gnaw Bone, but never dreamed I'd have a chance to actually experience being there. Dani, however, was reluctant to go out of our way. I tried to encourage her by pointing out the black dots along County Road 46, which indicated a scenic route. That proved to be a mistake.

"Look," she said, "the Triptik doesn't show Gnaw Bone, or indicate how we would get back on 65. Do we come to Ogilville, head for Jonesville, or just look for Bobtown? We might not be able to get to any of those places. Look how the Jonesville road passes under the Interstate. We could be going a hundred miles out of our way."

"Oh, it couldn't be that far," I argued.

"We don't have a state map, so how can you be so sure? I definitely don't want to get lost in Brown County and miss the start of my meeting."

We turned around.

Because we used a narrow linear map, I never got to explore the fascinating town of Gnaw Bone. In a similar fashion, Pattern 2 organizations that use narrow sequential methodologies often fail to explore the territory around their chosen route to project success. Or when they do explore, they often get lost and fail to arrive on schedule. As Humphrey says,

> *Unless they are introduced with great care, new tools and methods will affect the process, thus destroying the relevance of the intuitive historical base on which the organization relies.* Without a defined process framework in which to address these risks, it is even possible for a new technology to do more harm than good.[2]

This possibility—getting lost without a wide scale map—is another reason why Pattern 2 organizations tend to be so conservative about innovations. Given what they know, it's *smart* to be conservative.

7.1.4   Adding feedback to the methodology

More sophisticated methodologies, like the modified Waterfall Process Model in Figure 7-2, do attempt to deal with the possibility of nonlinear deviations by providing for feedback. Notice how some kind of feedback is indicated in that diagram in two areas: from the Program Design stage to the Software Requirements stage, and from the Testing stage to the Program Design stage.

These arrows in a process diagram say, in effect, "Under some circum-stances, we will go back and do this step over." In my experience, they don't mean much in practice because

1. There are many, many places besides the end of a phase when the con-troller gets information saying that the project is off course. These devia-tions, to paraphrase Agatha Christie, may seem completely unimportant. That is why they are so interesting. They are exactly the things real con-trollers need to notice if they are to act early, act small.

2. Getting back on course by recreating a design or a specification is such an enormous piece of work to do over that it's always a nonlinear disturbance.

3. Redoing a design or specification is such an enormous piece of work that managers seldom dare to actually do them over, lest they get lost in down-town Gnaw Bone.

4. The methodology doesn't provide any sense of what *information* is to be fed back from one stage to the other, so people don't really have a map of what they're supposed to do.

5. The methodology doesn't say anything about the dozens or hundreds of other feedback situations or how to handle them. The basic focus seems to dictate a choice: Either do it right or do it completely over (presum-ably right the next time). The methodology makes no small distinctions or corrections between doing it right and doing it wrong.

7.1.5   Keeping the feedback early and small

Recently, authors have attempted to correct some of these problems by cre-ating smaller feedback loops in their methodology. For instance, Humphrey[3] introduces the valuable idea of *basic unit cells* (Figure 7-4) from which a larger process can be composed. Each of these basic unit cells has feedback coming in from later cells and going back to earlier cells. By making these cells smaller, the nonlinearity is ideally minimized.

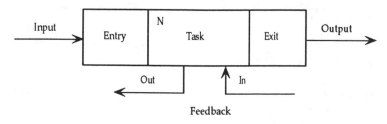

Figure 7–4.   By building processes from basic unit cells, Humphrey adds smaller-scale feed-back to a large-scale development process, thus creating a more stable process.

Another approach, which can be used in conjunction with Humphrey's basic unit cells, is Gilb's "Evolutionary Delivery Cycle."[4] As shown in Figure 7-5, work is done in "micro-projects," so that feedback cycles cannot grow too large or too big. At most, feedback can move from one micro-project to the next.

Humphrey and Gilb are just two of many examples of methodologists who are becoming aware of the importance of feedback. I recommend that you examine their important work, but I will not explore it further here because all such software methodology work still omits most of the important available feedback.

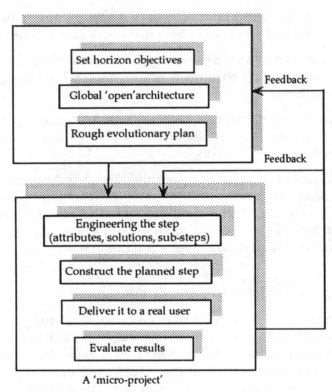

A 'micro-project'

Figure 7–5.   By building the entire product in small evolutionary units, Gilb ensures that feedback cycles must be shorter in time and smaller in impact.

7.1.6 Applying the feedback at different levels

Both basic unit cells and micro-projects address the problem of feedback, but still focus only on the *product* being built. The feedback they use is information about the product, not information about the process in general. An effective manager needs to know much more information, much earlier, than the product alone can provide.

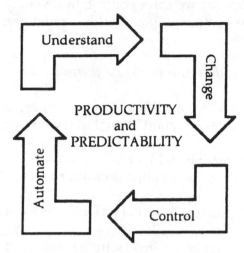

Figure 7–6.   By focusing on the process, Hewlett-Packard and other firms have been able to establish great gains in software quality and productivity. The cycle of process improvement is just like a product improvement cycle, but the process is the product.

A more general focus to improve software quality and productivity is on the *process,* as taught by Deming[5] and others and as practiced by Hewlett-Packard[6] (see Figure 7-6). In effect, these efforts define where the developers are and where they desire to go in terms of the *process,* not the product. In other words, the process *is* their product and is controlled by the same sort of feedback dynamics. An ideal improvement program combines this focus with the idea of small improvements to achieve successful change with a minimum of instability.

As we'll see later, this approach can also be carried out at the *cultural* level, above the level of particular processes, let alone the product level. Wherever we look, people are discovering that the same control model is needed at all levels; and with it, they are acquiring the ability to think and observe in terms of nonlinear effects and then to act in concordance with those observations and thoughts.

7.2   The Human Decision Point

Since models are always approximations, none is ever perfect; but they all should be *believable*. To use models effectively, we must be able to act as if we believe them, even while we remember that they are approximations.

We get into serious trouble with models when we *do* believe them. In particular, when a model says or implies that some action is impossible, we are not likely to consider attempting that action. Good intervention models will help us to understand what we can't control, but a faulty model may lead us to overlook some effective interventions. In this section, we'll examine how these oversights can happen.

7.2.1   Intervention models and invisible states

An intervention model says something like this (where B is the "bad" state I'm trying to change, and G is the "good" state I'm trying to attain):

> If the system is in state B and I do X,
> then Y will happen, which I hope is closer to state G.

To take a simple example, the Waterfall Process Model of Figure 7-2 says

> If the program design is finished (state B) and we do the coding (X), then we will be in the testing state (Y), which I hope is closer to state G.

Given the particular model, there's no suggestion that something that happens in coding may send the project further away from G, to some place like

1.   a previous step in the methodology, such as back to Software Requirements

2.   a state not mentioned in the methodology, such as a state in which

    a.   there are large numbers of difficult coding errors
    b.   project members are falsely confident
    c.   upper management wrongly believes the project is closer to completion
    d.   one of the key programmers has gotten sick from overwork
    e.   a programmer and a team leader have become bitter enemies

Software people are perhaps too familiar with methodologies (which are models of processes) and not familiar enough with effects models. This is one reason they're not very good at predicting the effects that are not directly based on the states of their methodology. Figure 7-7 is intended to clarify the distinction.

In the figure, I have superimposed on the Waterfall Process Model some measurements from a diagram of effects:

1.   "Errors Found in Test" is certainly associated with one and only one stage in the process model, but this measure may be *influenced* by other variables

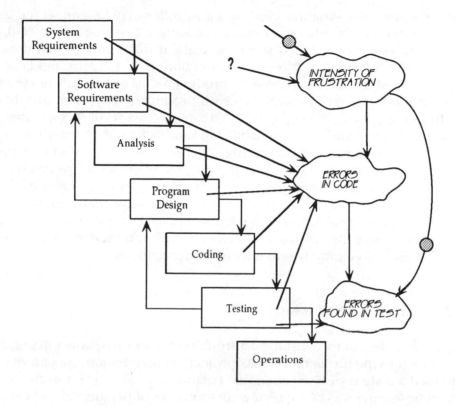

Figure 7–7.   The difference between a process model and a diagram of effects is shown by this
diagram of the Waterfall Process Model indicating where some measurements
may originate. The feeling of frustration may not originate in a specific step that
we can identify in the Waterfall Process Model, but may still be a critical variable
in the project's success.

seemingly not related to that stage. For example, "Intensity of Frustration"
throughout the project may lessen the effectiveness of the testing effort.

2.   "Errors in Code" may be associated with any stage in the methodology because errors can originate anywhere, including places not mentioned in
the methodology itself (for example, by someone in a different project cor-
rupting the source code database). They may also be influenced by other
variables, such as a feeling of frustration.

3.   Variables such as "Intensity of Frustration" may be influenced by any number of factors. We may have a hard time identifying these effects. Although
we generally won't be able to associate such variables with any particular
stage in the Waterfall Process Model, that doesn't diminish their importance. If anything, it increases it.

In other words, the variables used by a controller may be connected with the product (which is the ultimate interest) or simply be some of the "Other Outputs" we saw in Figure 4-4. If you look again at that figure, you'll notice who cares that the "Controller" takes input from *both* the "Software" and the "Other Outputs." Most methodologies are so product-focused that they never mention other outputs not *directly* connected with product quality, cost, or schedule.

To a great extent, managing to avoid a crisis consists of recognizing, nurturing, strengthening, and creating stabilizing feedback loops, then sitting back and letting them do the work of preventing collapse. It also depends on recognizing, discouraging, negating, and decoupling positive feedback loops (such as the effects from blindly adding more workers late in the project). Only by modeling your interventions can you avoid creating new positive feedback loops in your efforts to solve the problems created by old ones. If your process model doesn't even acknowledge the existence of certain states—if it renders them invisible—it has no chance of guiding you to effective interventions.

7.2.2   *Visualizing the invisible*

I once was called in to consult on a troubled project that was missing all of its goals, much to the puzzlement of its project manger, Simon. As part of my visit, I attended a code review meeting that (against my advice) Simon also attended. Herb, whose code was being reviewed, took a lot of personal abuse from Simon to the point where his eyes started watering. I called for a "health break," and during the break, Simon came up to me and asked, "Does Herb have something in his eye?"

"Why do you ask?" I replied.

"Well, I noticed that there was water coming out of his eye."

After studying the project, I came to the conclusion that the project was in trouble largely because almost all of the people were feeling totally discounted by their management. In Simon's model of the world, emotional states of people in his project simply didn't exist. If they had been visible, Simon would have seen there was trouble early and been able to act small to do something about it. Therefore, I could explain nothing to Simon until he learned some new models, so that he could see what was previously invisible.

If you are managing a software project and are considering an intervention to control something, you must first express your idea in terms of the intervention model by answering the following questions:

1.   What is the state of the system now (B)?

2.   What is the action I intend to take (X)?

3.   What will be the dynamic of a system in state B if I take action X?

4.   Is Y (where the dynamic will take the system) closer to G (the good state
      I'm trying to attain)?

To answer these questions, you probably need methods of making visible that
which has previously been invisible.

7.3 It's Not the Event That Counts, It's Your Reaction to the Event

Feedback loops in action sometimes seem to have a mind of their own. That's
because managers are blind to the key role that people—especially management
people—play in each feedback.

All of the loops that concern management contain *decisions by people.*

> **Whenever there's a *human decision point* in the system, it's not the event
> that determines the next event, but someone's reaction to that event.**

For some Pattern 2 readers, this maxim will be the hardest to swallow of all
the ideas in this book. They would like to believe that projects obey some set
of mechanical laws, like Newton's Laws of Motion, and that the manager's job
is to learn these laws, set up the project properly, and then let nature take its
course to success. This is an especially comforting idea to those managers who
are afraid of their own workers because it means that they can hide in their
offices and manipulate plans, rather than deal with real human beings. As long
as they deny the role of human action in project management, they'll never be
successful project managers.

The human decision points in our model *must* be identified because *they're
the places where we have a chance to prevent a crisis.* When Fred Brooks says,
"More software projects have gone awry for lack of calendar time than for all
other causes combined," he could have said, More software projects have gone
awry *because their managers didn't know how to respond to lack of calendar
time.* We'll never have complete control, but neither are we victims.

Of course, every system does have some laws of nature that we can't do anything directly about. In the back pain system, if we eat more, we gain weight—
that's a *physiological* law. It's also a physiological law that if we gain weight,
we're more likely to have back pain. To manage back pain, we need to learn
which relationships we *can* influence, and then act on them. For instance,
there's no natural law that says, "When you're in pain, eat something." Your
mother may have taught you that, but grown-ups don't have to do what their
mothers taught them.

You could decide to do what your mother said and increase your eating in
response to the pain, thus converting a possibly stabilizing loop into another
force for destabilizing. But you do have choices as to how back pain affects
your eating and exercise habits, and how your weight affects your exercise.

Therefore, you could just as well decide to *decrease* your eating when your back hurts, as many people do. Figure 7-8 shows Figure 6-6 redrawn to identify those effects lines that are within your control.

The lines are identified by adding a symbol that suggests the idea of a human control point. (Think of the square as being an "unnatural" human-made shape, as opposed to the circle, which more often appears in nature.) Inside the square we place the *direction* of the control: white for positive; gray for negative; and mixed, meaning the choice is still open. In the figure, I've modeled a person who responds to increased weight by *increased* exercise, and to work lost by *decreased* eating, but who could decide either way about how exercise will be influenced by lost work. Notice how many more stabilizing (negative) feedback loops have been created by explicitly taking charge of your role as a controller.

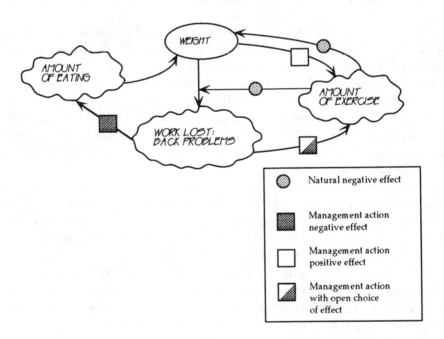

Figure 7–8.   Figure 6-6 redrawn to emphasize those effects that are human decisions (positive or negative). Reversing certain "natural" decisions produces a more stable, healthier system.

For the remainder of this volume, we'll work on describing many important *laws of software engineering management*. One of the most important tasks is not merely describing these laws, but in distinguishing which ones are

- "natural" laws that we'll have to learn to accept
- "human decision" laws that we'll have to learn to control

If you want to be the one who steers software, you'd better learn to pay attention to the difference.

7.4 Helpful Hints and Suggestions

1. When first working with the diagram of effects, be very sure that the people understand the difference between this diagram and a process model diagram such as that used in describing methodologies. It may help to have them brainstorm some measures that

   a. are directly connected with one product in their process model
   b. are directly connected with one stage in their process model
   c. are connected with more than one stage
   d. are connected with more than one product
   e. cannot be connected only with stages
   f. cannot be connected only with products

2. People may have to practice seeing things they don't ordinarily see, but the practice will usually pay off immediately in better control. For more on how to see what you're not seeing, refer to *The Secrets of Consulting*.[7]

3. People's language often reveals when they believe that they are victims of events, rather than having a choice of reactions to the event. For instance, people say things like these:

   a. "We *had to* ship the product on schedule."
   b. "The project was late, *so* we accelerated the testing."

   which *sound* like they are enunciating laws of nature. Learn to listen for falsely deterministic key words such as "had to" and "so." Then politely ask, "Could you show me the reasoning behind that statement?"

7.5 Summary

√ Many otherwise good, ideal methodologies fail to help prevent collapse because they don't prescribe negative feedback actions to be taken when the project deviates from the ideal model.

√ When the methodologies do prescribe feedback, they often speak only of the product level, or feedback steps that are too large. To be effective for control, feedback must operate in small increments, at all levels—personal, product, process, and cultural.

√   Software professionals often overlook the human decision point in models of effects. One reason is their inability to visualize certain states at all, often because they are other outputs of the process, and not directly connected with the product.

√   To control a project successfully, you have to learn that you need not be a victim of the dynamics. When human decision points are involved, it's not the event that counts, it's your *reaction* to the event.

7.6 Practice

1. Using a diagram of effects that you have developed to describe some software engineering behavior, label the diagram to show which are human decision points. Label these points to show how they are ordinarily decided in projects you have experienced.

2. Take the diagram from (1) and reverse one or more of the ordinary human decisions. Describe the resulting change in behavior.

3. Recall some dramatic event that forced you to make a quick decision. Looking back over that decision, list at least three alternatives you had. Describe the probable consequences of each, and compare them with the actual consequences of your decision.

4. For one day at work, carry a note pad and record every instance you hear of someone asserting a human decision law as if it were a natural law. What patterns do you see in these statements? What do they tell you about your organization?

8

Failing to Steer

*There's only one sin, and that's failing to
believe you have a choice.*
—Jean-Paul Sartre

In Chapter 4, we learned that to steer a software engineering project, the manager needs to

- plan what should happen
- observe what significant things are really happening
- compare the observed with the planned
- take actions needed to bring the actual closer to the planned (Figure 8-1)

Pattern 2 managers are able to plan what should happen. If they wish to move to Pattern 3, they need to learn to do the other three things. In this chapter, we'll study three dynamics that commonly stand in their way. Each of these dynamics is accompanied by a seemingly rational explanation:

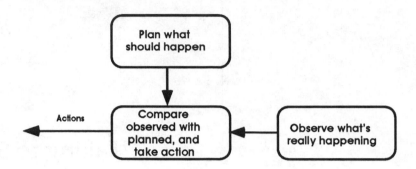

Figure 8–1.   Figure 4-5 repeated: What is necessary to steer a software engineering project.

- I'm just a victim.
- I don't want to hear any of that negative talk.
- I thought I was doing the right thing.

8.1   I'm Just a Victim

In 1956, I predicted that FORTRAN wouldn't last three years, and that was only the first of many gross mistakes I've made in my career. Let me tell you the story of how I almost made an even bigger mistake.

8.1.1   What distinguishes failures from successes?

In 1961, when I was at the IBM Systems Research Institute, I commissioned a student project to study software development projects that had failed. The students interviewed about a dozen project managers and derived a number of factors that had contributed to each project's failure. When we studied these factors, the only one they seemed to have in common was bad luck. There had been floods in the computing center, flu epidemics, essential employees leaving at crucial times, blizzards, lost source files, even an earthquake. Clearly, each of these project managers had been victims of natural laws.

The students wrote a paper documenting this astonishing but discouraging finding. I edited it, added a few thoughts of my own, and made a few calls to journal editors. One of these editors asked me whether we couldn't give the article a more positive tone by describing the factors that the *successful* projects had in common.

"We didn't study any successful projects," I said.

"Then how do you know they didn't also have bad luck?" (Click)

The "click" was the sound of his phone going dead and—a millisecond later—of my brain coming alive. We withdrew the paper until another group of students conducted a similar survey of successful projects. In each of these projects, too, there had been some natural disaster, but the results were entirely different.

Particularly striking was the contrast between two organizations that were hit by fires in the computing center. One project failed utterly, but the other recovered because it had been managed differently:

1. Backups of all source code had been stored off site, and were not affected by the fire damage. In the failed project, there were some backups, but nothing systematic.

2. Standard architectures had been used, so damaged hardware was readily replaced. In the failed project, a few thousand dollars had been saved by using "almost standard" hardware.

3. The entire staff was willing and able to pitch in and work overtime to clean up, restore files, and sort out project documentation. In the failed project, about twenty percent of the employees took the fire as an excuse and opportunity to leave for greener pastures.

4. Since everything had to be restructured anyway, consultants were brought in to help the successful project use the fire as an opportunity to reorganize. In the failed project, the only opportunity people saw was the chance to blame the fire for the failure they already saw was inevitable before the fire broke out.

In short, what made the difference was *not the event, but their reaction to the event.* The successful project reacted by acknowledging a tough break, then taking charge of the recovery, even seizing the opportunity to take advantage of the disaster. The failure, on the other hand, seized the opportunity to play victim. As the manager said, "What could I do? The whole place burned down."

8.1.2   Victim language

Since that time, I've never been asked to consult about a fire in the computing center, but I've certainly been called in to help many other troubled projects. In those cases, I always listen for victim language from the managers. If I hear any, I work with these self-described victims to develop diagrams of effects that clearly label points of potential human control.

A typical piece of victim language is when a manager says, "The project is behind schedule, and I can't do anything because Brooks's Law says I can't add people without making the project fall further behind." Let's examine how to reframe this from victim language into controller language.

Ardella was a project manager who added workers and then noticed that the project was falling behind. At that point, Ardella could have continued adding workers, which would have created a positive feedback loop that wouldn't have existed without management intervention, as we saw in Figure 6-4. When I was called in to help, the first thing I did was show Ardella why her own decisions were making the situation worse. This convinced her to stop adding workers, which was not exactly what I had in mind.

Figure 8-2 shows how I redrew Figure 6-4 to emphasize to Ardella that she had control in several areas.

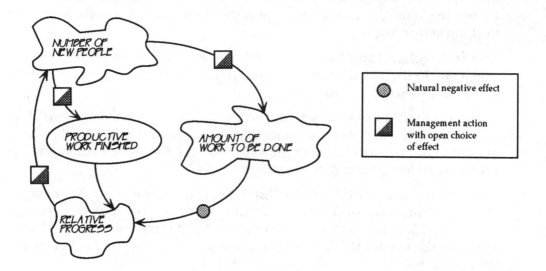

Figure 8–2.   The dynamics of Brooks's Law redrawn to suggest where a manager might look to prevent management-induced schedule delays. The difference between this figure and Figure 6-4 is the addition of human decision points.

The human decision points suggest ways to add people without disturbing the work of the experienced people and without increasing the coordination effort. It was Ardella's job to look for such ways, but that was the easy problem. Once she recognized that she was not a helpless victim, she took several steps to control the effect of "Number of New People" on "Productive Work Finished." For one thing, she assigned some newcomers to

- review designs and code
- update the project documentation
- create test cases
- do gopher work at the requests of the other workers

Thus, although she continued to add new people (her choice to do this is indicated by the gray square in Figure 8-3), she made their effect *positive* (as shown by the white human control square in the diagram of Figure 8-3). While doing so, Ardella did add some work burden to the experienced people, although she controlled this by giving strict instructions not to speak to the experienced workers without coming to her first. She also cut out a few work requirements that were not essential. Her partial control of the effect of "Number of New People" on "Amount of Work to Be Done" is indicated in Figure 8-3 by the half-and-half symbol.

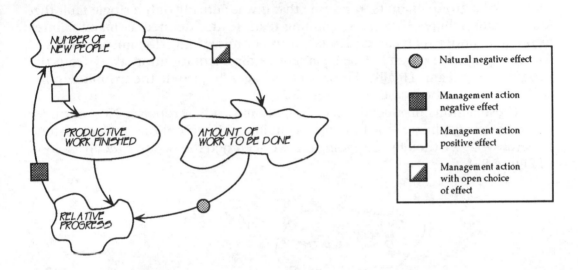

Figure 8–3.   Figure 8-2 redrawn to reflect Ardella's actual choices for managing the schedule problem.

In short, Ardella took charge of creating her own laws, as represented by the new diagram of effects in Figure 8-3. If you, on the other hand, prefer to have the certainty of natural laws, I can recommend one law of human behavior that has that kind of natural predictability. Any time you say, "I *can't* do that," you'll *always* be right. The trouble is, though, sometimes you'll also be an unnecessary victim.

8.2   I Don't Want to Hear Any of That Negative Talk

Even when managers are willing to take responsibility for their own control actions, they can't be effective unless they have accurate observations on which to base those actions. Accurate observation doesn't happen by accident, but only by conscious management decision.

Peter was a development manager who seemed to understand the software development process, but continually made inappropriate interventions to deal with a crisis of poor quality code. Our investigations of several projects under Peter's direction showed us that his poor decisions were based not on poor judgment, but on misleading information about the true state of software quality.

What caused the poor quality information? When the project started to experience quality problems, fear of what would happen if the problems were accurately reported led people to take actions that destroyed the accuracy of the reports. For example, the test engineers fixed some problems on the spot and did not report them through the official channels. Also, the test team leader reclassified some of the problems downward in severity. Third, the programmers fixed a group of faults, reporting that it was actually only a single fault that led to many failures. The programming team leader defined as many failures as possible under such categories as "customer misreading documentation" and "operating system glitch." These categories directed attention away from the programming team. Finally, the project manager "adjusted" the trouble reports with all sorts of "best case" interpretations.

These actions produced a set of highly misleading reports. No controller could have used them as the basis for an intelligent intervention. To demonstrate to Peter what we thought was going on, we sketched the positive feedback loop of Figure 8-4.

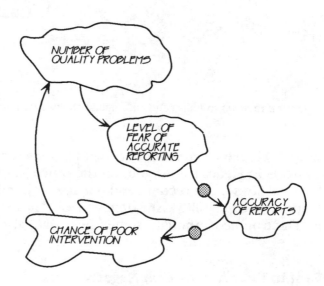

Figure 8–4.   Fear of consequences of accurate reporting of bad news leads to distorted trouble reports, making it unlikely the manager will implement meaningful interventions. This creates a positive feedback loop on poor quality.

When Peter saw this diagram of effects, he responded with victim language: "Well, if that's what's going on, there's nothing I can do about it. Look, there are no human decision points in the loop. People will naturally fear reporting accurately when there are lots of problems, and if they're afraid, they'll always find ways to make things look better. If the reports I get are inaccurate, there's nothing I can do to be effective, and if I'm ineffective, there will be more and more quality problems. So by your own modeling, I'm stuck in a positive feedback loop."

Peter was partially correct. If the diagram of Figure 8-4 was the total dynamic, he was indeed helpless. But a manager can always create a new diagram by adding something to the system. Together, we worked out the diagram of effects shown in Figure 8-5, which added the possibility that managers (perhaps unconsciously) could punish anyone who provided accurate measurements of quality problems, calling this sort of feedback "negative talk." This action creates yet another feedback loop that reinforces people's natural fear of giving a poor-looking report.

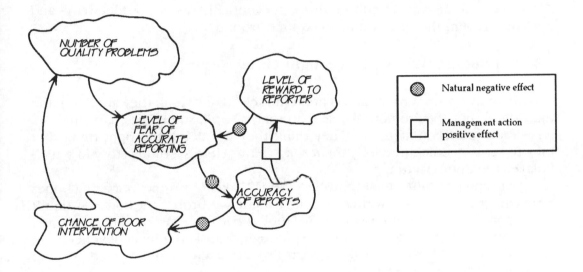

Figure 8–5.   One way a manager can react to reports of quality problems is to punish the reporter. A different approach is to reward accurate reports, which may not eliminate fear but will help keep it under control.

Though this second feedback loop seems to make matters worse, it *does* have a human decision point, so "worse" or "better" is subject to control. The managers do not have to punish people for providing accurate, but uncomfortable, information. If punishing messengers leads to the collapse of the information system, why not take steps to reverse this effect and *reward* accurate reports? Reversing this punishment effect creates a stabilizing negative feedback loop that prevents the natural fear of accurate reporting from getting totally out of hand.

I wish I could report that Peter corrected the situation immediately, but how could he? As we've seen, nonlinear situations like this are not easily reversible. Trust takes years to build, but it can be destroyed in a minute. Peter did inaugurate a program of management training, especially emphasizing communication skills. He set a good example by being the first to attend.

I worked with Peter's company long enough to hear him change some of his own unintended strong language, but not long enough to see whether he succeeded in undoing the Pattern 2 taboo against negative talk. As in all cases where *fear* is one of the variables, prevention would have certainly been sixteen times easier than cure. People are all too ready to fear the worst from their managers, so it doesn't take a very strong dynamic to set them off.

In the following chapters, we'll see many other examples of how such unconscious or uninformed management decisions can create the positive feedback loops that lead to an unproductive situation that's difficult to reverse. More important, we'll also see how managers can make conscious, informed decisions to create negative feedback that can eventually restore productivity—and perhaps prevent the situation the next time around.

8.3 I Thought I Was Doing the Right Thing

People often act on wrong intervention models. They think they are doing the right thing, but they're not. Worse than that, people sometimes have their intervention models *backward.* They think they are doing the right thing, but they're actually doing precisely the *wrong* thing. Here's a funny story in which I played the dumb victim:

Dani and I bought a dual-control electric blanket to protect our aging bones from the cruel Nebraska winter. The first night we brought it home, it didn't work, and we were both miserable. We took it back to Sears, and the salesman said he would happily take it back. First though, he asked if he could check the controls. He demonstrated that the controls were accidentally crossed, leading to the effects diagram in Figure 8-6.

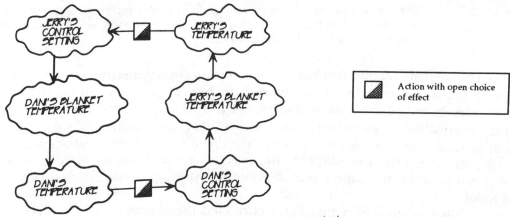

Figure 8–6.   How the dual-control blanket is cross-connected.

This dynamic is *not* a victim dynamic, but relies on our conscious actions, which happened to be based on our faulty models of how the blanket really worked. My model says, "When I turn my control down, my side of the bed gets cooler." Dani's model says, "When I turn my control up, my side of the bed gets warmer." These models work well, and we both should be comfortable unless the controls are crossed. Then the dynamic is a runaway to the maximum discomfort the blanket can provide.

Dani and I both had *backward* models of how the blanket actually worked. When she was too cold, she tried to improve the situation by turning up her control, but that resulted in my becoming warmer. As I was now too warm, my model dictated that I turn my control down, which actually resulted in Dani getting cooler. So in the end, her action to make herself warmer actually resulted in a boomerang effect, and she was colder than if she had left things alone.

It was very tempting for me to blame Dani for my discomfort (and for her to blame me), but it's meaningless in such a system to ask who's controlling whom. If anything, the person who connected the controls is controlling everybody, but it might be more accurate to say that our *ignorance is in control.* Perhaps that's why blaming is characteristic of many Pattern 2 organizations.

Certainly the cross-connected electric blanket exactly models many situations in Pattern 2 software organizations. Take another example. United Cigar Rentals was trying hard to move to Pattern 3. For instance, they had adopted Gilb's evolutionary approach for building an order entry system. Some of UCR's internal customers were not satisfied with the quality of their micro-project, nor were they happy that enhancements to the system were delayed to the next micro-project. They pushed the developer for speedy delivery. They also requested more functions, especially recovery functions due to the frequent software failures. They also reasoned they were waiting so long anyway, they wanted to get more for their patience.

In order to get all the new functions delivered on time, the development department then let quality slip in the next micro-project. The customer's faulty model of software development was thus confirmed, and another cycle started with the next micro-project. (See Figure 8-7.)

UCR worked their way out of this mess by implementing a three-part strategy: teaching both parties the dynamic model shown in Figure 8-7; showing each that they did have control points, but they were using them backward; and negotiating a period of trust, in which the customers reduced the pressure and developers cut back on promised functions while extending delivery times. The success of this strategy was aided by UCR's use of the micro-project approach, because none of these actions was too large for either party to accept.

One programmer suggested to me that his managers would be doing a decent job if only they would reverse every one of their management decisions. Unfortunately, it's not that easy. The electric blanket boomerang phenomenon was a favorite theme of Greek drama, thousands of years before there were elec-

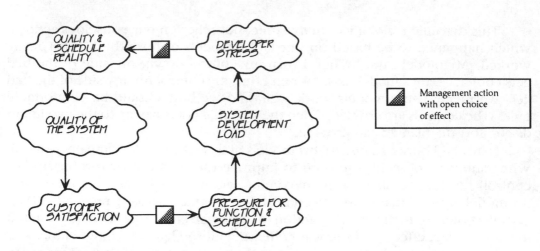

Figure 8–7.   It's possible for a software developer and a customer to get cross-connected just like an electric blanket.

tric blankets or software. Oedipus' father tried to avoid his prophesied death; yet his actions led to his death. Oedipus desired to see the truth, so his actions made him blind. To avoid such boomerangs, you have to understand feedback effects, and you have to do something about them.

8.4   Helpful Hints and Suggestions

1.   Tools do not determine how they will be used. Therefore, it's not the tool that counts, it's your reaction to the tool. Programming tools can be used to program without understanding, or they can be used to free the programmer's mind and hands for tasks that can't be made routine. Pattern 2 managers buy tools to force programmers to work in standard ways. Pattern 3 managers manage tools to empower programmers to work in effective ways.

2.   The same distinction can be made in managing software. Management tools (such as methodologies) can be used to manage without understanding, or they can be used to free the programmer's mind and hands for tasks that can't be made routine. The first is the Pattern 2 choice; the second, Pattern 3.

3.   When you hear two parties blaming each other, the chances are good that they are caught in a mutually destructive feedback loop. With improved understanding of the system that has them caught, they can usually work their way out—but only if things have not gotten so far that they want revenge more than they want the original solution.

8.5 Summary

√   Many project managers fail to steer well because they believe they are vic-
     tims with no control over the destiny of their project. You can easily iden-
     tify these managers by their use of victim language.

√   Brooks's Law doesn't have to be a victim law if the manager recognizes
     where the managerial control is and recognizes that this control can take
     different forms.

√   A common dynamic is punishing the messenger who brings accurate but
     bad news about a project's progress. This intervention avoids negative talk,
     but also diminishes the chance of the manager's making effective interven-
     tions needed to keep a project on track.

√   Since the beginning of time, people have not only gotten their interven-
     tions wrong, they've gotten them backward. Laying out a clear diagram
     of effects can help you sort out a situation in which two parties are driv-
     ing each other to destruction, all the while thinking they are helping the
     situation.

8.6 Practice

1.   Give three examples of victim dynamics from your own experience. Create
     a diagram of effects for each, and show some of the control alternatives
     available to the victim. In at least one of the examples, you should be one
     of the victims.

2.   Give three examples of negative talk situations from your own experience.
     How was the situation created? Was it ever corrected, and if so, by what
     means? How long did it take?

3.   Give three examples of electric blanket dynamics from your own experi-
     ence. Create a diagram of effects for each. In at least one of the examples,
     you should be one of the sufferers. How did you discover that you had
     things backward? How did you feel when you found out?

Part III
Demands That Stress Patterns

Organizations don't choose their patterns of management action at random. Each pattern is a response to a series of demands placed on the organization. There are the demands of their customers, the demands of the type of problem they are trying to solve, and the internal demands generated by the way they did things in the past.

It's the interplay of these demands that determines whether an organization even has a chance to succeed using its current pattern. In the following chapters, we'll see how the external demands—customer and problem demands—stress the organization's pattern, creating the problem that its internal organization must solve. We'll also see how organizations typically respond to these demands, and what happens for each response.

9

Why It's Always Hard to Steer

Some of the cornerstones of operational management simply fall apart when used for projects. A good example is the principle of economy of scale. We all have been taught that a bigger machine using more resources at a faster rate is more efficient than a smaller counterpart; that we can achieve more economy with a process producing 5,000 nuts and bolts an hour than one producing say, ten. This law applies well in a factory making nuts and bolts, but when we turn to the process of making the factory, we cannot use it. We have only one factory to be made.
—Robert D. Gilbreath[1]

In the previous chapter, we saw several common mistakes that managers make in trying to steer software projects. Why do they make such mistakes? Are they bad people? Are they stupid people? Or are they just people, like the rest of us?

The simple fact is that if they are bad or stupid, then we all are bad or stupid because everyone makes such mistakes when trying to play the *game of control*. In this chapter, we'll see why this game is always too hard for people to play unless they don't care too much about how well they play.

9.1 Game of Control

We are now in a position to understand an important distinction between two types of dynamics. We can speak of an *intervention dynamic* when an essential part of the dynamic is *the human decision about how to regulate part of the process*. Brooks's Law, for example, is an intervention dynamic because the manager could intervene differently and change the dynamic.

A *natural dynamic,* on the other hand, may involve human intervention, but in a situation where the decision has no power to alter the *form* of the dynamic itself. We may defy the Law of Gravity by lifting things or flying, but we have no power to change the law itself. Similarly, we can schedule programmers to work twenty-four hours a day, but it won't work for long because we can't change the laws governing the physiology of sleep. In other words, natural dynamics set limits on what intervention dynamics can accomplish.

9.1.1   *Square Law of Computation*

For those who would control software, the most important natural dynamic is the *Square Law of Computation,* which sets limits on what a mind can accomplish. To control any system, you need to be able to use your system models to compute the consequences of your planned intervention. As we've seen, these models can be expressed at least conceptually in terms of equations. Thus, every control system contains a "computer" of some sort capable of solving these equations and predicting what will happen. The computer might be a machine, but usually is a brain or a group of brains.

If a computer is to be involved, you may reasonably ask, "How big does that computer have to be?" The Square Law of Computation gives this answer:

> **Unless some simplification can be made, the amount of computation to solve a set of equations increases at least as fast as the square of the number of equations.**

Recall that the number of equations to describe a system is equal to the number of nodes with entering arrows, or approximately the number of measurements in the system. If system A has twice the nodes of system B, the computer for system A needs to be four times as powerful as the controller for system B.

Suppose that the computer happens to be *you,* a software manager. The Square Law of Computation says that to control the system, you must become four times smarter at solving control problems as the system size doubles (see Figure 9-1).

Do you know how to become four times smarter? If not, too bad because we can see that the dynamic of Figure 9-1 is natural. Why? Since it has no human decision points, you're not going to be able to do anything about it.

Now, suppose that the computer is an entire organization cooperating to control software development. In this case, the Square Law of Computation says the organization will have to grow a hundred times more effective if it wants to build systems that are ten times bigger! Is it any wonder that so many successful organizational patterns crumple under the stress of growth?

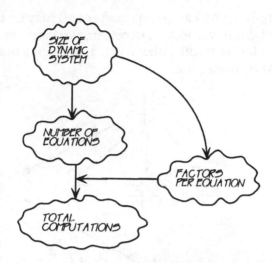

Figure 9–1.   The Square Law of Computation says that computation required to control a
                   dynamic system grows nonlinearly, which can be understood by this diagram of
                   effects for any controller computation.

9.1.2   Control as a game

Perhaps the question should be, How is it that any software organization manages to succeed? Games are simple examples of control situations in which we sometimes succeed in spite of their complexity. Perhaps the study of games can illuminate the question of success in the face of complexity.

How does a game model a control situation? The present position of the game is B, the initial (bad) state. Any winning position for the game is G, the good state you are trying to achieve. Your playing strategy is your way of getting from B to G, your control strategy.

Let's start with a very simple example. Tic-tac-toe is a *deterministic* game, so there are no random elements to contend with except for your opponent's moves. In terms of the cybernetic model, this means there is no Randomness input to contend with. Therefore, if your model of the game is better than mine, I can never beat you at tic-tac-toe. Your model tells you how to counter every move of mine with one that's at least as good. You can look ahead and see all possible consequences of each of your possible interventions. Thus, you are exactly in the position of the perfect controller.

In Figure 9-2, we see such a perfect controller's strategy starting from one position that may be obtained after four moves, two by X and two by O. As the complete game tree shows, this perfect controller can win every time from this position.

Tic-tac-toe, of course, does not provide a very complex regulatory situation, so your brain does not have to be very big to play a perfect game. At the

Nebraska State Fair, you can pay a quarter and play tic-tac-toe with trained chickens. The chickens never lose. Therefore, we can conclude that the complexity of tic-tac-toe is less than the capacity of a chicken's brain. No wonder we're not too impressed by tic-tac-toe.

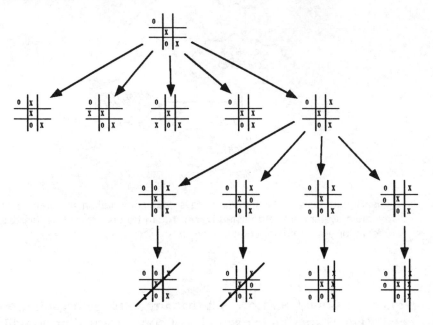

Figure 9–2.   Tic-tac-toe is a deterministic game, which means that in theory a player can look ahead and examine all possible moves, all the way to the end, to see which moves lead to a victory, loss, or draw. Here we see part of a game tree showing how X can achieve victory from one possible four-move position, regardless of what O plays.

9.1.3   How complex is chess?

What happens as the game gets more complex? Chess is obviously a more complex game than tic-tac-toe, but it is also deterministic because random changes in the board are not allowed. In some sense, that means chess is exactly the same game as tic-tac-toe, but one that requires a bigger computer.

In other words, your chess computer can think ahead through the game tree just as you can in tic-tac-toe. So far, however, nobody has taught a chicken how to play perfect chess, so perhaps it requires a computer bigger than a chicken's brain. Neither has anybody yet taught a mechanical computer to play perfect chess, although there are many excellent chess playing programs that use this look-ahead strategy. Figure 9-3, for instance, shows a position from which the chess program Deep Thought found a forced mate (a move tree in which every branch leads to victory) in 3.5 seconds.

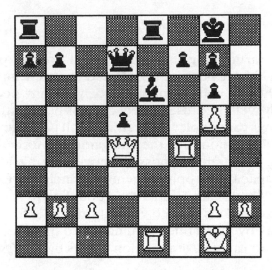

Figure 9–3.   Like tic-tac-toe, chess is a deterministic game, though it requires a larger com-
                puter. However, nobody has yet taught a chicken to play winning chess, though
                the computer program Deep Thought found a forced mate for White from this
                position in 3.5 seconds. Can you do better?

9.1.4   Computational complexity

The additional complexity of chess over tic-tac-toe is *computational* complexity, which arises because of combinatorics. In the tic-tac-toe position of Figure 9-
2, there are only five possible moves for X, each of which is followed by four
possible moves for O. Each of these is followed by three possible moves for X,
each of which has two possible moves by O (although the game may be lost
by then, which somewhat reduces the complexity). Thus, to examine all possible moves from this position requires consideration of $5 \times 4 \times 3 \times 2$, or 120
positions at most. Indeed, for all possible games of tic-tac-toe, there are at most
$9 \times 8 \times 7 \times 6 \times 5 \times 4 \times 3 \times 2 = 362{,}880$ sequences, which is one way to measure
complexity.

     Now consider the complexity of chess. From the chess position in Fig-
ure 9-3, White has 52 possible moves, each of which can be followed by a variable number of moves by Black. For instance, if White moves the king's pawn,
Black has 28 possible responses. If this is the average number of responses, then
there are $52 \times 28 = 1{,}456$ possible White-Black combinations. Thus, even a pair
of White-Black sequences has more than a million combinations, which is already far more complex than tic-tac-toe. Unlike tic-tac-toe, a chess game is not
guaranteed to end after a fixed number of moves, but if we estimate an average
game has 30 move pairs, and each move pair has 1,000 combinations, we would
estimate $1{,}000^{30}$ or 10^{90} different games.

9.1.5 Simplification by general principles

We know that no human being has ever learned how to play perfect chess; otherwise there would have been an undefeated chess champion. Perfect chess is probably beyond human computing capacity, yet many people do manage to play chess reasonably well. Because perfect chess is beyond their computational capacity, human beings cannot play by examining all possible moves in the game tree except in special situations like the end game or a forced mate.

Instead of trying to examine all possible moves, people increase their apparent computational capacity by applying general principles. Examples of general chess principles are "Castle early" and "Avoid doubling pawns on the same file." Although there are exceptions to each general principle, they help reduce computational complexity by restricting examination to the most promising moves. This is what the Square Law of Computation means by *"Unless some simplification can be made ... "*

For instance, one general principle of chess is "Don't give up your queen to capture a less powerful piece." This is an excellent principle that almost always leads to superior play because you don't have to consider such queen sacrifices. In the position of Figure 9-2, however, it is exactly such a "forbidden" move that leads to a forced mate for White.

Of course, White could probably win with a number of less powerful moves, but the point is clear. General principles of play allow us to play better with limited computational capacity *most of the time,* but the price is that we will miss the best play *some of the time*. This is the Square Law of Computation at work, forcing us to do the best we can with our rather limited resources—limited, that is, relative to the problem we are trying to solve.

9.1.6 Size/Complexity Dynamic

Now, what has this to do with software engineering? In the first place, I contend that developing perfect software is *much* harder than playing perfect chess, which is already well beyond human capacity. To deal with this complexity, the Square Law of Computation dictates that we have simplifying general principles.

If we are to have a fighting chance to produce *good* software, not to speak of *perfect* software, we need simplifications. These simplifications are what we call "software engineering." They include methodologies and effects models, both implicit and explicit. They also include such general principles as

- "Don't add workers late in a project in an attempt to catch up."
- "Never use GOTO statements in your code."
- "Always buy the best possible tools."
- "Don't write monolithic code; break it into modules."
- "Use the smallest possible team of the best possible people."

- "Never write any code until all the design work has been reviewed."
- "Don't punish the bearer of bad news."

Integrated collections of such methods, models, and principles are what we have been calling cultural patterns. Each cultural pattern contains its own large set of simplifications for playing the game of software engineering. Like the principle "Never sacrifice your queen," they are merely approximations that we need because of this dynamic:

Human brain capacity is more or less fixed, but software complexity grows at least as fast as the square of the size of the program.

This is probably the most important *natural software dynamic*. It combines the Square Law of Computation with the assumption that we cannot alter our brain capacity, at least in the short run. I call it the *Size/Complexity Dynamic*.

9.2   Size/Complexity Dynamic in Software Engineering

The Size/Complexity Dynamic is important because it appears everywhere in software engineering, though often in disguise.

9.2.1   History of software

Perhaps the most important occurrence of the dynamic is throughout the entire history of the software business, which could be summarized in the diagram of effects of Figure 9-4. This diagram shows that whenever the software development business has succeeded, we have raised our level of ambition. Thus, the problems we attempt to solve grow bigger until they become limited by the complexity of their solution because of the Size/Complexity Dynamic.

As we try to solve bigger and bigger problems, the Size/Complexity Dynamic drives us from a previously successful pattern to a new, untried pattern. Were it not for our insatiable ambition, we could rest comfortably with our present pattern until they carried us away in our rocking chairs. Many organizations have done just that, usually because their customers have no further ambitions for better software.

9.2.2   History of software engineering

Figure 9-4 shows that when there *is* ambition for more value in software, it quickly pushes against the barrier of the Size/Complexity Dynamic unless we can alter the capacity of our brain. Organizations sometimes do this by hiring smarter people, but there's a definite limit to that tactic. Several of the software organizations I work with have started complaining that there are not enough

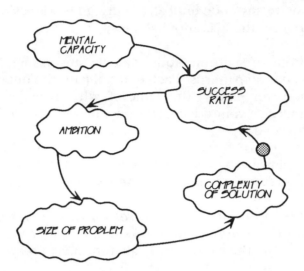

Figure 9–4.   The history of software development can be summarized in this diagram of effects, which shows how whenever we succeed, we raise our level of ambition.
Thus, the problems we attempt to solve increase until they become limited by the
complexity of their solution as a result of the Size/Complexity Dynamic.

top computer science graduates to go around, which has started a bidding war
for brains.

    We can't alter the capacity of our brain, but we can alter how much of that
capacity we use, as well as what we use it for. That's why software engineering
was invented. Figure 9-5 shows how software engineering attempts to simplify
the solutions to larger problems, thus raising the success rate in response to
increased ambition. It also shows if we examine its dynamics that as long as
our ambition is stimulated by success, we'll never finish the job of developing
software engineering.

    Conversely, Figure 9-5 also shows that once an organization reaches the
maximum level of ambition for software, there is no urge to adopt further software engineering practices, and the organization settles down into a comfortable cultural pattern. It's only when an organization reaches Pattern 4 that the
ambition for higher quality becomes internalized, at which point the cycle of
improved software engineering becomes self-sustaining.

9.2.3   Games against Nature

Each Size/Complexity Dynamic has two parts: the fixed human brain and the
complexity that grows with size. Each example of the complexity is a particular
instance of the Square Law of Computation. For instance, we always see the

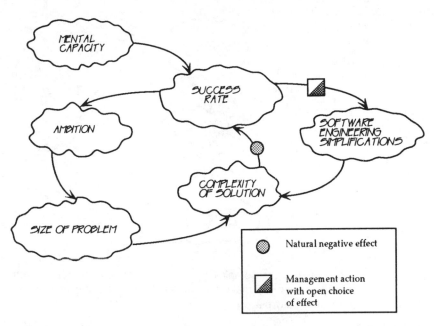

Figure 9–5.   The history of software engineering is the history of attempts to beat the Size/Complexity Dynamic by creating simplifications that reduce the complexity of solutions as problems grow bigger. Without ambition, there is no need for software engineering.

Size/Complexity Dynamic in any form of game, though the particular details will vary from game to game.

A game in this general sense is a situation in which there are two players (one of whom may be Nature, who dish up natural dynamics that we have to beat if we are to get from B to G). The two players more or less alternate moves, and because you must respond to your opponent's move, you get a two-move dynamic, as shown in Figure 9-6.

This diagram could also be used to describe the game of management, or the game of control. It matters not whether the opponent is Nature (Randomness) or the highly structured efforts of the other people in the organization. As controller, the manager has to respond to all moves that might start the project on a losing path. Good managers, like good poker players, don't believe in bad luck. They play well with whatever hand they're dealt.

9.2.4   Fault Location Dynamic

Figure 9-7 shows one of the most important ways that the Size/Complexity Dynamic applies to the building of large systems, software or otherwise. This is the *Fault Location Dynamic.* It shows why more labor is spent locating faults

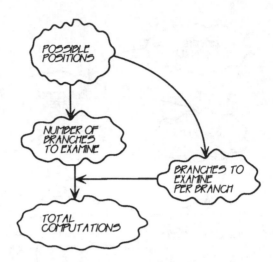

Figure 9–6.   The source of the complexity when the Size/Complexity Dynamic is applied to playing games. By making a bigger board, you can soon make the game too complex for any player.

as systems get more ambitious. You'll notice that nowhere in this model is there a measure of luck. Good programmers don't believe in luck either.

When Pattern 2 managers start to feel the barrier created by the Fault Location Dynamic, they may not understand that this is a natural dynamic. Instead, they may feel that it arises from some correctable inadequacy in the developers, like lack of attention or motivation. They don't understand that the Fault Location Dynamic describes finding faults in the *system,* not the management practice of finding faults with the *people* who are building the system and working against the troubles caused by the Fault Location Dynamic.

9.2.5   Human Interaction Dynamic

In order to beat the Fault Location Dynamic or other forms of the Size/Complexity Dynamic, Pattern 2 managers often acquire large staffs. When they do this, however, they encounter the dynamic in another of its common disguises: the *Human Interaction Dynamic.* The effects of this dynamic are well-known to social psychologists and project managers, who long ago observed that as the number of people increases, the ways they can interact tend to multiply faster than you can control them. The Human Interaction Dynamic, which we shall revisit many times, is shown in Figure 9-8.

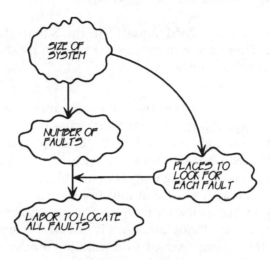

Figure 9–7.   The source of complexity when the Size/Complexity Dynamic is applied to the
                problem of finding faults in a system. If your development process creates faults
                at the same rate, your larger system will contain even more faults. Since the
                system is bigger, there are more places to look for each fault. Thus, total fault
                location labor grows nonlinearly. This is called the Fault Location Dynamic.

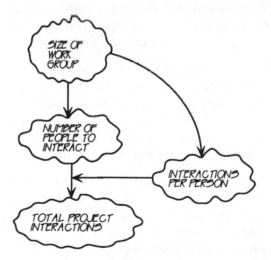

Figure 9–8.   The source of complexity when the Size/Complexity Dynamic is applied to the
                problem of coordinating a work group (which is part of the original Brooks's Law
                dynamic, as well as many others). The total number of interactions grows non-
                linearly with the number of people in a group, so that trying to work with bigger
                groups adds to the internal control work load. We call this the Human Interaction
                Dynamic.

9.3   Helpful Hints and Suggestions

1.   Don't take the word "square" in the Square Law of Computation too seri-
     ously. There are a number of reasons why the worst power could be less
     nonlinear. For instance,

     - The task (such as building software) is never totally mental. There are
       always things to accomplish that have nothing to do with the size of
       the mental task, such as the startup overhead for any project.
     - Projects are seldom working so far out on the curve that the nonlinear
       effects are being felt very strongly. Those that are, are probably failing
       and may not make it into the statistics.
     - Our best software engineering efforts are directed at reducing the non-
       linearity. Modularization is one of the strongest strategies for keeping
       the Square Law of Computation under control. This strategy fights
       complexity at the large project end, but adds work at the small project
       end, thus reducing the overall nonlinearity of the size/effort curve.

2.   Also, don't forget that it's possible to do much *worse* than the Size/Com-
     plexity Dynamic suggests. Whenever we create an intervention dynamic
     that contains positive feedback, we are in danger of making the Size/Com-
     plexity relationship not just nonlinear, but exponentially nonlinear. The
     Size/Complexity Dynamic speaks only of a limitation on good managers.
     Bad managers are unlimited in their potential to do mischief.

3.   There are many arguments to demonstrate that "perfect" control of soft-
     ware development is much harder than playing chess, but I'll give only
     one. On a typical computer, each machine instruction is represented by a
     pattern of 32 bits. Thus, one instruction can be written in 2^{32} or approx-
     imately 10^{10} ways. A sequence of two instructions can thus be written in
     10^{20} ways, and a program only 100 lines long can be written in 10^{1000} ways.

     For the program to be perfect, we must write the sequence of instructions
     exactly. Writing perfect programs of even 100 lines is thus far more com-
     plex than playing perfect chess. Remember, too, that a more typical size
     for a piece of commercial software may be 100,000 lines, with some run-
     ning more than 10,000,000.

4.   Do perfect programs have only one way to write them? It depends on the
     requirements. In chess, there are often two forced mates from the same
     position taking the same number of moves, so is one of them more perfect
     than the other? Perhaps winning every game would be perfect for most
     chess players. Perhaps winning every tournament, or winning only one
     tournament—the world title—could be perfect. What these arguments show

is that the more flexible we are in defining "perfect," the easier the job of control. In other words, if you're willing to give up some control at the outset, you increase your chances of staying in control at the end.

9.4 Summary

√ Human intervention dynamics are those over which we potentially have control, but a set of natural dynamics always puts a limit on how good a job any controller can do. A large part of the controller's job is devising intervention dynamics that can keep the natural dynamics under the best control possible, which can never be perfect.

√ The Square Law of Computation says that computational complexity grows nonlinearly as the number of factors in the computation grows.

√ Control can be thought of as a game that the controller plays against Nature. Even games of perfect information, such as tic-tac-toe and chess, require nonlinear increases in brainpower to play perfectly as the size of the board increases.

√ Simplification is always needed because controllers are always playing a game well outside their mental capacity. Simplification takes the form of rough dynamic models and approximate rules such as "Always break a project into modules."

√ Software engineering management is harder than chess because controlling a project is a game of imperfect information, and because the size of the "board" is not fixed.

√ The Size/Complexity Dynamic appears in many forms throughout software engineering, forms such as the Fault Location Dynamic and the Human Interaction Dynamic.

9.5 Practice

1. My colleague Tom DeMarco agrees that managing software development is harder than playing chess, but he says that my proof is wrong. He didn't, however, give his own proof. Give your own proof, by which I mean an argument that convinces you. Or if you're not convinced, give a proof of the converse.

2. Create a diagram of effects describing the "bidding war for brains": the attempt by organizations trying to push against the barrier of the Size/Complexity Dynamic by hiring more smart people. Show why, as one wag put it, "The growth of the software business has led to a flow of students from physics to computer science, which has resulted in an increase in the average intelligence of both fields." Do you believe it?

3.   The idea of a game can be generalized to more than two players. Discuss ways in which the arguments about control of software development can be generalized to a three-player game. Can you generalize to an N-player game?

10

What Helps
to Stay in Control

When you see someone coming to help you,
run for the hills.
—Henry David Thoreau

For those of us who continue to be ambitious about software, the Size/Complexity Dynamic says we're going to need a lot of help. In this chapter, we'll look at some of the characteristics of ideas and practices that will prove helpful for staying in control of software.

10.1 Reasoning Graphically About the Size/Complexity Dynamic

We know that models are helpful, but different people react to the same model in different ways. That's why it's always helpful to have different ways of representing the same ideas.

143

10.1.1   Size versus brainpower

Figure 10-1 shows the Size/Complexity Dynamic graphically in a form that often helps thinking about it. The curved line shows that the computational power needed to control a system grows nonlinearly with problem size. Each horizontal line represents an individual person's or organization's brainpower. Once the control curve rises above the brainpower line, that person can no longer play a perfect game of controlling in that problem situation.

Figure 10-1 is an antidote to people who become overly impressed with their own IQ. Notice how one person can be twice as smart as another (whatever that means), but not be able to solve twice as big a problem. As somebody once said, "IQ scores would be a lot more meaningful if you added 10,000 to each score."

Because the Size/Complexity Dynamic is a natural dynamic, the kinds of improvements we can make to our computational power—our thinking—cannot ultimately grow faster than the size of the programs we attempt to write. We may paraphrase this dynamic as

Ambitious requirements can easily outstrip even the brightest developer's mental capacity.

Let's return to chess to see why this is so. Suppose your "customer" gives you the requirement, "Write a perfect chess-playing program." And suppose you are smart enough to do it. All you must do to outstrip your machine's capacity is to define a new version of chess played on a larger board. A 25 percent increase to a 10 by 10 board means at least a 56 percent increase in the complexity of each move. If that isn't enough, you just have to increase the board to 20 by 20, or 100 by 100, until the machine as well as your program is outclassed.

10.1.2   Size versus effort curve

Figure 10-2 relates the curve in Figure 10-1 to software engineering.[1] A particular pattern for controlling software development can be conceptually represented by a single size/effort curve, where the effort is largely mental. Other patterns will be represented by other size/effort curves. Each curve shows how well its pattern *can* do on problems of different size. It doesn't show how well its pattern *will* do, because incompetent managers can always make a project go worse than it could have gone.

Each size/effort curve can be used as an estimating tool for a particular pattern. Suppose you were doing a project of size A, and were asked to increase the problem size by adding a few requirements. This would bring the project to size B, which you estimated to be about a ten percent increase in requirements. According to the estimating curve, developing B using the same cultural pattern

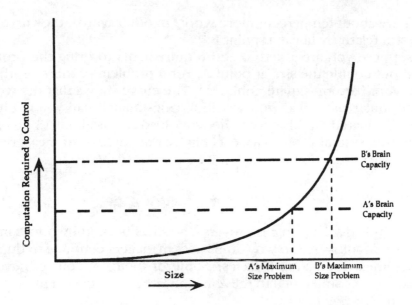

Figure 10–1. As the size of a system grows, the complexity required to control it grows nonlinearly (curved line). Any particular human brain, however, has a relatively fixed capacity, which can be represented by a horizontal line. Once the complexity curve
crosses that line, the system is too complex for that brain to control perfectly.

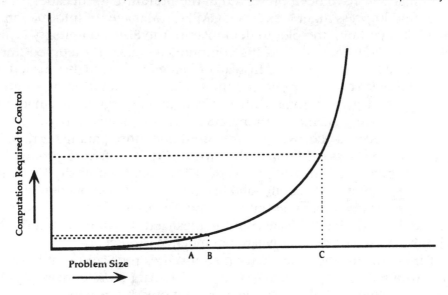

Figure 10–2. A particular software engineering method can be represented as a curve relating
size and complexity. Points A, B, and C represent three different size requirements, with B representing a ten percent increase over A, and C representing a
100 percent increase over A. Using this method, the complexity of solving B is
only about 10 percent greater than A, but C is about 1300 percent greater.

would require about ten percent more work. In other words, the curve for this pattern is still relatively linear at point B.

But suppose you are asked to add requirements to bring the problem to point C, about double the size at point A. For a problem of this size, the curve estimating your pattern is quite nonlinear. The curve shows that the work load will ascend much faster than you would have estimated had you extrapolated linearly. As estimated on this curve, the work load at C is about 13 times that at A, although the system is only twice as big by one method of measuring, such as lines of code or function points.

10.1.3   Variation and the Log-Log Law

The Size/Complexity Dynamic is universal and has been known for almost the entire history of software. So why do project managers continue to dupe themselves with linear estimation fallacies? Some of them, of course, never study history and so are condemned to relive it. But others are misled by two factors: *variation* and the *Log-Log Law*.

One of my clients, whom I'll call the Canadian American Border Fence Company (CABFC), decided to use a size/effort curve for estimating projects. Figure 10-3 shows their data from a dozen past projects. Their plot was typical of plots that have been presented in the literature for decades, so I thought they would impress Alger McKewan, CABFC's Manager of Information Systems. When I showed him the plot to demonstrate the Size/Complexity Dynamic, he gave me a blank look. I used his computer to make the curved line shown, which was a best statistical fit. Instead of being convinced, he pushed me aside, punched a few keys, and produced the straight line—another best statistical fit.

What had gone wrong with my convincing argument? Mathematically, the residuals were smaller with my curve (that is, it was a better fit), but that would be expected because my curve used one more parameter than his linear fit. The trouble was, of course, the *variability* in software productivity data, which has been well-known for decades. The Size/Complexity Dynamic is only a *tendency*—albeit a strong one—and just one of many factors that may influence the amount of work that goes into a particular project. Thus, any one organization may have difficulty visualizing the idealized dynamic within the real data, even if it keeps data on a fairly large number of projects.

Paradoxically, the other factor that obscures the Size/Complexity Dynamic arises from the attempt to make such variable data more convincing. For some years now, almost all of the public presentations of size-versus-effort data seem to be plotted on log-log scales. In Figure 10-4, which replots CABFC's data of Figure 10-3, you will notice how well this log-log straight line seems to fit the data. That's not surprising because the *Log-Log Law* says

Any set of data points forms a straight line if plotted on log-log paper.

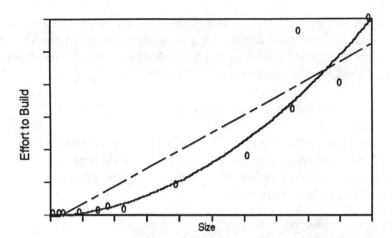

Figure 10–3.   Data from a dozen of CABFC's projects: Among all the variations in real data, it
                 may be hard to distinguish the nonlinear nature of the size/effort relationship.

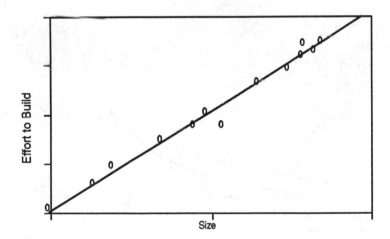

Figure 10–4.   The tendency to plot experimental data on a log-log scale tends to further ob-
                 scure the nonlinear nature of the size/effort relationship, especially to busy project
                 managers reading articles by glancing at the pictures.

Of course, the Log-Log Law is not strictly true, but is a fairly strong observation about the way the human eye senses data. By using a log-log plot, researchers can impress you that their data have meaning. In the process, however, they may obscure the most important meaning—that the relationship between size and effort is nonlinear. This log-log practice is especially misleading
for project managers who are too busy fighting the practical consequences of
the Size/Complexity Dynamic to read software engineering articles carefully.

10.2   Comparing Patterns and Technologies

One of the most important ways a manager tries to be helpful is by choosing technologies that will be part of the organization's cultural pattern and by ultimately choosing the entire pattern. Such choices can never be exact, but they are well suited for graphic reasoning.

10.2.1   Comparisons with a size/effort curve

Since a size/effort curve can be used to characterize a software engineering pattern, two different patterns can be compared by showing curves for the two approaches to solving the same set of problems. Figure 10-5 shows two general curves demonstrating how this is done.

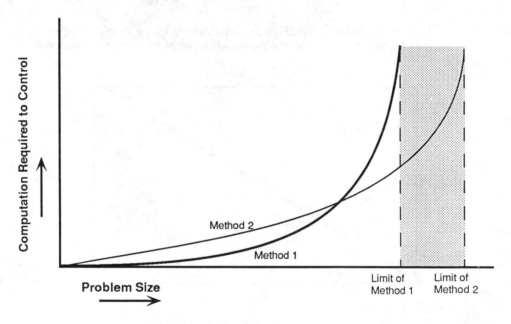

Figure 10–5.   The two software engineering methods can be compared by looking at their respective size/computation curves. Method 1 costs less for working with small systems, but reaches a limit first. Method 2 can control systems larger than anything Method 1 can control (in the shaded region); but because of the Size/Complexity Dynamic, Method 2 also eventually reaches an effective limit.

Methods 1 and 2 could represent entire patterns, such as Variable (1) and Routine (2). They could also represent parts of patterns, such as

- two programmers of different skill
- a programmer versus a programming team

- one organization's entire programming staff versus another's
- two different programming tools or languages
- an organization before and after adopting new practices

Regardless of what they specifically represent, Method 1 appears to be better for small problems, but runs out of computational capacity before Method 2. Method 2 can be thought of as the smarter method because it can control more complex systems. But no matter how much smarter one programmer is or what excellent practices are adopted, Method 2's curve has the same natural dynamic—the Size/Complexity Dynamic. Therefore, although Method 2 can push the complexity limit further to the right, it must always reach some limit of the system it can control.

10.2.2 Seeing through the data

Figure 10-6 shows a size/effort plot of some data taken from experiments with the Focus and COBOL programming languages,[2] which can be our Method 1 and Method 2. As usual, it's a bit hard to see exactly which method is better from among the scatter of data points, but Figure 10-7 shows the best linear fit to the two methods.

Looking at these two straight lines, we could easily be convinced that Focus is better than COBOL. Indeed, many software managers have come to such a conclusion about fourth-generation languages. But the data of Figure 10-7 were taken from relatively small-scale, though well-controlled, experiments. In actual practice when larger programs are attempted, the curves for Focus and COBOL probably look like Figure 10-5. At a certain point, the expressive and computational power of the fourth-generation language runs out of steam, and the clumsier third-generation language can still be pushed a bit further.

10.2.3 Combining two methods into a composite pattern

Because two methods may excel on problems of different magnitudes, we often find organizations using two or more methods for software development. In Figure 10-5, for example, Method 1 can be used for small jobs and Method 2 for large jobs, yielding the composite method shown in Figure 10-8. At least, that's the ideal. In many Routine (Pattern 2) organizations, Method 1 is used by those programmers and managers who know Method 1, and Method 2 by programmers and managers who know Method 2.

Employing a composite method burdens managers with an extra decision on each job. What is the choice point for choosing one method over another? A Steering (Pattern 3) manager is not afraid to have a tool kit of methods, even though that adds the task of choosing which method to use when. Routine managers living in a blaming environment prefer not to have this choice. That way

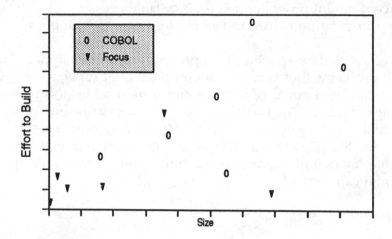

Figure 10–6.   Among all the variations in real data, it may also be hard to distinguish two different methods in a small set of experiments.

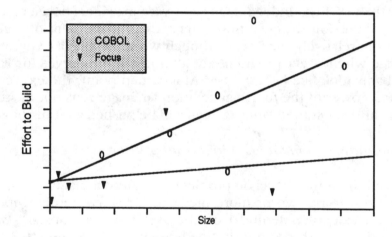

Figure 10–7.   The best-fit lines help us to distinguish the two sets of data, but may fool us into thinking this is a linear relationship rather than the early part of a nonlinear curve such as Figure 10-5.

when the project fails, they can plead, "Well, we followed the standard method all the way, so it's not my fault."

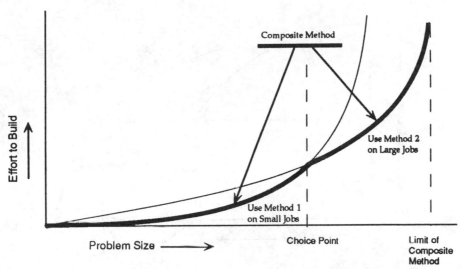

Figure 10–8.   When two methods differ greatly in their ability to handle different size problems, an organization may choose to use both, one for small problems and the other for large problems. This composite method consists of the two original methods plus a method for making the choice between them.

10.2.4   Choosing for reasons other than effort

This example suggests that managers choose methods for reasons other than the total effort they will require. Perhaps the most frequent reason other than effort is *risk*. Figure 10-9 shows a *size/risk graph* that can be used as an aid in this situation. A graph of this form highlights the maxim "Money can't buy everything" because each curve represents the best chance you have with the method, no matter how much you're willing to spend. At the size at which Method 1 has a 50 percent chance of success, Method 2 has about an 80 percent chance of success. Method 2 is obviously safer if we're willing to pay the price, although the graph says nothing about what this price is. For that, we'd need a *size/effort graph* to use in conjunction with the size/risk graph.

Figure 10-10 suggests another interpretation of Figure 10-9. Human beings take time to learn so whenever we use a new method, the first time costs more and is more risky. Figure 10-10 is a size/risk graph in which the two curves represent the first and second times we attempt to use a new method, which could be a new programming language, a new project management system, or even a new pattern.

10.2.5   Reducing the risk of change

This size/risk graph captures the idea in terms of risk that the first time is always hardest. Managers studying this graph may decide that their career

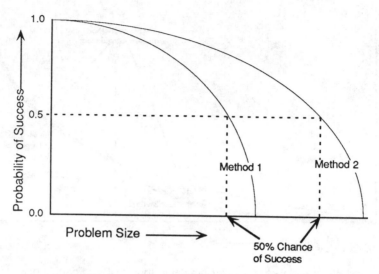

Figure 10–9.   A size/risk graph, showing how a project's chance of success depends on its size, for each of two methods. At the size where Method 1 has a 50 percent chance of success, Method 2 has about an 80 percent chance of success. Method 2 is obviously safer, though it says nothing about how much this safety will cost. For that, we'd need a size/effort graph.

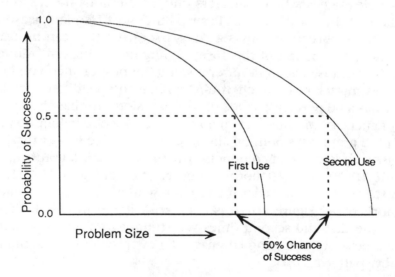

Figure 10–10.   A size/risk graph, showing how a project's chance of success depends on its size the first and second times a new method is used.

progress cannot afford this level of risk, so they'll let someone else be first. The decision to be second almost always makes sense to the individual manager. Thus, in order to move from one method to another, the risk on the decision maker has to be reduced. There are several tactics to help this change happen:

1. *Move the decision to a higher level of management.* For a higher-level manager, this will be only one risk of many so the risk is spread. It may, however, be difficult to find a lower-level manager willing to accept this project.

2. *Reduce the size of the first project.* This is the concept behind the *pilot project*. Unfortunately, many pilots forget this concept and choose a big project in order "to attract attention to the new technology." This is a poor strategy because the first time has a high risk of failure. If it's attention you want, get it on a project that succeeds, rather than one that fails. To do that, dedicate the first pilot to *learning* and the second to attention-getting. The first pilot can then only fail if you fail to learn from it.

3. *Reduce the criticality of the first project.* This is another concept behind the pilot project. It's fine to say that you're dedicating the first pilot to learning, but that won't work if users are depending on the first pilot to make millions. If you fail, you may not be given the opportunity to apply your learning to the next project.

Tactics such as these help raise the chance of successful technology transfer, but nothing can guarantee success with a new technology, no matter how helpful it promises to be. The use of graphical reasoning, however, guarantees that you don't fail because you failed to consider some important trade-off. That's all you can ask from a management tool.

10.3 Helpful Interactions

Now we can better understand the questions

1. How is it we keep doing harmful things over and over, even when we know better?

2. How can we be more helpful more consistently?

10.3.1 Do no harm

We do harmful things because we're trying to control systems that are beyond our mental capacity to control perfectly. That means we may not really know better because what we know may only be a simplification like "Never sacrifice your queen" that we've carried over from simpler control situations.

It also means we may not be able to see the true dynamics of a situation because so many dynamics combine to produce data with a high degree of variation. Only after we bring one dynamic after another under our control will this randomness start to disappear, and our process will become easier to understand. This kind of stability is what we need to move from Pattern 2 to Pattern 3.

With all this confusion, the short-term effects of our actions may be helpful; but the long-term effects are harmful, and we are not smart enough to see the connection. This kind of dynamic can create an *addiction,* which need not be to drugs. We can be addicted to any behavior, such as patching code directly in machine language. All such addictions are ultimately based on faulty intervention models—diseases of misguided intelligence.

10.3.2 Helpful Model

We are always trying to make sense of our world, to control it as much as we can, but the world is naturally more complex than our brains. We have simplifying models to help us measure what's going on and determine what to do about it. Because our models are only approximations, there are many ways we can fail. Or you can fail when I don't.

Sometimes, though, you are not failing at all. It's just that your models are not necessarily the same as mine, and in fact may be exact opposites. So when I see you doing something that seems to be making the situation worse, I don't immediately assume that you are trying to do harm. Instead, I apply what I call the *Helpful Model:*

No matter how it looks, everyone is trying to be helpful.

I often see interventions so bizarre that I get the impression people are attempting to sabotage the project and make me miserable. My Helpful Model leads me to see where other people's models of being helpful are going wrong and to deal more rationally with my own feelings of paranoia. The Helpful Model works for me because it takes away blame and lets me look at the dynamics independent of anybody's intention.

It also explains why people persist in doing something that wasn't helpful. Even when people's models are the same, they may be pursuing different *objectives.* Believing their intervention is helpful, they persist with enough strength to create a new intervention dynamic. Nobody has that much energy or patience for sabotage.

Using trade-off graphs such as size/effort and size/risk helps make these objectives available for public discussion; but why would people want to discuss trade-offs with someone they feel is trying to sabotage their efforts? If you're trying to save money while I'm secretly trembling with fear of project failure, my contributions are not likely to seem helpful to you. Always start by calling upon the Helpful Model.

10.3.3   Principle of Addition

To get rid of dysfunctional intervention dynamics, people's models must be changed. In a computer, you can simply erase the memory and load a new program, but people's brains don't work that way. Everything you have ever known is stored somewhere in your brain, so you can never eliminate mental models; you can only *add* to them. That's why this book is based on the *Principle of Addition:*

> **The best way to reduce ineffective behavior is by adding more effective behavior.**

That's ultimately the way I help organizations move from one pattern to another. As they add more effective models, they find them used more and more, and this simply leaves less opportunity for the ineffective ones to be used. Here's an example: Organizations get addicted to certain practices that are harmful in the long run, but relieve their pain in the short run. The more the organizations do them, the worse they feel, and the more they seek the relief of their addictive practices.

To counter such an addiction, add a long-range component to the organization's model. You need to measure things in the long range, and reward and punish behavior in the long range. Thus, if you find an organization addicted to some short-sighted intervention, you have to look for what rewards (explicit or implicit) are given for short-run success in this behavior. Then remove those if you can and supplement them with rewards that are tied to long-run success.

One organization was cured of code patching by a combination of interventions. First, I could see that patching was rewarded because the procedure seemed so much simpler than using the official configuration management system. I suggested providing a better configuration tool to make patching only marginally simpler than using the standard procedure.

Second, I observed that programmers were often rewarded for getting a product shipped on time even if they did it through bypassing the organization's procedures. Rather than trying to subtract this reward, I taught the managers to give even greater praise to programmers who conformed to the standards and still shipped on time.

10.3.4   Adding to the repertoire of models

By such a process of adding new systems of reinforcement, you may extinguish an addictive behavior. By adding a different model, however, you can do even better: You may prevent the addiction in the first place. That's because of the strong role that models play in people's behavior.

The way people behave is not based on reality, but on their *models* of reality.

Here's an example: I was working with a manager on the case of a "problem" employee. I was trying to get him to see that he was placating the employee, and by not confronting him, he was creating a co-dependent situation. I got nowhere and finally told the manager that I was going to stop, as I couldn't help him on this problem. The manager agreed.

As we were walking out of the room, the manager asked, "Now that that's done, can you help me with a personal problem?" We went back into the room to work on his "personal problem." As a new manager, he felt he was losing his technical abilities, and he lacked confidence. Once we got somewhere with his level of confidence, he stopped seeing the "problem" employee as a problem. The manager did what I suggested he do in the first place, but under a different model of what he was doing.

People with appropriate, effective models will never get hooked whether by drugs or code patching or problem employees. Ultimately, implanting a more effective model is the most helpful intervention.

10.4   Helpful Hints and Suggestions

1. Pattern 1 and Pattern 2 people are often found accusing one another of being destructive. Programmers believe that managers can manage best by staying out of their way, while managers believe that programmers try to avoid responsibility. They would both benefit from the Helpful Model, which reminds them that Pattern 2 people are often trying to do bigger things than Pattern 1 people. Often, the Routine managers are trying to enlarge products that were initially developed in a Variable culture. This effort brings them up against the Size/Complexity Dynamic, which may account for some of the "bizarre" things they try to inflict on programmers.

2. Routine cultures, when done well, often create Variable (Pattern 1) environments within themselves to do things that they don't do well, such as conducting small projects or those requiring creative breakthroughs. These Pattern 1 environments may be composed of individuals, teams, or third-party developers. Rather than being accused of recognizing that Variable culture is better, perhaps they should be congratulated for trying to be helpful and for their understanding of the dynamics of software engineering. They are a good step along the way to a Steering culture, and ought to be encouraged.

3. When buying software tools, ask the vendor to provide a size/risk graph showing their experience with a number of projects. If all problem sizes have a hundred percent chance of success, the vendor is either ignorant, stupid, or totally lacking in scruples. Don't buy a tool from a fool, a mule, or a ghoul.

4. If you ask Routine managers (or survey them) to draw size/risk curves for their organizations, you'll tend to get an overestimate of their prowess because they don't know what's happening in their organization. Thus, again, Pattern 2 may look on the surface as capable as Pattern 3. Ask them to put some data points on the graph and see how they correspond to their curves. If they can't supply data points, ask them why not?

5. If you ask managers to create size/effort curves or size/risk curves, they may start an argument over which measure of size they ought to use. Don't let yourself get involved in such arguments. Apply the Principle of Addition and create a separate graph for each person who is willing to support a favorite measure with a little data gathering effort. If they're not willing to gather data, politely ignore their arguments. You'll probably find that all the graphs look more or less alike. If not, you'll learn something very useful.

10.5   Summary

√   Our brain will never be big enough for our ambitions, so we'll always need thinking tools, such as size/effort graphs.

√   Size/effort graphs can be used to reason about the Size/Complexity Dynamic, such as when estimating a project or comparing the impact of two different technologies. However, such graphs as log-log graphs can also distort or conceal the nonlinear nature of the dynamic. We must learn to see the stable meaning through the variations in the data and the method of presentation.

√   Because of the Size/Complexity Dynamic, it's easy to write requirements that the most competent programmers cannot satisfy.

√   A single method or tool is seldom the best over the entire range of problem sizes. Size/effort graphs can help managers combine two methods into a composite pattern that adopts the best range for each one.

√   The bottom line doesn't dictate all technology choices. Managers are often willing to pay a lot on the bottom line to reduce the risk of failure. The size/risk graph can help in reasoning about these choices especially when used in conjunction with the size/effort graph.

√   If you set out to change an organization, the first rule should be the one given to physicians by Hippocrates: "Do no harm."

√   We are all subject to the Size/Complexity Dynamic, so interactions intended to be helpful often wind up being irrelevant or actually destructive. It's a good idea to assume that regardless of how it looks or sounds, everyone is trying to be helpful.

√   We can help most when we apply the Principle of Addition to add more effective models to a person's repertoire.

10.6   Practice

1.   Give an instance when you thought someone was being disruptive but it turned out the person was only trying to be helpful. How did you discover the true intention? How can you do it earlier next time?

2.   Give an instance when someone thought you were being disruptive when you were only trying to be helpful. What could you do next time to ensure that people know you're actually trying to be helpful?

3.   Draw a size/risk curve for your own organization's culture. How big a problem can you solve in a satisfactory manner at least fifty percent of the time? At least ninety percent of the time? At least often enough to meet your customers' tolerance for risk?

11

Responses to Customer Demands

When printing stylized text (shadow or outline) in large point sizes on the ImageWriter LQ and the Laser Writer IIsc, some characters may not print. This problem only occurs with a Mac-Plus, or SE, and varies depending on the application, font, font style and font size being used. When this happens, Apple recommends plain text.
—from Apple Computer's *Change Histories* for Macintosh System 6.02®

You can often tell an organization is in crisis by the attitudes expressed toward its customers and other outsiders. An organization in crisis is so entangled in its internal problems that it forgets its fundamental reason for existence. Up until now, we have considered the dynamics of the software organization as if it were a more-or-less *closed* system, which is the way many software organizations see themselves. In this chapter, we want to introduce a jolt of reality by relaxing that assumption and seeing how outside influences contribute to the instability of a development process.

11.1 Customers Can Be Dangerous to Your Health

In Chapter 3, I introduced the concepts of *customer demands* and how they influence the organization's need to move to new patterns (see, for example,

Figure 3-1). Just what do I mean by customer demands, and how exactly do they press upon an organization's choice of pattern?

11.1.1   More customers increase the development load

You know your software development organization is in trouble when you hear such complaints as

- "We have too many customers."
- "If only our customers didn't bother us, we could have a great system."
- "Why do they need all this stuff? We know what's best for them."

These complaints are justified. If you believe adding workers to a project is bad, think about what happens when you add *customers*. Figure 11-1 shows a natural dynamic underlying the trouble with customers. Since no two customers are identical, each new customer potentially adds requirements, which increases the size of the system and invokes the Size/Complexity Dynamic. This in itself would be a nonlinear effect, but some of those added requirements don't just differ among customers—they conflict.

Conflicting requirements add to the labor needed to build a system through one or more of the following:

- labor to resolve the conflict
- labor to explain why the resolution went one way and not the other
- labor to create and maintain multiple systems that satisfy everybody

11.1.2   More customers increase the maintenance load

Even if you increase the number of customers of an existing product without changing the way you do business, you may collapse your cultural pattern, as suggested in Figure 11-2.

This type of collapse has actually befallen several of my clients, as in the following case: I was called in to consult with a software organization that had been an independent software vendor until its acquisition eight months earlier by a much larger company known for its aggressive marketing. Its product, Zodiacal Business Forecasts (ZBF), was full of attractive features—on paper. Most of the features didn't work very well if at all, a fact that was known to most of the forty original customers. These customers had bought ZBF in the full knowledge that most features didn't work in order to get the one or two other features that worked reasonably well. These customers weren't delighted with ZBF's present buggy condition, but they believed they were getting value for their money, and had never been misled about its condition.

The same could not be said for the 110 new customers the parent organization brought into the ZBF fold in the first six months of aggressive marketing.

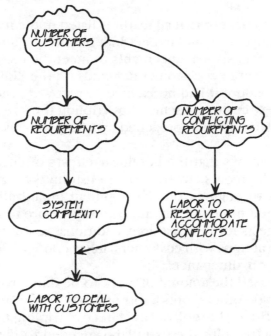

Figure 11–1.   As the number of customers increases, the development labor needed to deal with customer requirements grows nonlinearly.

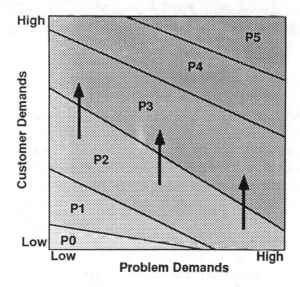

Figure 11–2.   The growth in the number of customers can by itself push an organization into a new region requiring a new cultural pattern. This kind of growth usually takes place faster than an organization can change its culture, so the organization must take steps to reduce the effective number of customers, or else break down.

They had been led to believe that all features listed in the marketing documents were working, as anyone would expect in a mature product. Moreover, many of them had been promised enhancements to meet their *real* needs.

When this wave of new customer demands hit the ZBF organization, it collapsed. Just to make sure it had no chance of recovery, the new management helped meet the new customer demand by tripling the size of the development staff. Two months later, I was approached by a desperate user group to see what I could do.

This example shows that the nonlinear effects of customers are not confined to initial development activities. More customers for ZBF meant increased customer demands throughout the development organization, including more field failures reported more quickly; increased pressure to repair these failures quickly; more requests for new features; additional requests for changes to old features; more interactions with customers; more configurations to support; and more releases under maintenance.

All these increased the amount of work to be done, while reducing the resources available to do other work—a sort of Brooks's Law applied to customers. Added to this was the real Brooks's Law effect of tripling the number of developers in a few months, plus the extra labor needed to create a new working relationship with the new customers. These changes could not be handled by the existing culture, so either the culture had to be changed or the number of customers reduced. Later, in Section 11.2.3, we'll see that because the culture couldn't be changed fast enough, ZBF set in motion a program of reducing the *effective* number of customers while the organization worked to get back on its feet.

11.1.3   Close contact with customers can be disruptive

If we imagine the software development organization as an organism, then the customers have many of the characteristics of *disease carriers*. For example, if we get in too close contact with them, we can become "infected"; and if we are "infected," we cannot do a good job of producing software. In order to regulate the system's output, the controller must keep the system healthy and so must deal with these "outside" forces (Figure 11-3).

11.1.4   The organization can be disruptive to the customers

Of course, the customers can look at your software organization the same way with equal justification. Perhaps we can improve the analogy by thinking of the customers as *mates*. Your organization needs intimate contact with them for survival of the species, but close contact may expose the organization to some terrible disease, or at least a common cold. Like mates, customers do not intend to cause diseases. It's in their best interest to have a healthy mate. The same

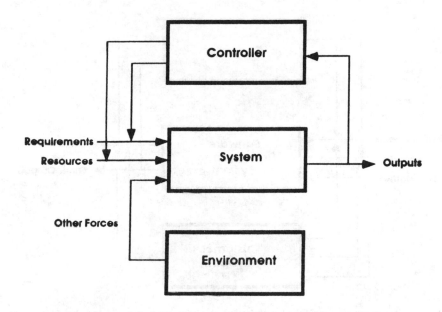

Figure 11–3.   The feedback model of a system can be elaborated by showing that part of the system is dedicated to regulating outside forces, such as disease carriers.

goes for your development organization. If you make your customers sick, then you go out of business.

Figure 11-4 shows a more complete interpretation of the *Mate Model,* in which the "Customer System" needs the outputs of the "Software Development System." To get these outputs, it supplies "Requirements" to indicate its needs and "Resources" to empower the development system to produce them. In the process, it also supplies some "Randomness," or "viruses," which are a potential threat to getting what it wants. The "Customer System" cannot always know which inputs are which primarily because many of the inputs serve more than one purpose.

Notice that in this view the customer looks just like a controller, as indeed it *is.* The customer's attempts to control the software development system are sometimes in concert with the system's own controller, but not always. When they are not synchronized, the customer's organization is actually working against its own ultimate purposes, but doesn't know it. It's easy to see how that situation can contribute to instability, as in the case of the electric blanket.

11.1.5   What happens when there are many customers?

The situation is even worse if we add yet another level of reality. Figure 11-5 suggests the effects of having more than one customer. The development sys-

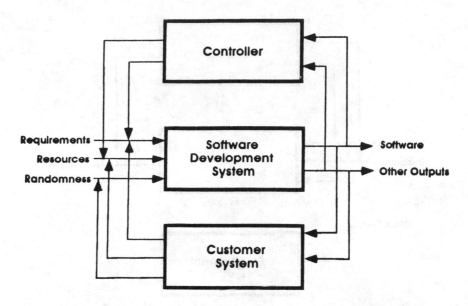

Figure 11–4.   The feedback model of a software development system can be elaborated with
                 an interpretation of the customer's role as a supplier of external inputs. Some
                 of these inputs are necessary requirements, but others are seen as random
                 disturbances.

tem *wants* multiple customers because it can obtain more resources from them;
but in return it gets multiple requirements, some of which conflict, and lots of
extra randomness, as we saw in the ZBF case.

11.2   The Cast of Outsiders

Customers are not the only dangerous outsiders. There are so many outsiders
who threaten the stability of software development that it is useful to lump
them into several major categories: customers and users, the marketing function, other surrogates, programmers, testers, and unplanned surrogates.

11.2.1   Customers and users

Sometimes, it's helpful to distinguish customers from "users" (users include everyone affected by the system. You may not need to satisfy all of the users as
you do the customers, who have the right to define quality by giving you requirements. Even so, the users are out there interacting with the system, and
that in itself will eventually produce some sort of extra requirements. At the
very least, the users will experience failures. When these failures come back to
your organization, they become requirements about faults to locate and fix.

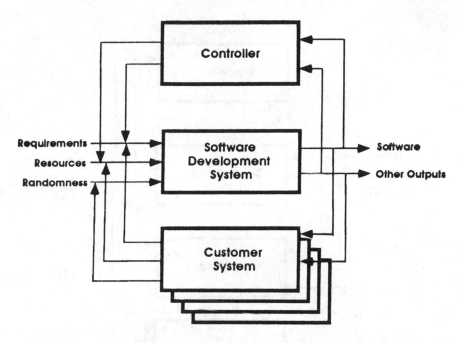

Figure 11–5.   With multiple customers, there are more potential resources. There are also
multiple requirements, which may conflict, and lots more randomness.

11.2.2 Marketing function

In development organizations that sell their products, we often find a *marketing
function*. Marketing is not the customer of the development organization, but
a *surrogate* that *represents* the customer, sometimes well and sometimes badly.
If you satisfy the customers, you don't really have to satisfy marketing; but if you
don't trust marketing, you have a problem.

   If customers are like disease carriers, marketing is like a hypodermic injection of medicine. We create a marketing function to stand between the disease
carrier and the system to reduce the flow of disturbances (Figure 11-6). "Marketing" in this sense may include a variety of roles, such as developing product
requirements, aiding in the installation of new systems, training users, and ser-
vicing any problems that arise at the customer's location.

   In return for this reduction of disturbances, however, we put another group
of people—the marketing staff—nearer the core of the system, under the skin
("hypo-dermic") as it were. Because of this position of marketing, *their* disturbances bypass all other defenses. There may be fewer disturbances, but each
one is harder to deal with because they are already "inside." The effect of these
people wandering among the development staff is like a strong medicine wandering inside your body. They act faster, and they act undiluted. You may get
side effects that are worse than the original disease. That's why the marketing

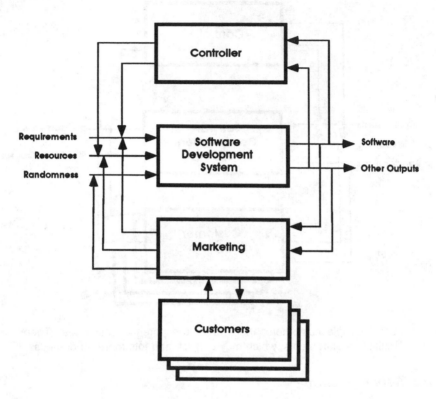

Figure 11–6.   A marketing function is created to stand between the customers and the development organization to filter inputs and outputs. In reducing the flow of disturbance, this role is helpful; but because it is closer to the core of the development organization, it has great potential for harm.

organization, like any medicine, can so easily stop being a solution and start being a problem.

11.2.3   Other surrogates

Marketing isn't the only surrogate. Even when the product is not sold but developed internally, organizations create the position of *customer liaison* to stand between the developer and the customer. The effect of all such surrogates is to change the actual number of customers to an "effective number"—the number with which the development organization has to deal (Figure 11-7).

Another common surrogate is the *customer service function,* which is sometimes considered part of marketing, sometimes part of development, and sometimes independent. An independent customer service function serves the filtering need best if it truly cannot be co-opted by development or marketing. This is the approach I used at ZBF, although ZBF met great resistance from the

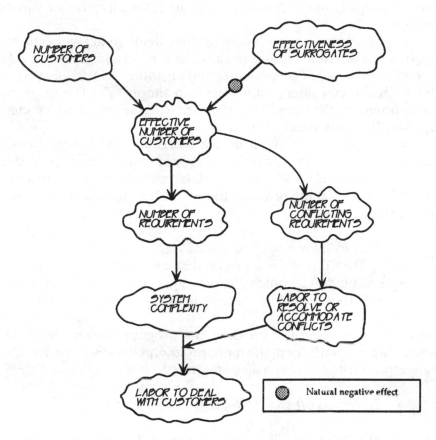

Figure 11–7.   The surrogate, if acting effectively, reduces the effective number of customers, thus reducing the nonlinear effects of the number of customers.

old-time developers who wanted to give the customers "personal service," as they had in "the good old days." The initial result was a reduction in the amount of interference from the new customers, but it took more than a year and a complete change in the phone system before even half of the old customers stopped calling the developers directly.

11.2.4   Programmers as self-appointed user surrogates

Programmers appoint themselves as user surrogates. In that sense, they are "inside outsiders." If they're not satisfied, they have the power to stop the system from working, just like the customers—only faster. If marketing is like a hypodermic injection of medicine, programmers are even worse; they're like an injection of viruses that migrates directly to the inside of cells. From there, they can do awesome things—awesome in their creativity or awesome in their destructiveness, or both. It is this destructive potential that so strongly motivates Routine (Pattern 2) managers to get rid of all traces of Variable (Pattern 1) culture.

Paradoxically, programmers are not likely to act as customer or user surrogates in a Variable culture because of the close, one-to-one relationship that often exists between programmer and customer. If Variable programmers wonder what the customers want, they can simply ask. The more customers they have, however, the more likely they are to make decisions for customers on the fly, whether authorized or not.

One of the marks of an unstable organization is how frequently the programmers are making unauthorized, and often unnoticed, decisions about what the customer really wants. Making decisions for customers is a tempting shortcut when the pressure mounts. You can almost hear the programmers muttering,

- "They'll love this neat trick."
- "They'd never want to do that anyway."
- "This will be much clearer, especially to the smart ones."
- "If they don't like this feature, they don't deserve it."

Sometimes, even most of the time, the programmers are right. But what about when they are not? Then, the more programmers you have, the more potentially dangerous customer surrogates you have.

11.2.5   Testers as official and unofficial surrogates

Testers, of course, are official surrogates of the customers, attempting to faithfully replicate customers' use of a system before they have to suffer from its slings and arrows. If effective in this role, testers can dampen the effects of increased numbers of customers; but being closer to the developers than the customers, they often fail to act as effective surrogates. Rather than annoy a developer, they will all too easily agree with the developer who argues, "What customers in their right mind would want to do that?"

Unofficially, then, testers are incessantly making implicit decisions about what customers would and what they wouldn't do. This implicit decision making is characteristic of Pattern 2 organizations, and tends to thwart the best-laid testing plans.

11.2.6   Unplanned surrogates

Liaisons and customer service people are planned responses to increased customer demand, but outsiders may appoint themselves customer surrogates, just as the programmers do from the inside—to be helpful. One customer may speak or claim to speak for a group of customers. A so-called user group is a surrogate for a group of customers. Members of the press may take it upon themselves to act on behalf of a group of users or even potential users. And, I shudder to think of it, the people in some branch of the government may decide that only they know what's best for the users.

Each of these surrogates can gather information that would be difficult to obtain elsewhere and, like marketing, can provide filtering factors for excessive amounts of feedback. Yet they can also provide additional doses of trouble for the unstable organization to handle. From the dynamic point of view, the critical questions about any outsider, surrogate or otherwise, are these:

1.   Where do they interact with the system—close in or far away?

2.   With what force, or volume, do they interact?

3.   With what frequency do they appear?

Let's examine a few important interactions, keeping in mind that they probably were intended to be helpful.

11.3   Interactions with Customers

As the number of customers increases, the most obvious dynamic change is that the number of interactions with customers must change. How does the number of interactions grow, and how does this growth affect the productivity and quality of the organization?

11.3.1   Dynamics of interruption

An hour of work is not an hour of work if you are interrupted during the hour. DeMarco and Lister studied the effect of interrupt-free time on productivity. They cite a metric[1]

$$E\text{-factor} = \frac{\text{Uninterrupted Hours}}{\text{Body-Present Hours}}$$

In one instance, they recorded a range of E-factors in their coding experiments from 0.10 to 0.38. The people in the first instance need 3.8 times as many body-present hours to accomplish the same work as those in the second instance.

This is a very approximate measure of the effect of interruptions. A more precise way of looking at this information is to consider the lasting effect of an interruption. DeMarco and Lister introduce the concept of "reimmersion time":

> If the average incoming phone call takes five minutes and your reimmersion period is fifteen minutes, the total cost of that call in flow time (work time) lost is twenty minutes. A dozen phone calls use up half a day. A dozen other

interruptions and the rest of the work day is gone. This is what guarantees, "You never get anything done around here between 9 and 5."[2]

11.3.2   Interrupted meetings

Of course, interruptions don't always come when we're working alone. De-Marco and Lister cite IBM's Santa Teresa study[3] as showing that software developers spend thirty percent of their time working alone, fifty percent working with one other person, and twenty percent working with two or more others.

How does interruption affect the working-together times? In our consulting, Dani and I observe that reimmersion time is greater the more people in the group who are interrupted. If, for instance, a meeting of seven people is interrupted for one person to take an emergency call, the other six people scatter out of the meeting room to attend to various tasks. The meeting then stays interrupted until the *last* of the seven returns, which can be a long time. These two factors create a nonlinear effect of number of people on wasted time, as shown in Figure 11-8.

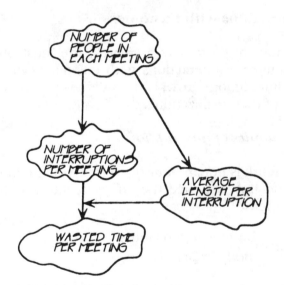

Figure 11–8.   The more people in the meeting, the more interruptions there are and the longer each interruption is, so that wasted time is a nonlinear effect of the size of the meeting.

Once they are all together, there is still more time needed to get them all on the same track. Usually, this period is extended because some of the people need to discuss what happened when they were out of the room.

For one client, I kept track of a series of review meetings we were holding with seven people. Over six meetings, there were 13 interruptions when one of the people was called out of the room. The time between the call and the meeting to get back on track ranged from 13 minutes to 47 minutes, with an average of 21 minutes. (In the 47-minute interruption, two of the people never came back, but the meeting went on in a fashion without them after waiting 47 minutes.)

If this pattern is typical and if the average meeting had seven people, then this client was wasting $21 \times 7 = 147$ work-minutes every time a meeting was interrupted. Some of that time was undoubtedly put to good use, but I would estimate a loss of two full hours of work time for each meeting that was interrupted. At a burdened labor cost of $50 per hour, each interruption cost about $100. We created a sign asking

IS THIS INTERRUPTION WORTH $100?

to hang on the door of each review meeting. It seemed to have some effect, for the interruptions decreased.

11.3.3   Meeting size and frequency

McCue's observations are of one organization (IBM) doing one type of work. My own observations show that these numbers vary from organization to organization, depending on a number of factors. Among these factors is the number of customers.

The number of customers affects both the frequency of meetings and their average size. I have observed that the number of meetings grows as the number of customers grows, but reaches a maximum at about ten to twenty customers. Up to that point, increasing the number of customers has even greater nonlinear effects on wasted time than suggested by the dynamic of Figure 11-8. In that case, the effects are better illustrated by Figure 11-9.

Why doesn't the complexity grow after ten to twenty customers? This curious pattern seems to arise from the customers' expectations. When a software organization serves a small number of customers, each customer's organization feels that it deserves to be given individual attention. This is the typical pattern in several situations:

- an in-house application that serves only a few customers because several departments have the same function to perform, like physical inventory
- a consortium arrangement, whereby the software developers serve a few organizations for cost savings; for instance, the Bellcore organization develops software for the former Bell operating companies
- a start-up organization that has its first few customers

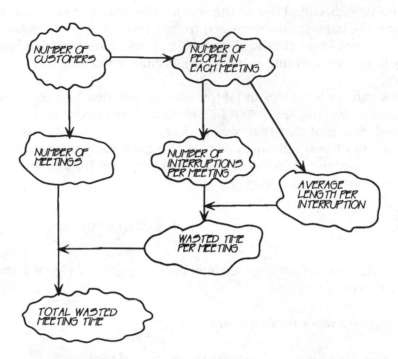

Figure 11–9.   The more customers, the more meetings, and the larger those meetings are. These factors combine to create even more nonlinearity in the amount of wasted time as the number of customers grows.

In each of these cases, the people who decide to have one software package for several customers believe their needs are similar. When considered in detail, however, every customer's needs are different. A software organization must spend time meeting with each customer to discover its exact needs and to adapt the package to those individual needs.

When the number of customers grows much larger, however, it becomes physically impossible to serve each one's needs exactly. Moreover, most customers don't really *expect* that they will get the package modified to their exact needs. In any case, the software organization begins to treat customer needs *statistically,* so that they no longer need an ever-increasing number of customer meetings.

11.4   Configuration Support

More customers can mean more hardware configurations for the software to support, because marketing wants to reach everybody. What are some of the effects of supporting multiple hardware configurations?

11.4.1   Effects on test coverage and repair time

The number of configurations tends to grow exponentially over time, since all it takes to differentiate one configuration from another is to change *any one component* touched by the software product. Consider this example:

UGLI Software had one software product for a personal computer intended for use with 15 different CPUs (some of which were called IBM compatibles but were in fact slightly different from the IBM original), 21 different printers, 16 different disk drives, and 4 different networks. This led to $15 \times 21 \times 16 \times 4 = 20,160$ different configurations, without counting different software that the word processor had to work with.

Of course, not all these configurations could be tested. Although most of them worked quite well, not a day would pass without some customer calling UGLI's technical service department with a problem on a configuration the technician had never seen before. And when such customers did call, UGLI often couldn't reproduce the configurations in the test lab and had to work on locating the problem without having the actual hardware configuration the customer was using. Even when UGLI could reproduce them, the set-up time added considerably to the time to fix the errors.

Having different configurations means that test coverage is less thorough, which means more faults to repair. But different configurations also means that each repair will take longer and that each repair becomes a multiple repair—the multiplier being perhaps as great as the number of configurations supported. Therefore, the number of repairs can be much greater than the number of faults in the software, and also grows nonlinearly with the number of customers. Total repair time, of course, is total repairs multiplied by the time per repair. The overall effect is shown in Figure 11-10.

Obviously, in practice, any software culture that produces high numbers of faults could never keep up with all the potential configurations. They are thus forced either to change their culture or lower their support level for configurations. They generally choose the latter, for reasons that will become obvious in the analysis in the following section.

11.4.2   Analyzing the test situation externally: An Apple example

The Apple quote at the beginning of this chapter is a typical example of what happens when any developer attempts to continue to support multiple feature combinations on multiple-hardware configurations. I know the story of the Apple release 6.02 only as a devoted Macintosh user, not as an insider, so it makes a good example of analyzing a situation externally.

At the time of this system release, if I'm counting correctly, Apple was supporting seven Macintosh CPUs, and seven official Apple printers, for at least 49 different relevant hardware configurations. (People with non-Apple printers

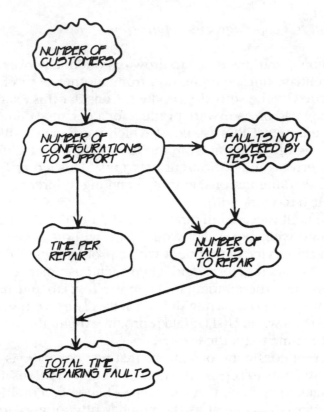

Figure 11–10.   A large number of customers has a nonlinear effect on the amount of time spent repairing faults because of the larger number of potential configurations.

and CPU upgrades presumably had already learned to take their own chances on what would work and what wouldn't.)

On the software side, the problem was much worse. There is no limit to the number of fonts, but just counting fonts released with its printers, Apple had perhaps 10 to support. The style menu offered 7 options besides Plain—Bold, Italic, Underline, Outline, Shadow, Condensed, and Extended. The first 5 of these can be used in any combination, which makes 32 different combinations, of which Plain is only one instance. Any of these can be Normal, Condensed, or Extended, which means there are $3 \times 32 = 96$ styles for each font. Font size can be just about anything—I have used from 4 point to 72 point—but let's say we consider 8 to be a typical number shown on the font menu. Not even worrying about what might happen if we superscripted or subscripted a 72 point Zapf Chancery Condensed Italic Shadow font, Apple has to test $10 \times 96 \times 8 = 7,680$ font combinations.

But the memo states that the results vary "depending on the application." There are hundreds of Macintosh applications, but suppose that Apple only tested the top 100. They would now have 100 applications, times 49 hardware configurations, times 7,680 font combinations, for a grand total of 37,632,000 configurations to test for proper printing. Assume that with highly automated testing techniques, Apple could test one configuration in the amount of time it took to print a page. Then, with the seven different printers working simultaneously, it would require more than five years to test all of these configurations. If ten tests could be printed on a page, the output paper would stack about as high as a 120-story building, and somebody would have to check each paper carefully to see which characters did not print.

What this analysis shows is that neither Apple nor anyone else in a comparable situation can actually expect to test all the configurations Apple theoretically supports. As a result, the company can expect a continuing stream of complaints from customers who try "bizarre" combinations of features. Indeed, I myself found a certified hardware error in my LaserWriter Plus when trying to print Extended Outline Times font in a header. It worked swell on the first page, but not on the second. Perhaps they only tested the first page. Or only tested footers, and didn't test headers at all. Would you be surprised?

11.5 Releases

This Apple problem appeared in Release 6.02 of the system software. A *release* is a point at which a piece of work passes from one group to another. More specifically, a *software release* takes place when the work actually begins to be used for some productive work. The 6.02 means (probably) that this was the second "minor" revision of the sixth major release. We can't be sure because marketing departments play tricks with release numbers so their software development culture doesn't look quite so shabby.

11.5.1 Pre- and post-release dynamics

The release concept is critical to software quality dynamics because at the moment of release, the dynamic structure changes. For instance, for a particular software product, more than one version of the software exists, and each version must be accounted for at all times. As a result, developers are not really working with one system, but with N systems, which threatens to multiply the workload by N right off the bat. Sometimes N can be very large. Also, errors flow into the development organization at a much faster rate in a much less organized fashion, because there are more people finding errors.

The urgency of correcting errors is much greater because once the product is in real use, it must typically continue in use uninterrupted. Thus, part of the development organization is now driven by an external clock, perhaps many external clocks, rather than being largely in control of its own pace. The cost of an incorrect change is much greater, sometimes millions of times greater, because effects are no longer confined to the development organization's boundaries. Costs are incurred in the customer's own business as well, and more than one business has been driven into bankruptcy by released errors. Only software companies fail because of unreleased errors.

11.5.2   Multiple versions

With only a single customer, the release concept doesn't really apply as there is only one physical copy of the software in use, which effectively defines the current state. You may, of course, have another version in ongoing development. With more customers, you need releases, or else you would have to maintain as many versions of the system as there are customers. If you have discrete release points, in theory there will be only as many versions to maintain as there are active releases, plus those releases that are in use internally.

In practice, more customers means more versions than the release concept would imply. If a release hits a major customer and doesn't work, the software organization will often send a patch to that customer. Different customers soon have different collections of patches, each one amounting to a somewhat different release. Again, this effect is most pronounced with a moderate number of customers, and tends to disappear when there are enough customers to treat them statistically with no special favors.

More releases in operation at any given time means more trouble with repairs because each repair must work with every release in use. In theory, this implies that every repair must be tested against every release; but in reality, this conservative approach may be shortcut under pressure, which increases the chances of introducing new errors.

With more customers, people will be installing the releases at many different times, so that repairs may accumulate and not be applied in the right order or some not applied at all. This adds to the complexity of understanding failure reports.

Once an item—a single patch or a whole system—is released to the customers, it follows a different dynamic than an internal item. Customers start using the item to do their work; and if it fails, the urgency to repair is much greater than for a similar failure inside the development organization.

Moreover, failures in the development cycle tend to occur at times when the organization is prepared for failures, with people dedicated to fixing them and getting on with the development. Failures after release to many customers come in on an almost continuous basis, interrupting all other work at any stage.

11.5.3   Release frequency

Management often tries to cut down on the failure load by slowing down the repair releases; but this means that distribution time gets longer, and so the same failure is reported more often. On the other hand, as the number of customers increases, the pressure to release more frequently increases, which tends to balance the pressure to make the release time longer. Perhaps that is why we often find software products in mature organizations released exactly twice a year, regardless of the application, the number of customers, or any other factor. If release frequency varies a great deal from twice a year, it may be a sign of instability and suggests that deeper examination of the dynamics would be profitable.

11.6   Helpful Hints and Suggestions

1. The liaison is supposed to represent the customer to the developers and the developers to the customers, filtering demands from each and reducing the effective numbers of customers. Often, the liaisons get co-opted by one side or the other, whereupon they serve as amplifiers—rather than filters—of disturbance.

2. There is a dynamic of the difficulty of satisfying customers versus the number of customers. Factors in this dynamic include the customers' expectations of getting all their requirements satisfied, the developer's standards for satisfying customers, and the difficulty of satisfying multiple requirements. As the number of customers goes up, after a certain point most customers no longer expect to have all their wishes satisfied. Similarly, the developers don't imagine that they can satisfy each of 100,000 customers' exact requirements.

    The result is a hump-backed curve, which my own observations indicate usually peaks at around nine customers. This is the kind of thing you get when a consortium of single customers decides to share work to save development costs. Each expects to get his or her own way in everything because the price paid is still much higher than for that of a custom software product.

3. As the number of customers grows even further, the developers first try to satisfy all of them, but eventually are unable to do this. In self-protection, they start to assign importance to different customers, perhaps on the basis of how much they are paying or perhaps on how nice (or nasty) they are in dealing with the developers. Once the number of customers gets large enough, any individual customer is written off with a shrug of the shoulders and the remark, "You can't satisfy every bizarre request."

4. Fred Brooks was the first to my knowledge to write about the difference between a program and a program product.[4] A product must have more function and also be "bulletproof," so the amount of work goes up nonlinearly. Managers who have successful programs often are tempted to make them into products, without realizing this dynamic, let alone the dynamic of releases and of combinatoric configurations.

11.7 Summary

√ The relationship with customers is the second important factor driving organizations to adopt particular software cultural patterns.

√ Simply increasing the number of customers can wreak vast changes on an
organization, such as

- increasing the development load
- increasing the maintenance load
- disrupting the pattern of development work

√ On the other hand, a software development organization can be extremely
disruptive to its customers. That's why customers try to be controllers of
the software development organization, leading to a situation of multiple
controllers. The more controllers, the more randomness there appears to
the other controllers.

√ The cast of outsiders who may influence software development is enormous, including such roles as

- customers and users
- marketing function
- other surrogates
- programmers as self-appointed user surrogates
- testers as official and unofficial surrogates
- unplanned surrogates

√ Many of these outside roles are planned as attempts to reduce the effective
number of customers.

√ Because some of the surrogates are much more intimate than others with
the development system, they may negate their reduction of the effective
number of customers with the force and frequency of their interactions.

√ Interactions with customers are fraught with peril as the number of customers grows: Interruptions increase; meetings increase in size and frequency; and time lost because of interrupted meetings increases. All of
these increases are nonlinear.

√ With more customers comes more configurations to support. More configurations means additional coding, more complex testing, less effective test
coverage, and longer repair times.

√   Releases are needed whenever there are multiple customers. As soon as a product is released to customers, it assumes an entirely different dynamic than when it was held in the shadow of the development organization.

√   Multiple versions of a software product complicate maintenance enormously, but more customers means more versions, whether official or unofficial. Frequent releases complicate the development/maintenance process, but so do infrequent releases, such that almost all software cultures tend to stabilize releases at around two per year.

11.8   Practice

1.   Draw a diagram of effects, similar to the Brooks's Law diagram, showing how increasing the number of customers affects a development organization. Are there any self-limiting feedback loops in your diagram?

2.   What forces affect the identification of a customer service organization with the customers? What forces affect its identification with the developers? Can you diagram these forces?

3.   Explain why it's usually faster to reduce the effective number of customers than to change the culture of a development organization.

4.   Propose a set of guidelines that could reduce the effect of the number of customers on meeting size and frequency.

5.   Propose a set of guidelines that could reduce the effect of the size of meetings on the amount of time wasted. What difficulties do you foresee in applying these guidelines in your own organization?

Part IV
Fault Patterns

Three of the great discoveries of our time have to do with programming: the programming of the human mind (psychoanalysis), the programming of inheritance through DNA, and the programming of computers. In each case, the idea of *error* plays a central role.

Sigmund Freud's development of psychoanalysis opened the twentieth century and set a tone for the other two. In his introductory lectures,[1] Freud opened the human mind to inspection through the use of errors—what we now call "Freudian slips."

The second of these discoveries was DNA.[2] Once again, key clues to the workings of inheritance were offered by the study of errors, such as mutations, which were mistakes in transcribing the genetic code from one generation to the next.

The third of these discoveries was the stored program computer. From the first, the pioneers considered error a central concern. John von Neumann[3] noted that the largest effort of natural organisms was devoted to the problem of survival in the face of error, and that the programmer of a computer need be similarly concerned.

In all three of these great intellectual innovations, errors were treated not as lapses in intelligence, or moral failures, or insignificant trivialities—all common attitudes in the past. Instead, errors were treated as *sources of valuable information*.

The treatment of error as a source of valuable information is precisely what distinguishes the feedback (error-controlled) system from its less capable predecessors—and thus distinguishes Steering software cultures from Patterns 1 and 2. Organizations in those patterns have more traditional—and less productive—attitudes about the role of errors in software development, attitudes that they will have to change if they are to transform themselves into Pattern 3 organizations. So, in the following chapters, we'll explore what happens to Pattern 1 and especially Pattern 2 organizations as they battle those "inevitable" errors in their software.

181

12

Observing and Reasoning About Errors

Men are not moved by things, but by the views which they take of them.
—Epictetus

One of my editors complained that the first sections of this chapter spent "an inordinate amount of time on semantics, relative to the thorny issues of software failures and their detection." What I wanted to say to her and what I will say to you is that semantics is one of the roots of "the thorny issues of software failures and their detection." Therefore, I need to start this part of the book by clearing up some of the most subversive ideas about and definitions of failure. If you already have a perfect understanding of software failure, then skim quickly, and please forgive me.

12.1   Conceptual Errors About Errors

12.1.1   Errors are not a moral issue

"What do you do with a person who is nine hundred pounds overweight who approaches the problem without even wondering how a person gets to be nine hundred pounds overweight?" This is the question Tom DeMarco put to me when he read an early version of the upcoming chapters. He was exasperated about clients who were having trouble managing more than ten thousand error reports per product. So was I.

More than thirty years ago in my first book on computer programming, Herb Leeds and I emphasized what we then considered the first principle of programming:

The best way to deal with errors is not to make them in the first place.

In those days, like many hotshot programmers, I meant "best" in a moral sense:

1.   Those of us who don't make errors are better than those of you who do.

I still consider this the first principle of programming, but somehow I no longer apply any *moral* sense to the principle, but only an *economic* sense:

2.   Most errors cost more to handle than they cost to prevent.

This, I believe, is part of what Crosby means when he says, "Quality is free." Even if it were a moral question in the sense of (1), I don't think that Pattern 3 cultures, which do a great deal to prevent errors, can claim any moral superiority over Pattern 1 and Pattern 2 cultures, which do not. You cannot say that people are morally inferior because they don't do something they *cannot* do, and Pattern 1 and Pattern 2 software cultures, where most programmers reside, are *culturally incapable* of preventing large numbers of errors. Why?

Let me put Tom's question another way: "What do you do with a person who is rich, admired by thousands, overloaded with exciting work, nine hundred pounds overweight, and has 'no problem' except for occasional work lost because of back problems?" Tom's question *presumes* that the thousand-pound plus person perceives a *weight* problem, but what if that person only perceives a *back* problem. Weight, *per se,* is not a problem unless you perceive it as a problem—perceive its connection to your other problems.

In the same way, my Pattern 1 and 2 clients with tens of thousands of errors in their software do not perceive they have a serious problem with errors. They are making money, and they are winning the praise of their customers. On two products out of three, the complaints are generally at a tolerable level. With their rate of profit, who cares if a third of their projects have to be written off as a total loss?

If I attempt to discuss these mountains of errors with Pattern 1 and 2 clients, they reply, "In programming, errors are inevitable, but we've got them more or less under control. Don't worry about *errors*. We want you to help us get things out on *schedule*." They see no more connection between enormous error rates and two-year schedule slippages than the obese person sees between nine hundred pounds of body fat and pains in the back. Can I accuse them of having the wrong moral attitude about errors? I may just as well accuse a blind person of having the wrong moral attitude about the rainbow.

But it is a moral question for me, their consultant. If my thousand-pound client is *happy,* it's not my business to tell him how to lose weight. If he comes to me with back problems, I can show him through a diagram of effects how weight affects his back. Then it's up to *him* to decide how much pain is worth how many chocolate cakes.

12.1.2   Quality is not the same thing as absence of errors

Errors in software used to be a moral issue for me, and they still are for many writers. Perhaps that's why these writers have asserted, "Quality is the absence of errors." It must be a moral issue for them, because otherwise it would be a grave error in reasoning. Here's how their reasoning may have gone wrong. Perhaps they observed that when their work is interrupted by numerous software errors, they can't appreciate any other good software qualities. From this observation, they conclude that many errors will make software worthless—that is, zero quality.

But here's the fallacy in that thinking:

Though copious errors guarantees worthlessness, having zero errors guarantees nothing at all about the value of software.

Let's take one example. Would you offer me $100 for a zero defect program to compute the horoscope of Philip Amberly Warblemaxon, who died in 1927 after a 37-year career as a filing clerk in a hat factory in Akron? I doubt it, because to have value, software must be *more than perfect*. It must be *useful to someone*.

Still, I would never deny the importance of errors. First of all, if I did, Pattern 1 and Pattern 2 organizations would stop reading this book. To them, chasing errors is as natural as chasing sheep is to a German Shepherd dog. And as we've seen, when they see the rather different life of a Pattern 3 organization, they simply don't believe it.

Second of all, I do know that when errors run away from us, we have lost quality. Perhaps our customers will tolerate 10,000 errors; but, as Tom DeMarco asked me, will they tolerate 10,000,000,000,000,000,000,000,000,000? In this sense, errors *are* a matter of quality. Therefore, we must train people to make *fewer* errors, while at the same time managing the errors they do make to keep them from running away.

12.1.3 The terminology of errors

I've sometimes found it hard to talk about the dynamics of errors in software because there are many different ways of talking about the errors themselves. One of the best ways for a consultant to assess the software engineering maturity of organizations is by examining the language they use, particularly the language they use to discuss errors. To take an obvious example, those who call everything "bugs" are a long way from taking responsibility for controlling their own process. Until they start using precise and accurate language, there's little sense in teaching such people about basic dynamics.

Faults and failures

First of all, it pays to distinguish between *failures* (the symptoms) and *faults* (the diseases). Musa et al. give these definitions:[1]

- A "failure" is "the departure of the external results of program operation from requirements."
- A "fault" is "the defect in the program that, when executed under particular conditions, causes a failure."

For example, an accounting program had an incorrect instruction (fault) in the formatting routine that inserted commas in large numbers such as $4,500,000. Any time a user printed a number greater than six digits, a comma could be missing (a failure). Many failures resulted from this one fault.

How many failures result from a single fault? That depends on where the fault is, how long the fault remains before it is removed, and how many people are using the software. The comma insertion fault led to millions of failures because it was in a frequently used piece of code, was in software that had thousands of users, and remained unresolved for more than a year.

When studying error reports of various clients, I often find that they mix failures and faults in the same statistics because they don't understand the distinction. If these two different measures are mixed into one, it will be difficult to understand their own experiences. For instance, because a single fault can lead to many failures, it would be impossible to compare failures between two organizations that aren't careful in making this semantic distinction.

Organization A has 100,000 customers who use its software product for an average of three hours a day. Organization B has a single internal customer who uses its software system once a month. Organization A produces one fault per thousand lines of code, and receives more than a hundred complaints a day. Organization B produces a hundred faults per thousand lines of code, but receives only one complaint a month.

Organization A claims it has better software developers than Organization B. Organization B claims it has better software developers than Organization A. Perhaps they're both right. Perhaps each knows how to develop software that's best for its own customers.

System trouble incident

Because of the important distinction between faults and failures, I encourage my clients to keep at least two different statistics. The first of these is a database of *system trouble incidents* (STIs). In this book, I'll mean an STI to be an incident report of one failure as experienced by a customer or simulated customer (such as a tester).

I know of no industry standard nomenclature for these reports except that they invariably take the form of TLAs (Three Letter Acronyms). The TLAs I have encountered include

- STR for software trouble report
- SIR for software incident report or system incident report
- SPR for software problem report or software problem record
- MDR for malfunction detection report
- CPI for customer problem incident
- SEC for significant error case
- SIR for software issue report
- DBR for detailed bug report or detailed bug record
- SFD for system failure description
- STD for software trouble description or software trouble detail

I generally try to follow my client's naming conventions, but I also try hard to find out exactly what is meant. I encourage every organization to use unique, descriptive names. It tells me a lot about a software organization when it uses more than one TLA for the same item. Workers in that organization are confused, just as my readers would be confused if I kept switching among ten TLAs for STIs. The reasons I prefer STI to some of the above are as follows:

1. It makes no prejudgment about the fault that led to the failure. For instance, it might have been a misreading of the manual, or a mistyping that wasn't noticed. Calling it a bug, an error, a failure, or a problem tends to mislead.

2. Calling it a "trouble incident" implies that once upon a time, somebody, somewhere, was sufficiently troubled by something to bother making a

report. Since the definition of quality is "value to some person," someone who was troubled implies that it's *worth* something to look at the STI with the assumption that people don't like being troubled.

3. The words "software" and "code" also contain a presumption of *guilt,* which may unnecessarily restrict location and correction activities. We may correct an STI with a code fix, but we may also change a manual, upgrade a training program, change our ads or sales pitch, furnish a help message, change the design, or let it stand unchanged. The word "system" says to me that any part of the overall system may contain the fault, and any part or parts may receive the corrective activity.

4. The word "customer" excludes troubled people who don't happen to be customers, such as programmers, analysts, salespeople, managers, hardware engineers, or testers. We should be so happy to receive reports of troublesome incidents *before* they get to customers that we wouldn't want to discourage anybody.

Similar principles of semantic precision might guide your own design of TLAs, to remove one more source of error, or one more impediment to their removal. Pattern 3 organizations always use TLAs more precisely than do Pattern 1 and 2 organizations.

System fault analysis

The second statistic is a database of information on faults, which I call *system fault analysis* (SFA). Few of my clients initially keep such a database separate from their STIs, so I haven't found such a diversity of TLAs. Ed Ely tells me, however, that he has seen the name RCA for *root cause analysis.* Since RCA would never do, the name SFA is a helpful alternative because, first, it clearly speaks about faults, not failures. This is an important distinction. No SFA is created until a fault has been identified. When an SFA is created, it is tied back to as many STIs as possible. The time lag between the earliest STI and the SFA that clears it up can be an important dynamic measure.

A second reason for choosing SFA is that it clearly speaks about the system, so the database can contain fault reports for faults found anywhere in the system. Finally, the word "analysis" correctly implies that data is the result of careful thought, and is not to be completed unless and until someone is quite sure of their reasoning.

Fault does not imply blame

One deficiency with the semantics of the term "fault" is the possible implication of *blame,* as opposed to *information.* In an SFA, we must be careful to distinguish two locations associated with a fault, but neither of these implies anything about whose "fault" it was:

- *origin:* at what stage in our process the fault originated
- *correction:* what part(s) of the system will be changed to remedy the fault

Pattern 1 and 2 organizations tend to equate these two notions, but the motto "You broke it, you fix it" often leads to an unproductive "blame game." "Correction" tells us where it is wisest under the circumstances to make the changes, regardless of what put the fault there in the first place. For example, we may decide to change the documentation not because the documentation is bad, but because the design is so poor, it needs more documenting and because the code is so tangled we don't dare try to fix it there.

If Pattern 3 organizations are not heavily into blaming, why would they want to record the origin of a fault? To these organizations, origin merely suggests where action may be taken to *prevent* a similar fault in the future, not which employee is to be taken out and crucified. Analyzing origins, however, requires skill and experience to determine the earliest possible moment of prevention in the process. For instance, an error in the code might have been prevented if the requirements document had been more clearly written. In that case, we should say that the origin was in the requirements stage.

12.2   Misclassification of Error Handling Processes

By the term "error handling process," we'll refer to the overall pattern that has to do with errors, a pattern that can be resolved into several activities. Once we understand the distinction between these component activities, we'll be able to describe the dynamics of each in a way that will suggest improvement. Characteristically, however, Pattern 1 and Pattern 2 organizations are not very adept at knowing just precisely what their error handling process is. If you ask, the typical answer will be "debugging." With that sort of imprecise speech, improvement in error handling is unlikely.

12.2.1   Detection

Detection of faults is achieved in different ways in different software cultures. Pattern 1 and 2 organizations tend to depend on faults being detected by *failures* in some sort of machine execution of code, such as machine software testing, beta testing, and operational use by customers. These are the STIs.

Pattern 3 organizations also detect faults through failures, but they tend to prefer going *directly to faults* by some process that does not require machine execution of the code. These mechanisms include accidents (such as stumbling on to an error while looking in the code for something else); technical reviews of great variety; and tools that process code, designs, and requirements as analyzable documents, suggesting failures without machine execution of the code itself. These methods result in SFAs that don't necessarily correspond to any STI, if they were applied early enough to prevent any failure resulting from the fault.

12.2.2 Location

Location, or isolation, is the process of matching failures with faults. Even when a fault is found directly, as in a code review, good practice dictates that the SFA contain a trace forward into the set of failures known to exist. Only by forward tracing can unsolved failures be cleared out of the STI database. If a great many unsolved STIs remain, managers and programmers tend to discount all of them, which makes location of truly active STIs more difficult.

12.2.3 Resolution

Resolution is the process that ensures that a fault no longer exists, or that a failure will never occur again. A failure may be solved without having its fault or faults removed. Removal of faults is an optional process, but resolution is not. Resolution of an STI *may* be performed in several ways:

1. Remove the fault that led to the STI. This is the classic way of debugging.

2. Define the STI as unimportant, such as "too minor to fix," or "non-reproducible."

3. Define the STI as not arising from a fault in the system, but usually as a fault in the person who reported it.

4. Define the fault as not a fault, such as by following the Bolden Rule: "If you can't fix it, feature it."[2]

In troubled Pattern 2 organizations, the majority of STIs are resolved by (2), (3), and (4), while management believes they are resolved by (1).

12.2.4 Prevention

Prevention may seem a pie-in-the-sky approach to people buried deep in Pattern 1 and Pattern 2 organizations. The history of other engineering disciplines assures us that some schemes for preventing errors will ultimately prevail, but these seem a long way from where most of my clients are standing today. When I show them articles about Pattern 3 organizations, they say they're not applicable to their organizations. When I show them articles about cleanroom software development[3] or other Pattern 4 techniques, they simply chuckle in disbelief.

In fact, however, most of the error work in a software development organization is actually preventive work, though Pattern 2 managers don't understand this. Only after they become rather sophisticated in analyzing software engineering dynamics do they realize that most of their activities are in place to *prevent* errors, not fix them. Just to take one example, ask people why they follow the practice of doing design before code. Very few of them will recognize this rule as an error prevention strategy dictated by the war against the Size/Complexity Dynamic.

12.2.5   Distribution

In Pattern 2 organizations, *distribution* of errors is an important and often time-consuming activity. By distribution, we mean any activity that serves to prevent attributing errors to one part of the organization *by moving them to another place*. For example, developers quickly throw code over the wall to testers so that errors are seen as somehow arising during testing, rather than from coding; or the organization skips the design reviews so that design faults are seen as coding faults; or testers pass code into operations so that problems can be classified as maintenance faults.

These three examples are the type of distribution activity that prevents *blame;* they arise in response to measurement systems that are used to punish rather than to control activities. When you don't know how to prevent errors, what else can you do but prevent blame for errors? Of course, because workers are playing hot potato with faults, they have that much less time to do actual productive work. We'll see more about the hot potato phenomenon later when we study the dynamics of management pressure.

Not all distribution activities are disguised forms of hot potato. When blame is not the name of the game, distribution actually serves useful purposes. Pattern 3 organizations tend to distribute the faults *earlier* in the process than Pattern 2 organizations and derive some benefits from doing so. For instance, requirements work and design work are seen as ways of catching faults early in the development process, rather than later when they will be more costly to resolve; and user manuals are written early on in the process as a way of revealing faults in interface requirements and of generating the basis for acceptance tests. Again, this unburdens the later parts of the development cycle.

12.3   Observational Errors About Errors

Failure detection is a process of *noticing differences* between what is desired and what exists. When we consider the cybernetic model of control, we understand how important seeing differences—failure detection—is to a feedback controller.

Giving things labels is a *substitute* for noticing. That's another reason I always emphasize the importance of the words controllers use. It's all too easy not to notice important differences if you name two things the same, or to see a difference where none exists if you name them differently.

12.3.1   Selection fallacies

There is a whole class of common mislabelings that I call *selection fallacies*. These occur when a controller makes an incorrect linear assumption about an observation that says

> "I don't have to observe the full set of data, because a more easily observed set of data adequately represents it."

It's a fallacy because it doesn't take into account that the processes of selecting the two groups of data may be different, and thus conclusions drawn from one group may not apply to the other. Selection fallacies are easy to spot after the fact, and easy to fall into before, especially if we have some reason to *want* one conclusion more than another. In this section, I'll discuss three typical fallacies.

Completed versus terminated projects

Here's an example of a common selection fallacy in software: A client surveyed the number of faults produced per thousand lines of code (KLOC) in 152 projects. The study was done very carefully, using the SFA database for each project. The study concluded that the projects produced a range of 6 to 23 faults/KLOC, with an average of 14. They felt that this was in line with other organizations in their industry, so they had no strong motivation to invest in further reductions.

   Listening to the presentation of this careful study, I could have easily missed the selection fallacy; but always being cautious, I asked, "How did you choose the 152 projects?"

   "Oh, we were very careful not to bias the study," the presenter said. "We chose *every* project that was completed in a three-month period."

   "You emphasized the wrong word," I said, now seeing the selection fallacy.

   "What do you mean?" he asked.

   "You should have said, 'We chose every project that was *completed* in a three-month period.' How many projects here are started that *never* complete?"

   The presenter didn't know, and neither did anyone else in the room. I got them to give an approximation, which was later verified by a small study. Historically in this organization, 27 percent of initiated projects were never completed. These projects accounted for more than 40 percent of their development budget, because some were not abandoned for a long, long time. A sample of these projects showed a range of 19 to 145 faults/KLOC, with an average of 38. Later, when the average was weighted by project *size,* it grew to 86. The two biggest projects also had the highest faults/KLOC.

Where had they gone wrong? In presenting *completed* projects as representative of *all* projects, the presenters had committed a common selection fallacy that led the organization to believe that they were not too bad in their fault-producing performance. Then, when they presented *all failed projects* as typical of their *worst* projects, they committed the same fallacy in reverse. The second fallacy led them to miss the fact that they simply didn't know how to develop large projects, probably because they couldn't deal with the faults they generated.

Early versus late users

A second common selection fallacy involves STIs over time. For example, a software organization shipped an update to product X and tracked the STIs that arrived during the first two months. The organization used this set of early STIs to make a linear projection of the STI load it would have to handle in subsequent months. Its estimate of the number of STIs was quite accurate, but the total work load generated by those STIs was underestimated by a factor of 3.5.

This organization had committed several selection fallacies, all based on the assumption that early STIs would be typical of later STIs. They were not, though, because, for one thing, later STIs had a far higher failure/fault ratio; more customers were using the system and encountering the same failures multiple times. The company had no efficient way of resolving these multiple reports of the same failure.

Second, early users of the update were not typical of later users. Early users tended to be more self-reliant, and worked around a number of failures that later users had to report as STIs in order to get help. Although the failures were easy to work around, their underlying faults were not necessarily easy to resolve.

Third, early users also tended to use a different set of features than later users whose work was much more extensive, both in features covered and number of people having access to the system. These attributes meant that their installation procedure was more complex, thus slower, which is why they were later users. More people accessing the system and using more of the features meant many more STIs.

"He's just like me."

The selection fallacy works not only on the observations, but also on the *observers*. Here's a continuation of the story about Simon, the project manager who couldn't recognize tears.

After Simon asked me whether there was something in Herb's eye, I said, "Well, I really don't know. Why don't you ask him?"

"Oh, it's not really important enough to take the time," Simon replied. "I need to ask you how you think the project is going? I'm really pleased at what a great job Herb did, getting that program ready just a week late, after it was in so much trouble."

"Really?" I said. "I thought you were rather upset about the late delivery."

"Oh, that. Sure, I'd like to have had it on time, but it's no big deal."

"I think Herb thought it was a big deal."

"What makes you think that?"

"I believe he was upset when you yelled at him."

"Oh, no. Herb knows me too well to be upset, just because I raised my voice a little. He's just like me, so he knows I'm just an enthusiastic guy."

Simon committed a selection fallacy by assuming "he's just like me." The managers in a software organization are not just like the rest of the people— else why were they selected to be managers, and why are they being paid more money? Why not observe the other person instead of assuming the two of you are exactly alike?

Any manager who can't or won't see or hear other peoples' feelings is like a ship's captain trying to navigate at night without radar or sonar. Feelings are the radar and sonar of project life—reflections off the reefs and shoals and shallow bottoms on which your project can run aground. You can't do it with your eyes and ears closed, just using a map inside your own head, if only because you're not just like everyone else.

12.3.2   Getting observations backward

It's one thing to fail to observe something correctly. It's quite another to observe correctly but then to interpret the observations *backward*, so that black is labeled white and white is labeled black. Some people have a hard time believing that a highly paid software engineering manager could actually label observations backward, so here are a few examples of hundreds I've observed.

Who are the best and the worst programmers?

A software development manager told me that he had a way to measure who were his best programmers and who were his worst. Fascinated, I asked him how he did it. He told me that he observed who was always out asking questions of users and other programmers. I thought this was a terrific measure, and I discussed it with him with great excitement. After a few minutes, however, I realized that he thought the programmers who spent the most time asking questions were his worst ones. I, on the other hand, thought that they were probably the best programmers in his shop.

Which is the high-quality release?

When she received her first monthly STI summary for a newly released product, the vice president of software technology waved it at me and said, "Well, we've finally put out a high-quality release." As it turned out, the release offered so little new function that essentially nobody bothered to install it. Hence, there were virtually no troubles reported. Later, when people did have to install it, they found it was just as full of errors as all the previous releases.

Why is someone working late?

A programming team manager told me, "Josh is my best programmer. The reason he starts work in the afternoon and stays late at night is so he won't be disturbed by the less experienced programmers." It turned out that Josh was so ashamed of the poor quality of his work that he didn't want anyone to see how much trouble he was having.

Who knows what's right and wrong?

Another team leader told me, "Cynthia is angry because I showed her what was wrong with her program, and how it should have been done in the first place. I suppose you're going to tell me I have to learn to be more tactful." Cynthia showed me the program and what the team leader had said was wrong. It wasn't wrong at all. Cynthia said, "What ticks me off is working under a boss who's not only technically illiterate, but doesn't know how to listen. He approaches every problem with an open mouth."

Which process is eliminating the problems?

A project manager told me, "We've abandoned technical reviews in this project. They were valuable at first, and we found a lot of problems. Now, however, they don't find much trouble—not enough to justify the expense." As it turned out, the reason there were no problems was that the programmers were conducting secret reviews to hide their errors from the manager, who berated anyone whose product showed errors in the review. They had not abandoned technical reviews; they had abandoned the practice of telling their manager about their technical reviews.

Feedback controllers use observations of behavior to decide upon actions to eliminate undesired behaviors. They feed these actions back into the system and thus create a negative feedback loop to stabilize the system, as shown in Figure 12-1.

When the feedback controller gets the meaning of the observation backward, however, the designed actions create a *positive* feedback loop, actually encouraging the undesired behavior, as shown in Figure 12-2.

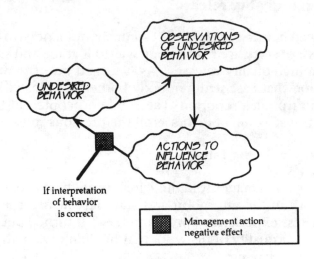

Figure 12–1.   The feedback controller uses observations to decide upon actions to stabilize the system's behavior.

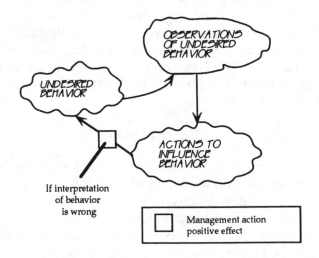

Figure 12–2.   Getting the meaning of an observation backward creates an intervention loop that promotes what it should discourage and vice versa.

12.3.3 Controller Fallacy

The example of eliminating technical reviews illustrates another common observational fallacy. Even if it is true that reviewers no longer found errors, is that sufficient reason to abandon them? Technical reviews serve many functions in a software project, but one of their principal functions is to *provide feedback information to be used in controlling the project.* In other words, they are *part of the controller's system.*

It is the nature of feedback controllers to have an inverse relationship to the systems they attempt to regulate.[4] For example, we spend money on a thermostat so we *won't* spend extra money on fuel for heating and cooling; we keep the fire department active so that fires will be *inactive;* and we put constraints on the powers of government so that government *won't* put unnecessary constraints on the governed.

One result of this inverse relationship is

The controller of a well-regulated system may not seem to be working hard.

But managers who don't understand this relationship often see lack of obvious controller activity as a sign that something is wrong with the control process. This is the *Controller Fallacy,* which comes in two forms:

If the controller isn't busy, it's not doing a good job.

If the controller is very busy, it must be a good controller.

Managers who believe the second form are the ones who "prove" how important they are by being too busy to see their workers.

The first form applies to the reversed technical review observation. If the technical reviews are not detecting a lot of mistakes, it *could* mean that the review system is broken. On the other hand, it could also mean that the review system is working *very* well, and preventing faults by such actions as

- motivating people to work with more precision
- raising awareness of the importance of quality work
- teaching people how to find faults before coming to reviews
- detecting indicators of poor work before that work actually produces faults
- teaching people to prevent faults by using good techniques they see in reviews

12.4 Helpful Hints and Suggestions

1. Usually there are more failures than faults, but sometimes there are faults that produce no failures, at least given the usage of the software up to the present time. Sometimes, it takes more than one fault to equal one failure. For instance, there may be two that are "half-faults," neither of which would cause trouble except when used in conjunction with the other. In other cases, such as in performance errors, it may take an accumulation of

small faults to equal a single failure. This makes it important to distinguish between functional failures and performance failures.

2. *Proliferation* of acronyms is a sign of an organization's movement toward Pattern 2, where name magic is so important that a new name confers power on its creator. *Care in designing* acronyms and their nonproliferation is a sign of an organization's movement toward Pattern 3, where communication is so important.

3. You can almost count on the fact that first customers aren't like later ones. Managers often commit a selection fallacy in planning their future as software vendors based on initial favorable customer reactions to a software system. The first customers are first because they are the ones the requirements fit for. Thus, they are very likely to be "like" the original designers/developers. Developers and customers communicate well, and think alike. This is not so as the number of customers grows, and explicit processes must be developed to replace this lost "natural" rapport.

4. Selection fallacies are everywhere. Whenever someone presents you with statistics to prove something, you can protect yourself either by wearing garlic flowers around your neck, or by asking, "Which cases are in your sample? Which cases are left out? What was the process by which you chose the cases you chose?"

12.5 Summary

√ One of the reasons organizations have trouble dealing with software errors is the many conceptual errors they make concerning them.

√ Some people make errors into a moral issue, losing track of the business justification for the way in which they are handled.

√ Quality is not the same thing as absence of errors, but the presence of many errors can destroy any other measures of quality in a product.

√ Organizations that don't handle errors very well also don't talk very clearly about them. For instance, they often fail to distinguish faults from failures, or they use faults to blame people in the organization.

√ Well-functioning organizations can be recognized by the systematic way they use faults and failures as information to control their process. The system trouble incident (STI) and the system fault analysis (SFA) are the fundamental sources of information about failures and faults.

√ Error handling processes come in at least five varieties: detection, location, resolution, prevention, and distribution.

√   In addition to conceptual errors, there are common observational mistakes people make about errors, including selection fallacies, getting observations backward, and the Controller Fallacy.

12.6 Practice

1.   Here are some words I've heard used as synonyms for "fault" in software: lapse, slip, aberration, variation, minor variation, mistake, oversight, miscalculation, blooper, blunder, boner, miscue, fumble, botch, misconception, bug, error, and failure. Add any words you've heard to the list, then put the words in order according to how much responsibility they imply on the people who created the fault.

2.   When an organization begins the systematic practice of matching every failure with a known fault, it discovers that some failures have no corresponding fault. In Pattern 3 organizations, these failures are attributed to "process faults"—something wrong with their software process that either generates fictitious failures or prevents the isolation of real ones. List some examples of process faults commonly experienced in your own organization, such as careless filling out of STI records.

3.   For a week, gather data about your organization in the following way: As you meet people in the normal course of events, ask them what they're doing. If it has anything to do with errors of any kind, note how they label their activity: debugging, failure location, talking to a customer, or whatever. At the end of the week, summarize your findings in a report on the process categories used for error handling in your organization's culture.

4.   Describe a selection fallacy that you've experienced. Describe its consequences. How could a more appropriate selection have been made?

13

The Failure
Detection Curve

Throughout the history of the software business, people have been frustrated by the ever-receding end of a project after it reaches "ninety-nine percent complete." In Pattern 2 organizations, the receding end is blamed on anyone who will stand still long enough to become a target. Pattern 3 organizations, on the other hand, know that another dynamic is really at work, the Difference Detection Dynamic. In this chapter, we'll study the light this dynamic throws on the "ninety-nine percent complete" situation.

13.1 The Difference Detection Dynamic

Selection fallacies can have enormous consequences. A fascinating story of a worldwide selection fallacy is contained in an article by Root and Drew on "The Pattern of Petroleum Discovery Rates."[1] For many years, analysts had seriously overestimated oil recovery from regions, based on early drilling success. They had hypothesized all sorts of explanations for the failure of their models, but Root and Drew finally demonstrated that the failure of the models could be explained by a selection fallacy: "First, most of the oil and gas discovered in a region is contained in a few large fields; and second, most of the large fields are discovered early in the exploration of the region."

Obviously, if you drill holes at random, you're more likely to hit oil somewhere in one of the big fields than in one of the small ones. With trillions of dollars at stake, why did it take so long to discover this selection tautology? Are petroleum engineers stupid? Before laughing at the petroleum engineers, save a chuckle for ourselves, the *software* engineers.

13.1.1   The Root-Drew Fallacy in difference detection

The Root-Drew Fallacy is committed every day in software development in trying to predict how long testing will take based on early returns from testing. To understand how this happens, start by taking the psychological test in Figure 13-1. This test nicely simulates all sorts of processes in which differences are detected, including the process of software testing. For instance, I often use such twin pictures to simulate testing processes for software engineers. Once we separate the fault location process, what we call "testing" is detecting differences between software requirements (written or unwritten) and software performance.

If many people "test" a pair of pictures such as in Figure 13-1, they do not all find the same differences in the same order. In a recent workshop, for instance, I had 47 people perform this experiment. No two found the differences in the same order.[2] It's from observations such as this that people conclude there's no order or system to software testing, and particularly to software failure detection.

There is order, however, but we must look at the data in a different way to see it. If we gloss over *which* differences are found, and instead plot *how many are found in how much time,* we find a great consistency among people. Figure 13-2 shows *this* order in the form of a curve plotting the percentage of differences found versus time. I call this curve the *Failure Detection Curve,* because it is a universal description of the process of discovering differences or, in software terms, failures.

As it turns out, of course, the Failure Detection Curve is exactly parallel to Root and Drew's observations about the discovery of oil fields. The easiest oil fields to find are found first, and so are the easiest picture differences. We could paraphrase Root and Drew and give a description of Figure 13-1 by saying

First, the smallest amount of the test time is spent on a few easy problems; and second, most of the easy problems are found early in the test cycle.

This is the *Difference Detection Dynamic*.

Figure 13–1.   Compare these two pictures and record as many differences as you can find. Keep track of the time it takes you to find each difference.

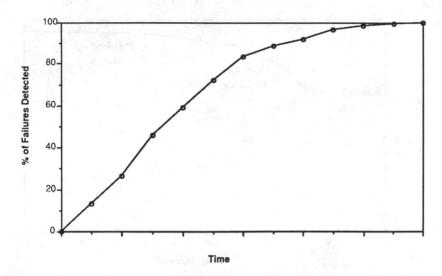

Figure 13–2.   The rate of finding differences between the paired pictures shows remarkable consistency over a great diversity of people, yielding an S-curve.

13.1.2   Why we misestimate failure detection

In Figure 13-3, I have labeled the time intervals of the Failure Detection Curve to indicate the tautological nature of the Difference Detection Dynamic:

- Failures are not equally easy to detect.
- The easiest (shortest time) failures, by definition, will be detected first.
- The hardest (longest time) failures, by definition, will be detected last.
- Therefore, the average detection time will keep rising throughout the project.

This selection fallacy explains why testing seems to get harder and harder as it progresses. It also explains why so many projects lose their schedules in testing, when things are "ninety-nine percent complete" for month after month. Figure 13-4 shows the results of an estimating exercise based on the paired pictures. First, I tell the participants that there are exactly sixteen differences. At the end of two minutes, I ask them to estimate how long it will take them to find all remaining differences. The average estimate is right around four minutes, which corresponds closely to a linear projection of their experience so far.

At four minutes, I ask them to estimate again, and they again use a linear projection, which takes them to six minutes. At six minutes, they estimate ten minutes. At ten minutes, the group tends to divide in three:

- One group continues to estimate that they are ninety-nine percent complete.

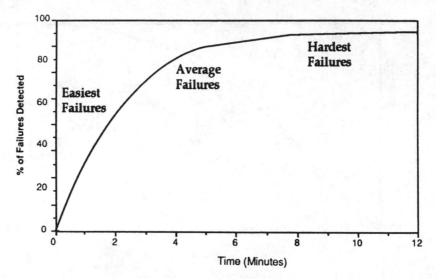

Figure 13–3.   The Failure Detection Curve is a tautology because the failures that are hardest to find are found last. That's what "hardest to find" means.

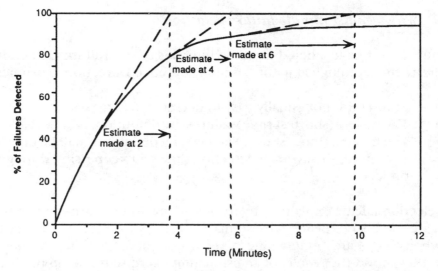

Figure 13–4.   At each moment in the detection process, estimators tend to use a linear projection of their most current experience.

- One group estimates that they are a hundred percent complete (and that I lied about the sixteen).
- One group estimates that they will *never* be complete.

In my experience, these three groups correspond to personality types that exist in all real projects. In real projects, of course, nobody could truly know how many failures are yet to be detected, but managers can always find someone to give them the answer they want—once the project has been ninety-nine percent complete for a few months.

13.1.3   *The bad news about the Failure Detection Curve*

The Failure Detection Curve is a characteristic curve of all failure detection technologies, such as

- desk checking by the developer
- desk checking by some other person
- technical reviews by the inspection technique
- technical reviews by the walkthrough technique
- hand-generated test sets
- machine-generated test sets
- beta testing by selected customers
- field testing by thousands of customers
- random tests

Each technology has a curve of this same shape. The exact placement of the curve will be different for different technologies, but there will always be that long, long, long tail for "the last failure." The tail explains why the correct answer to "How many more failures are there?" always seems to be "one," no matter how many have been removed. The bad news in the Failure Detection Curve is

There is no testing technology that detects failures in a linear manner.

There is also good news. Although every technology has the same shape curve, they each have different "easiest" and "hardest" failures to detect. Just like humans looking at the two pictures, no two testing processes will detect failures in exactly the same order. That provides the good news:

Combining different detection technologies creates an improved technology.

Figure 13-5 shows what happens to the Failure Detection Curve when we combine two technologies, such as adding technical reviews to machine testing or using two beta testers instead of one. The combined curve has to be better than either of the individual curves. Unfortunately, no matter how you add them, the combined curve still has the long tail of a Failure Detection Curve. That means it represents a natural dynamic, and we'll have to find ways to live with its tail.

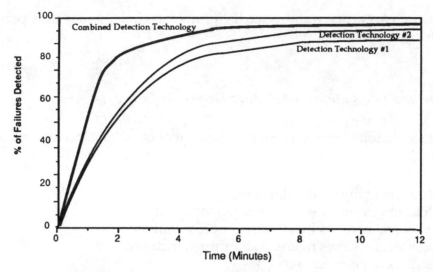

Figure 13–5.   The sum of two Failure Detection Curves is another Failure Detection Curve, which will be better as long as the two failure detection technologies are not identical.

13.2   Living with the Failure Detection Curve

Like the Size/Complexity Dynamic, the Failure Detection Curve is a limiting condition of software engineering. You can do worse than it says, but you can't do better. Pattern 1 and 2 organizations often do *much* worse than the Failure Detection Curve allows, which is bad enough, but they also continue to predict that they can do much *better*. Thus, the discrepancy between what they promise and what they deliver grows larger.

13.2.1   Failure Detection Curve as a predictor

Pattern 3 organizations learn how to use the Failure Detection Curve to predict future patterns of software failure.[3] In order for these predictions to be possible, you need at least three conditions:

1.   The entire error handling process must be reasonably stable. For instance, if software test procedures differ in practice from project to project, Failure Detection Curves between projects will not be comparable.

2.   The test coverage must be reasonably complete. If one part of a system is tested much more thoroughly than another, there will be two rather different Failure Detection Curves, not one. If certain aspects of the system are not tested at all, then no prediction can be made about their future failure history.

3.   The software pattern must take a system engineering attitude toward failures, not a moral attitude. The system engineering attitude considers failure rate, mean time between failures, or other failure measurements as parameters to be traded with other parameters such as cost, schedule, and functionality to deliver maximum value to customers. The moral attitude considers failures as signs of personal decay, and thus must insist on zero defects. There is no way a Failure Detection Curve can predict the moment of zero failures. It can, on the other hand, predict finite failure levels—such as when you will reach a certain mean time between failures—with reasonable precision if the conditions of stability and diversity are met.

Given the conditions required, such predictions are not really available to Pattern 2 organizations. Their process tends to be unstable in just those projects where schedule prediction is desired, and those very projects cannot exert reliable control over their test coverage. In many Pattern 2 organizations, the moral attitude toward failure prevents them from improving the situation by small increments.

13.2.2   Undermining test coverage

For the Failure Detection Curve to be useful as an estimating device, test coverage must be reasonably complete. Intelligent planning is necessary to produce adequate test coverage,[4] but intelligent planning is not sufficient. Several phenomena tend to destroy even the best-planned test coverage, including blocking and masking faults and delivering late releases to test. I'll discuss each below.

Blocking faults

Here's an example of a blocking fault. The Common Ordinary Works for Software (COWS) was running late on delivery of release 9.0 of their dairy herd management software (DHMS). Everyone in the testing lab was under a lot of pressure to get their test scripts executed and the STIs back to the developers for resolution.

Unfortunately, release 9.0 of DHMS contained a new database interface routine that was supposed to allow the product to be sold to customers owning a wide variety of disk drives. The database interface routine was delivered to the test lab on time, but it didn't work very well. Indeed, it prevented many functions of the system from being tested effectively for seven weeks.

In the COWS situation, there are, in effect, two different parts of the system: the part to which access is blocked by the faulty database interface routine, and the part that isn't. In this situation, the Failure Detection Curve actually looks like Figure 13-6. This was not the Failure Detection Curve that management was expecting, however, but was a sum of two curves: one for the unblocked part that started on time, and one for the blocked part that started seven weeks later.

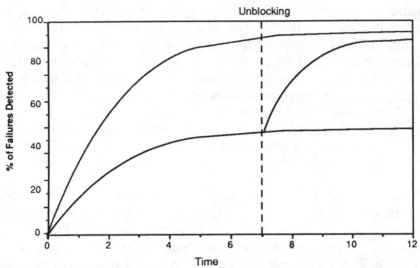

Figure 13–6.   The Failure Detection Curve in a blocking fault situation does not follow the ex-
                 pected upper curve, but follows the lower curve that is the sum of two curves,
                 one of which only begins to rise after access to certain failures is unblocked.

If estimated completion time were based on the assumption that test coverage
was uniform over the entire test period, the upper curve in the figure would
have been used, and the predictions would have been far off. They would have
been at least seven weeks off for the late start, but the atmosphere of growing
pressure and frustration led to all sorts of shortcutting of the prescribed test procedures, resulting in an even slower test process and incomplete test coverage.

Masking faults

Masking faults are similar to blocking faults in producing the effects shown in
Figure 13-7. The difference is that management—Pattern 3 managers, at least—
can take action to unblock a blocking fault and/or work around it as soon as they
become aware of its existence. In the case of masking faults, though, management may never become aware of its existence, as in the following example:

After COWS finally delivered release 9.0, things seemed to be going quite
well. A few STIs came in from the field, but nothing extraordinary. Four months
later, however, a flood of STIs crashed through the doors. Every new function in
the system seemed to be full of faults, but nobody in development could figure
out why if things were so bad they hadn't heard earlier.

Management created a team to investigate the situation. The team discovered that the packaging department had not received the new manuals on time,
so had shipped release 9.0 without manuals. Customers were able to use their
release 8.0 manuals, but had no systematic way to learn of the new features

of release 9.0. When the release 9.0 manuals finally arrived, customers started using the new features—or at least *trying* to use them—and experienced failures.

In effect, COWS depended on their customers to finish their failure detection process, but parts of the system were masked from the customers until their new manuals arrived. Those parts were, therefore, blocked psychologically by a fault in the shipping procedure as effectively as if they had been blocked physically by a fault in the database interface routine.

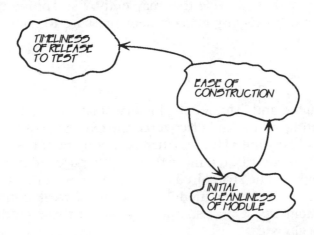

Figure 13–7.   If the coding of a module gets off on the wrong foot, its subsequent correction may lead to a positive feedback loop that makes it even worse.

Late releases to test

Pattern 2 organizations are distinguished by their orderly process plans for assembling large systems out of smaller modules. In the course of events, however, some of the modules are not completed according to plan and thus are released late to the testing process. The testers may respond by stretching the schedule, but this is seldom allowed by management. Instead, the time planned for test coverage of late modules is reduced. To do the same amount of testing in less time, you must either go faster (and perhaps miss failures or misrecord them) or truncate the tests themselves. In either case, late-arriving modules violate the assumption of equal test coverage of all parts of the system.

13.2.3   Late-finishing modules

Why are modules released late to test? Of course, there are many possible reasons, but most are released late because the developer had trouble reaching an acceptable level of unit test. That's the result of four likely problems: poor coding, fault-prone modules, management decision, or bad luck.

A cycle of poor coding

In many cases, the developer is caught in a positive feedback loop such as that shown in Figure 13-7. Perhaps starting with a poor design or poor understanding of the problem, the developer writes some code that is not very clean. The uncleanliness of the code makes it difficult to work with, and corrections have a high probability of making it even dirtier. This creates a cycle of patching and then patching the patches—a cycle that may end by scrapping the design and starting over, but more likely by management pressure to hand over the code to test.

Fault-prone modules

In 1970, Gary Okimoto and I studied the history of faults in many releases of the IBM OS/360 operating system and discovered the existence of *fault-prone modules*. These modules accounted for less than two percent of the code in OS/360, but over their life had contributed more than eighty percent of the faults. Since 1970 was in the midst of the structured programming movement, we attempted to explain the existence of these modules in terms of weak control structures, such as GOTO statements. Our assumption was that these modules had been poorly coded to begin with.

We had limited success in our search, but people continued to notice the fault-prone phenomenon all over the world. Recently, we have begun to realize that in most cases, fault-prone modules are modules that for one reason or another never received their planned test coverage. And most of these were late releases—or not released at all—to test. Of course, if they were not full of faults when they were released to test, the lack of test coverage wouldn't matter. As indicated in Figure 13-8, fault-prone modules are the result of at least two factors—test coverage and initial cleanliness.

The management decision point

The dynamics of Figures 13-7 and 13-8 are related, and they can be put together to create the diagram of effects shown in Figure 13-9. This diagram illustrates that test coverage and cleanliness are not independent, but that the nature of their dependence is a result of management decision. In the diagram, we show the typical Pattern 2 management decision:

"Don't worry if we're behind schedule; we'll make it up in test."

Pattern 2 managers hope to make up the schedule on poor modules by "getting lucky" in test, but the diagram of effects shows that just the opposite tends to happen. Late modules tend to be fault-prone modules or, if you like, "unlucky"

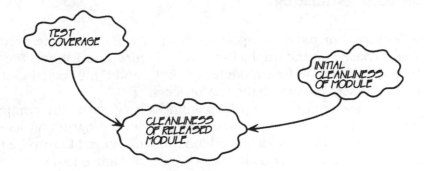

Figure 13–8.   To create a released fault-prone module, you must have an unclean module to begin with, and you must fail to give it adequate test coverage.

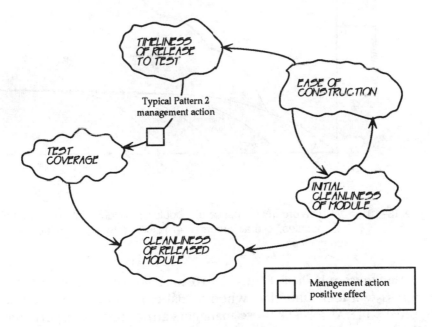

Figure 13–9.   The dynamic created by the Pattern 2 management slogan "Don't worry if we're behind schedule; we'll make it up in test."

modules. Cutting or squeezing their test coverage ensures that they will remain "unlucky" when they go out the door.

Pattern 3 managers, understanding this dynamic, don't count on luck. They understand that late delivery of a module to test gives them *information about the cleanliness of that module*. Therefore, they reverse the Pattern 2 decision and insist on giving that module *greater* test coverage, not less.

"Bad luck" estimating

The Pattern 2 manager compounds this problem by making predictions of test progress based on the original schedule. Figure 13-10 shows the Failure Detection Curve based on four modules (A, B, C, and D), of equal cleanliness, being introduced sequentially to the test process.

If the assumption of equal cleanliness holds true, the composite curve of Figure 13-10 can be used to track the project's progress on its schedule. But we've just seen that late-delivered modules are more likely to be fault-prone, so a better picture of the situation may be that of Figure 13-11.

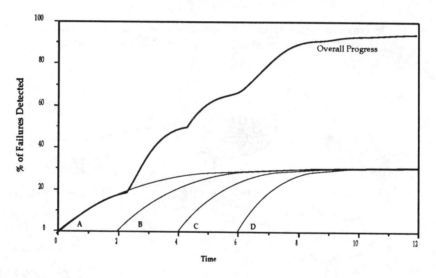

Figure 13–10.   With an orderly sequence of modules introduced into test and uniform cleanliness of modules, overall progress in failure detection can be used to estimate test completion.

Managers who use Figure 13-10 to make predictions of failure detection progress will feel "unlucky" when actual experience is more like the curve of Figure 13-11. As long as these managers attribute this experience to luck, they will remain stuck in Pattern 2. The first step toward Pattern 3 management is always management's acceptance of responsibility for poor project performance.

When a project doesn't make its estimates, it's not because of bad bugs or bad luck, and it's certainly not because of bad programmers or bad testers. The project was either managed badly or estimated badly or both. In either case, it's the responsibility of management. As they say in the Army,

There are no bad soldiers; there are only bad officers.

Perhaps we should modify this for software management:

There are no bad programmers; there are only managers who don't understand the dynamics of failure.

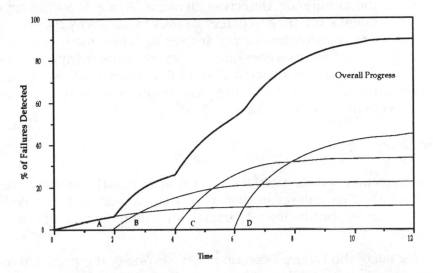

Figure 13–11.   When management decisions mean that late modules are likely to be fault-prone modules, the Failure Detection Curve is likely to be stretched out much worse than it could be, leading to seriously optimistic estimates of failure detection progress.

13.3   Helpful Hints and Suggestions

1. Not all failures are created equal. Therefore, one way to beat the Failure Detection Curve is to create a testing process that correlates the earliest failures with the most important failures. For instance, faults in deeply embedded routines on which other routines depend are likely to block more testing than less deep routines, so a testing process that scours these routines first may have increased favorable impact on the schedule. Similarly, test scripts that are based on actual customer usage will have a more favorable impact on customer acceptance than mathematically generated test scripts that cover all logical cases regardless of their value to customers.

2. If there is a correlation between which failures are hardest to detect and which faults are hardest to locate and resolve, this would add to the effect of misestimating the entire detect-locate-resolve cycle. I don't know of any hard data supporting this correlation, but it does seem to fit with my clients' experience.

3. The Failure Detection Curve can be S-shaped, as in Figure 13-2, or without the little curve at the beginning, as in Figure 13-3. The curve at the beginning is "start-up time," and will be found to the extent that the testing activity is new to the organization. In an experienced organization that has put many projects through the same testing procedures, the tail disappears.

4. Of course, the Difference Detection Dynamic is not the only set of effects that influence the time to detect failures. That's why there are other explanations as to why the correct answer to "How many more failures are there?" always seems to be "one"—no matter how many have been removed. For instance, any dynamic that results in new faults being added to a system will stretch out the Failure Detection Curve, as will any process that slows down the error handling process generally.

13.4 Summary

√ Failure detection is dominated by the tautology that the easiest failures to detect are the first failures to detect; so that as detection proceeds, the work gets harder, producing a characteristic Failure Detection Curve with a long tail.

√ The long tail of the Failure Detection Curve is one of the principal reasons managers misestimate failure detection tasks.

√ Because the Failure Detection Curve represents a natural dynamic, there is nothing we can do to perform better than it says. We can, however, perform much worse if we're not careful of how we manage the failure detection process.

√ The Failure Detection Curve is not all bad news. The pattern of detected failures over time can be used as a predictor of the time to reach any specified level of failure detection as long as nothing is happening to undermine test coverage.

√ Some of the things that can undermine test coverage are blocking faults, masking faults, and late releases to test.

√ Late-finishing modules may arise from a cycle of poor coding, which means that they are more likely to be fault-prone modules. Management policies designed to speed testing of late-finishing modules may actually make the problem worse, and may account for much so-called bad luck estimating.

13.5 Practice

1. Gather data on modules in a project you have available to study. For each module, record when it was delivered to test compared with when it was

originally scheduled to be delivered to test. Also record the number of failures recorded in its testing, as well as the number of faults, if available. If the failure/fault history after delivery is available, record that too. Then produce a study correlating delivery to test with various measures of module cleanliness.

2. Give a feasible explanation of how fault-prone modules could also have the property of concealing faults—that is, making them harder to uncover in normal testing. Then show the impact of this property on predictions of failure detection progress.

3. Give an example of a blocking fault from your experience. What was done to minimize the impact of blocking on the schedule? With the wisdom of hindsight, what could have been done?

4. Give an example of a masking fault from your experience. What finally stripped off the mask? What could have been done to strip off the mask earlier?

13.6   Chapter Appendix: Official Differences Between the Pair of Pictures in Figure 13-1

- "Untied States" instead of "United States."
- On the right border of #2, one ribbon weaves over rather than under like the rest.
- In the left-hand band, one drummer has no drumstick.
- The flags in the two pictures have a different numbers of stripes.
- One eagle looks left, the other looks right.
- In #2, the bottom straight border touches the woven border.
- Virginia is dotted differently.
- Iowa is striped differently.
- One border is missing between New Hampshire and Vermont.
- The persons in Oklahoma are different sizes.
- The trees in Alabama are different.
- The N arrows are different.
- The southeast corner of Missouri is missing in one picture.
- The flag in Oregon is reversed.
- Long Island, New York, is missing in one picture.
- In New Mexico, one van touches the Texas border and one doesn't.

14

Locating the Faults Behind the Failures

. . . complex systems will evolve from simple systems much more rapidly if there are stable intermediate forms than if there are not. The resulting complex forms in the former case will be hierarchic.
—Herbert A. Simon[1]

Quite possibly the hardest part of error handling is *fault location*. Pattern 2 organizations seldom realize how much effort they are putting into fault location because they lump it with some other activity. Some organizations lump fault location with failure detection under the title "testing." Others lump it with fault resolution under "debugging," although that title is also used for all three activities—detection, location, and resolution.

Pattern 3 organizations, however, examine their processes more carefully, and know that the most troublesome and time-consuming error handling activity is tracking each failure back to the fault that is its progenitor. Sometimes the relationship between failure and fault is obvious; but when it's not, extremely long delays can result, often for reasons we'll develop in this chapter.

14.1   Dynamics of Fault Location

Figure 14-1 shows figures for three typical clients who measured fault location as distinct from failure detection. The three pie charts show the relative amount of effort each spent detecting failures, locating faults, and resolving them. (Of course, these figures still exclude the unrecognized prevention and distribution activities, which may be even larger.) Location time was the biggest recognized expenditure for all three. Why does this happen?

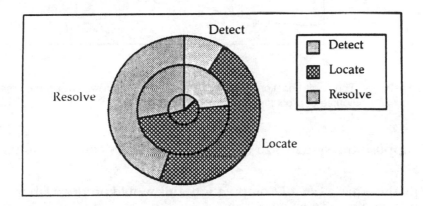

Figure 14–1.   Typical software organizations spend as much effort on fault location as they do on detection and repair together.

14.1.1   Direct effects of system size

We've already seen the Failure Detection Dynamic, which is a special case of the Size/Complexity Dynamic (shown in Figure 9-7). In a given software cultural pattern, the cleanliness of individual parts remains in a more or less constant range. Therefore, as the number of parts increases, the number of faults increases. When there is a failure and we have to look for one of these faults, we have more places to look, so the time to look is longer. Thus, the time spent locating all faults grows at least as fast as the square of the size of the system because there are more faults and more places to look (Figure 14-2). Several consequences of this dynamic are clear in the organizations I have studied.

14.1.2   Divide and Conquer to beat the Size/Complexity Dynamic

The Size/Complexity Dynamic also has less direct effects on the time to locate faults. In order to beat the dynamic, software engineers adopt the strategy of "Divide and Conquer."[2] A numerical example of the reasoning goes like this:

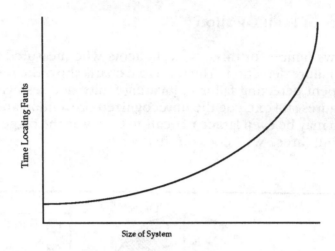

Figure 14–2.   The Fault Location Dynamic: As the system grows larger, the time to locate the source of problems grows nonlinearly.

1. Suppose the system size is 1,000 units. (Units could be hours, weeks, or years.)

2. By the Square Law of Computation, this would produce labor proportional to $1,000^2$, or 1,000,000.

3. Divide the system into 10 parts of 100 units each.

4. Each 100 unit part requires labor proportional to 100^2, or 10,000.

5. There are 10 units, so total labor is proportional to $10 \times 10,000$, or 100,000.

6. Thus by dividing in this way, we reduce total labor by a factor of 10.

Of course, this reasoning makes certain optimistic assumptions. In practice we don't achieve quite this good a result. Although we reduce the labor per part, we add a new source of labor, the labor to *integrate* the parts (see Figure 14-3). It's this integration labor that prevents us from carrying the Divide and Conquer argument to its outrageous limit, which would be to build a million lines of code by dividing the system into a million modules!

The actual decision on how many parts to create is a complex design problem, but the gross dynamics of the problem are easy to understand if we express them graphically as in Figure 14-4. Total effort is part-building effort plus integration effort. Both of these components are nonlinear functions of the number of parts. They move in opposite directions; so as we gain in one, we lose in the other. Somewhere between one big part and a million little ones, we find the optimal division that minimizes total labor to solve the problem.

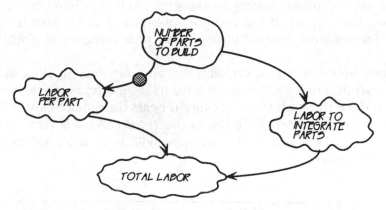

Figure 14–3.   In an attempt to beat the Size/Complexity Dynamic, we resort to a variety of process improvements. The major tactic is Divide and Conquer.

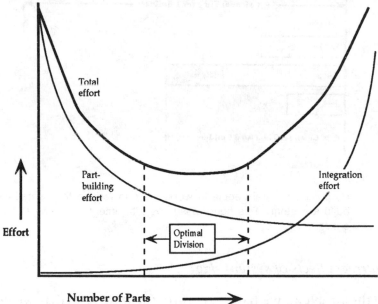

Figure 14–4.   The more parts we divide the system into, the more linear the labor of each part becomes. On the other hand, the more parts, the more integration effort grows nonlinearly. Eventually, there would be so many small parts that the integration effort would be greater than the building effort.

14.1.3   Divide the labor to beat delivery time

From a software engineering viewpoint, however, the Divide and Conquer strategy has another component. If we had all the time in the world, we would allow one programmer to apply Divide and Conquer to each project. In order to get done faster, however, we may decide not just to divide the work, but to divide it among several programmers working in parallel. Then, instead of the total time being the sum of all the component-building times plus integration time, it is the *largest* component-building time plus integration time, as shown in Figure 14-5.

Figure 14-5 shows that dividing the problem and dividing the responsibilities are two different tactics, each with its own effects. Dividing the *problem* tends to reduce the *total work* because it beats the Square Law of Computation. Dividing the *responsibilities* reduces the *total calendar time* because it uses resources in parallel. But neither of them will work at all unless the process is controlled properly.

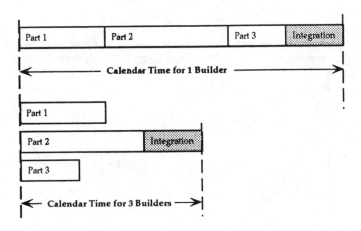

Figure 14–5.   By putting several people to work, we can reduce the overall calendar time to build a system. This figure assumes total integration time is the same in both cases.

14.1.4   Indirect effects of system size

In dividing the problem, we have to control the *design* so that we don't lose the advantage gained by adding so much integration work. In dividing the responsibilities, we have to control the *process* so that we don't lose the advantage gained by adding so much process work. Process work is added because of the necessity to coordinate the activities of different people. Figure 14-6 shows how the process overhead adds both to the calendar time and the total labor. It always costs more to have more people working on a project, but it *may* be faster. In order for the division of responsibilities to fulfill its promise of faster completion, it must be well-managed. As usual, to manage it well, you need to understand the dynamics. Figure 14-7 shows four kinds of additional work the division of responsibilities creates that affect the time to locate faults:

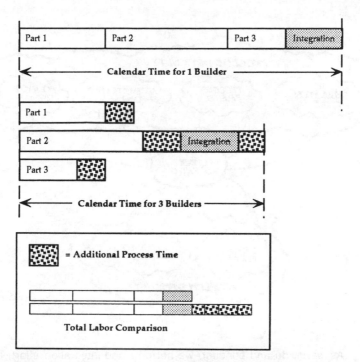

Figure 14–6.   More realistically, however, the more people, the more process time is needed because of coordination problems among the people, in addition to integration effort between the models. This additional process time means losing some of the savings in calendar time and also spending more total labor.

- STI circulation time
- process faults
- administrative burden
- political time

The dynamics of each of these demonstrates a way we can lose the benefits of the Divide and Conquer strategy through process complexity and poor control. We shall look at each in turn, especially to see how they may indicate it's time for a Pattern 2 organization to think seriously about what it will take to move to Pattern 3 in order to cope with increasing problem demands.

14.2   Circulation of STIs Before Resolution

Suppose we receive an STI that stems from a code fault. Since it has to be resolved by changing code, the STI must eventually reach the hands of a person responsible for the code in which the repair will be made. If there is only one programmer, this is no problem. With more people, however, each is responsible for only a part of the whole.

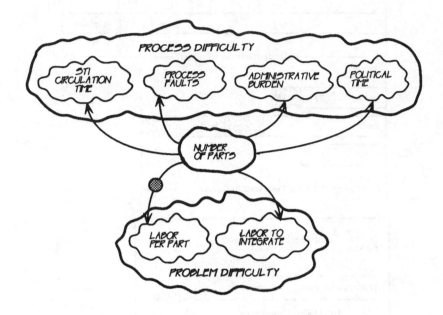

Figure 14–7.   As we divide and conquer, we not only add integration effort, but we create a more complex process.

How STIs are handled becomes a sensitive test of the organization's software culture. As systems grow larger, STIs no longer tend to be handled by the first person who sees them. In an organization under the stress of increasing customer and problem demands, many STIs cycle around from desk to desk, some for months or even years. Let's look at the dynamics of location, circulation, and resolution of STIs, in the next sections.

14.2.1   Resolver location time

A first and easy measurement for an organization is the time between its receipt of an STI and the *time to locate the right person to solve the problem,* which we call the *resolver location time* (RLT). Even if there is no SFA database, this measure is easy to determine from almost any sort of routing slip. For example,

John   10/10/8am
Mary   10/12/4pm
Paul   10/13/9am
John   10/13/2pm
Joan   10/17/11am

The STI first arrived in John's office at 8 A.M. on October 10, and after a circuitous route, found its way to Joan at 11 A.M. on October 17. Joan must have resolved the issue because hers is the last name on the slip. Therefore, the time to reach the resolver is the difference between the first and last times, or seven days and three hours. The RLT doesn't say anything about how long Joan took to *resolve* the STI, only the time it took to reach her; and can thus be quite different from the *incident resolution time* (IRT), which does depend on how long Joan took.

If the average RLT starts to grow, or if the *longest* RLT starts to grow, something is breaking down. Pattern 3 organizations routinely monitor the distribution of RLTs, because they are sensitive indicators of loss of control. The RLT doesn't necessarily tell *why* control is breaking down—it may be the code, or the way in which the STI is being handled—but the distribution of these times gives a clue as to where to look further. In any case, a rising mean or maximum RLT is a sign for management action.

14.2.2   Circulation dynamics

Figure 14-8 illustrates the STI circulation dynamics and the effect of system size on the STI circulation problem. Because of the Size/Complexity Dynamic, organizations are more likely to experience the nonlinearity of this effect as they attempt to solve bigger problems. With more total faults, there will be more STIs circulating. With a bigger system, more time will be needed to locate faults (even without the circulation effect). In other words, problem demands get you off to a bad start; and once you are behind, it's hard to catch up.

Because of the circulation dynamic, uncontrolled STI circulation is an easy way to spot a Pattern 2 organization that is feeling the push of growing problem demands. Initially, the circulation feeds on the number of faults produced; so if the organization doesn't improve the cleanliness of individual modules, they'll be sucked into this maelstrom as the number of modules per system expands.

Figure 14-9 presents the results of a teaching simulation based on the circulation dynamic of Figure 14-8. It shows the time to clean up all the outstanding STIs in two systems, one with 90,000 lines of code and one with 100,000 lines of code. In this simulation, an 11 percent increase in the system size led to a 28 percent increase in the time to locate the last STI.

There's an instructive story behind this finding: YES Systems was a third-party software developer that bid on and won a 90,000 LOC project. It was well underway when the project leader was asked by his manager to add 10,000 lines of new function. In estimating how much additional time to ask for, the project leader increased the fault location time by 11 percent, from 53 to 60 working days.

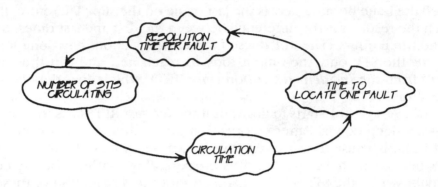

Figure 14–8.   The circulation dynamic used for the simulation model of Figure 14-9.

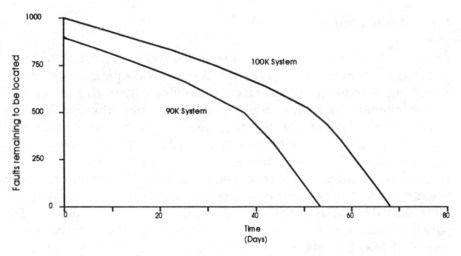

Figure 14–9.   Because STIs circulate, the time to locate all STIs in a system grows even faster than the square of the system size, even if the time to fix an STI is zero.

Later, YES managers asked me to help them figure out why the total project had been four months late. I developed some diagrams of effects to teach the managers what went wrong. Then I put their own numbers into a rough simulation[3] for fault location.

This simulation modeled the test efforts needed for a first release, and assumed (far too optimistically, of course) two things: one, that no new faults are introduced when correcting the ones located; and second, that located faults are resolved instantly. The model also assumed 10 faults per thousand lines of code (10 F/KLOC) going into prerelease testing, based on YES's previous experience on similar systems, and it assumed exactly one STI per fault (which was very optimistic). In the simulation, then, the larger system thus starts with 11 percent more code and 11 percent more faults and generates 11 percent more STIs. But, of course, it takes much more than 11 percent longer to find all of them.

In this case, 69 work-weeks were needed instead of the 60 that the project leader predicted on the basis of the 90,000 line system. Because there were about three to five programmers involved in location activities at any moment, the model proposed that two or three weeks of the lateness was just because of size and circulation effects. Actual measurements showed that fault location took approximately 75 days (and did not actually remove all faults).

How much cleaner code would YES Systems have had to produce to negate the effect of an 11 percent increase in system size? In order to have matched the time of the 90,000 line system, the entire 100,000 line system would have had to have been written with no more than 7 F/KLOC. This was an unlikely improvement over YES's normal experience, and showed it would have had to make significant changes in its development process to compensate for increased problem demands.

One of the interesting effects of this simulation was that it motivated YES Systems to make some measurements. It discovered that the late-added 10K actually showed a discovered fault rate of 17 F/KLOC, almost double the usual experience. This was the first time YES had an actual measure of how much poorer its code was when written quickly, under pressure.

This rough simulation was very different in motive from the kind of precise simulation that a Pattern 4 organization runs to optimize its operations. The purpose here was educational: to help a Pattern 2 organization learn what sorts of changes it needed to make to transform itself into Pattern 3.

14.3   Process Faults: Losing STIs

In Pattern 2 organizations that are losing the battle with customer and problem demands, STIs don't just circulate, they get "lost." Some become lost forever. People hope they will go away. Perhaps simply getting STIs off their desks will make them disappear.

Losing STIs may be a conscious reaction to overload, or it may be unconscious, as the following story illustrates: At First Federal Fidelity Financial, each STI was represented by a dump averaging half an inch thick. One programmer, Emery, had a stack of dumps next to his desk approximately seven feet tall, which contained about 170 unfinished STIs. (This was about average, apparently, as they had 40 programmers and something over 6,000 STIs, though they weren't really sure how many as their database had broken down.)

When I asked Emery how he decided which dump to work on next, he explained that he used a first-in-first-out method. He knew he could never handle all the STIs, so he felt that this was the "fair" way to proceed. When he received an STI, he placed it on top of the stack. When he finished one, he took his next one from the bottom.

This seemed fair enough until I observed what Emery did when he received a call from a loan executive asking about an STI in the middle of the stack. After much awkward fumbling, Emery managed to locate the dump about a foot from the bottom of the stack. He looked at it a bit, explained some of the problems to the executive on the phone, and replaced the dump *on top of the stack*.

When I questioned him about this procedure, Emery seemed genuinely unaware of what he had done. He was shocked to discover that his "fair" system had the effect of punishing anyone who happened to inquire about the status of an STI. In fact, you don't need a simulation to see that if you inquired often enough, your STI would *never* get out of the stack. It would be, in effect, lost in the system—circulating forever, like the Flying Dutchman.

14.4 Political Time: Status Walls

The problem of getting an STI into the right hands is not merely a matter of awareness and logic. In the culture of most large organizations, there is a *status hierarchy* that tends to obstruct the simple logic of fault location. For example, the programmers who work on the operating system often have a higher status than those who work on applications.

When an STI arrives that doesn't obviously go in one place or another, it tends to get bumped quickly to the lowest-status group that can imaginably be responsible. In such an organization,

1.   operating system errors tend to wind up in the application area

2.   application errors tend to wind up in the documentation group

3.   documentation errors tend to get shipped back to the customers with instructions to "use the system correctly"

Such an incorrect initial routing tends to add a constant delay to the time to locate the fault, amplifying the effect we've already seen in the simulation. Unfortunately, the status hierarchy not only leads to initial misclassification, but creates strong walls of defense between areas. These walls grow stronger as the stress on a project grows, so it becomes very difficult to get a problem out of a wrong area once it has fallen in.

Of course, as the system grows more complex, many faults are the result of miscommunication between areas and cannot truly be said to be in one area or the other. Moreover, they cannot be properly resolved without considering both areas. But as the status walls grow higher and stronger, it's hard to get the people together from the different areas to pinpoint these boundary problems, let alone to resolve them.

In some Pattern 2 organizations, management attempts to accelerate the processing of STIs by keeping score on each group. Managers count the number of STIs being held by each group each week, and punish groups who can't keep their score down. To avoid blame, the idea is *not* to be caught with the hot potato at the end of the week. This leads to fast processing of STIs at each stop on their journey, but a long, long journey before they find their way home— another backward effect of management intervention.

14.5   Labor Lost: Administrative Burden

In troubled Pattern 2 organizations, all this cycling plus the growing backlog swells the administrative burden on the developers. They spend little time actually resolving STIs, and more time

- looking for lost STIs
- working with the wrong documentation for the particular STI
- answering queries about what happened to particular STIs
- complaining about the customers or the testers who generate STIs
- arguing so that they won't be blamed for STIs
- playing games like hot potato to beat the management measurement system

All this work leaves them little time or appetite for truly important administrative work. For example, tracing each resolved fault back to all relevant STIs in order to clear the STI database is important administrative work that only the developers can do. It reduces the size of the STI database, and thus reduces both stress and further administrative burden.

This kind of administrative burden affects all programmers' work, and particularly adds to the average time to locate the true fault behind any failure. No wonder many organizations reach the point where they decide to handle their 10,000 outstanding STIs by scrapping the lot and starting over. In doing so, they relieve the pressures of circulating STIs; but if they don't get to the root cultural cause, they will soon have another 10,000 STIs circulating.

What they really need to do is sit down and ask, "What is this enormous load of circulating STIs trying to tell us about our culture?" Having obtained the answer, the next question should be, "What do we propose to do about it?"

14.6   Helpful Hints and Suggestions

1.   A handful of routing slips tabulated each week can adequately estimate RLT for the organization. The average number of stops on each slip also gives a good estimate of the level of hot potato being played.

2. If the nonlinear effects of circulating STIs are considered, it's not a bad idea to scrap unresolved STIs as a first step in getting the organization back under control. This should be done systematically, however, and not done just as an emotional response to actual collapse. A reasonable policy is that any STI not resolved in, say, two months is simply sent back to the originators. If they still care enough, they can just send it back. In my experience, the resubmission rate is less than ten percent, although it may be low because people are disgusted with the programmers.

3. If STIs are sent back to originators, it's a good idea to send them along with a polite note. For example, one of my clients uses this message:

> "After two months of effort, we have been unable to locate the fault that led to STI #99999 (attached). It is possible that this fault was resolved in processing a different STI, in which case, you won't experience it again.
>
> "If you wish, however, you may simply resubmit the STI. Of course, it would help us if you added any new information you may have discovered in the meantime. Please accept our apology for not being able to resolve this problem in a more decisive manner."

4. Even though the underlying dynamics are the same, the kind of consulting advice an organization needs depends critically on its cultural pattern. Consider the case of circulating STIs:

- If your organization is at the seven-foot-stack-of-dumps level of keeping track of STIs, the first thing you should do is notice that the Divide and Conquer strategy applies very nicely to stacks of dumps. As I suggested to Emery, two five-foot stacks of dumps are much easier to search than one seven-foot stack. On the basis of that advice, he decided I was a genius.

- If your organization is at an automated database level of keeping track of STIs, one of the first things you should do is consider "groupware," which would allow any number of people to share the STI information at the same time. But the introduction of groupware into Emery's organization could prove a disaster, as Emery would now have all 6,000 STIs to think about, not just the 170 stacked up by his desk. This illustrates an essential principle of culture change: You can't go from Stone Age tools to Space Age tools in one step.

14.7 Summary

√ System size has a direct effect on the dynamics of fault location, but there are indirect effects as well. We use the Divide and Conquer strategy to beat the Size/Complexity Dynamic, and we also divide the labor to beat delivery time. These efforts, however, lead to indirect effects of system size on fault location time.

√ You can learn a great deal about an organization's culture by observing how it handles its STIs. In particular, you can learn to what degree its cultural pattern is under stress of increased customer or problem demands.

√ An important dynamic describes the circulation of STIs, which grows non-linearly the more STIs are in circulation.

√ Process errors such as losing STIs also increase location time.

√ Political issues, such as status boundaries, can contribute nonlinearly to extending location time. Management action to reduce circulation time by punishing those who hold STIs can lead to the opposite effect.

√ In general, poorly controlled handling of STIs leads to an enlarged administrative burden, which in turn leads to even more poorly controlled handling of STIs. When STIs get out of hand, management needs to study what information that provides about the organization's cultural pattern; then take action to get at the root causes, not merely the symptoms.

14.8 Practice

1. Draw a diagram of effects for the game of hot potato with STIs. One of the variables should be "average number of names on routing slips." Show how the management intervention could be changed to reverse this undesirable effect.

2. Show how increased customer demands—such as doubling or tripling the number of systems sold—affects STI circulation. In particular, incorporate the effect of each fault being experienced many times by multiple customers.

3. A field service staff—sometimes several levels of staff—is often added to marketing to filter out some of the customer's STIs before they reach developers. Each level of field organization, however, tends to slow down the transit of an STI from the customer to the developers. The longer this delay, the more STIs are found for the same fault, while the customers wait for the organization to find it, resolve it, and distribute the fix. Use a diagram of effects to show how this delaying effect limits the effectiveness of the multilevel STI filtering process.

15

Fault Resolution Dynamics

"I hope they won't uglify the house," sighed Lady Laura. "People generally do when they try to improve a sweet, picturesque old place."
—Mary Elizabeth Braddon
Miranda, Book II

Substitute the word "program" for the word "place" and Lady Laura could have been a modern-day software developer. It's one thing to detect failures and locate faults. When it comes to fixing those faults and actually producing an improvement, that's another kettle of fish—or as the industry cliché has it, another bowl of spaghetti. Just as with sweet, picturesque old houses, aging systems get more and more difficult to improve. Thus, a Pattern 2 organization that seems to have a stable customer environment can experience growing problem demands—the demands of keeping the sweet, picturesque old software working. In this chapter, we'll see some of the reasons this happens, and what they tell us about an organization's software culture.

15.1 Basic Fault Resolution Dynamics

If the quality of individual parts is held constant, as the number of parts increases, the time spent fixing problems grows at least as fast as the square of the size of the system. This is because there are more faults, each fault takes longer to fix, and there are more possible side effects to consider. This dynamic is very similar to location time dynamics, which is not surprising as they both are versions of the Size/Complexity Dynamic. (See Figure 15-1.)

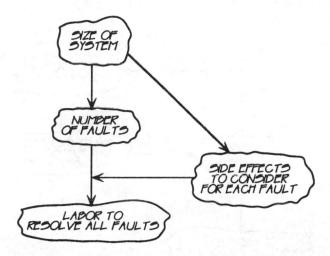

Figure 15–1.   The Size/Complexity Dynamic applied to the problem of resolving faults in a system. If we create faults at the same rate, there are more faults as the system size increases. Since the system is bigger, there are more possible side effects to consider when resolving a fault. Thus, total fault resolution time grows nonlinearly.

Another fault resolution dynamic is the selection of easier problems to fix first. This may be unintentional, as when faults that are difficult to locate are also difficult to fix; or intentional, as when programmers put aside tough problems in order to cope with time pressure. The effect of either type of selection is more or less the same—a prolongation of the time to resolve faults well beyond any simple extrapolation of the faults removed so far.

These basic fault resolution dynamics are quite similar to the dynamics of detection and location because they don't yet take into account the way that resolution differs from detection and location; namely, that resolving a fault usually results in *changes* and changes to code, like any new code, are subject to faults themselves. Not every resolution is an improvement.

The consideration of these faulty resolutions slows down the resolution process. As the system gets more complex, *side effects*—inadvertent changes to the code when correcting faults—grow more likely. Thus, when we fix one thing in a bigger system, there are more things to consider. More things to consider means the Size/Complexity Dynamic comes into play, which means increased time to make fixes correctly, as shown in Figure 15-1.

Even when we take as much time as we like, nobody's perfect, least of all when writing programs. We could try to beat the dynamic of Figure 15-1 by ignoring possible side effects, but that's no solution. If we don't consider side effects carefully, we will feed new faults into the system through the fault correction process, thus complicating and prolonging the work in a different way, as Figure 15-2 indicates.

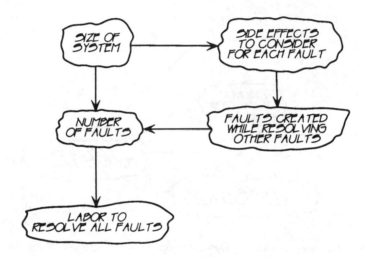

Figure 15–2.   Can we beat the Size/Complexity Dynamic by resolving faults without considering possible side effects? If we do that, we create new faults while resolving old ones. Thus, there are even more faults to fix, and total fault resolution time grows nonlinearly.

Side effects do not always show themselves immediately, nor do they always show themselves as faults. Possible side effects include increases (sometimes, decreases) in code size, destruction of code quality, loss of design integrity, and documentation obsolescence. All these side effects lead to a decay of maintainability.

15.2   Fault Feedback Dynamics

The most obvious nonlinear result of side effects is simply the creation of more faults to fix. Faults put into a system when attempting to correct other faults is called *fault feedback,* and those dynamics reflect the ability of a culture to deliver high-quality products.

15.2.1 Fault feedback ratio

One very sensitive measure of a software culture is the number of problems created per fix or the *fault feedback ratio* (FFR). The formula is

$$FFR = \frac{\text{Faults Created}}{\text{Faults Resolved}}$$

The FFR can be approximated historically by counting the number of faults found in code that was created as part of the resolution of an earlier fault. Although this approximation underestimates the FFR, since there will be more faults that haven't yet been located, that doesn't diminish its usefulness.

Figure 15-3 shows the changes in the FFR over time in a six-month project that was headed for serious trouble. Management noticed the growth in the FFR and introduced "fix reviews" to remedy the situation. Because of the backlog of old, non-reviewed fixes, it took several weeks before the impact of this change started to show in the FFR. With the benefit of hindsight, management agreed that it should have instituted a retroactive review of all *previous* fixes. This insight showed it was on its way to Pattern 3 thinking.

The FFR is a critical parameter measuring the quality in any software organization. It's easily measured, it ought to be measured, yet it's seldom measured. When it is measured, we find that the average fix creates somewhere between 0.1 and 0.3 new problems. When it's not measured, the FFR is probably higher because the cultures that need to measure it are just the ones least likely to do any measuring.

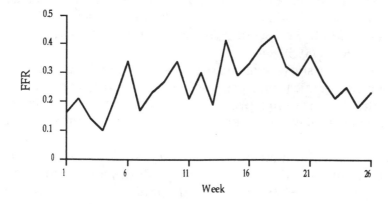

Figure 15–3.   The fault feedback ratio (FFR) is a sensitive indicator of trouble in a project. In this project, management noticed the growth in FFR and introduced fix reviews to remedy the situation.

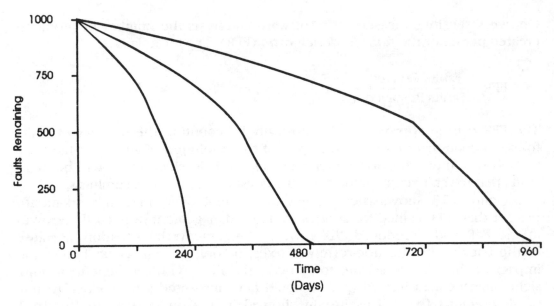

Figure 15–4.   The time to finish removing faults is critically dependent on the fault feedback ratio. The two simulations differ only in their feedback ratios. A 20 percent difference in feedback ratio leads to an 88 percent difference in completion time, but the next 10 percent increase leads to a 112 percent increase.

15.2.2   Impact of the FFR

Why is the FFR so important? The ratio is a sensitive indicator of the fault resolution process. The three curves in Figure 15-4 show the results of a teaching simulation of the feedback of side effect faults. The first curve (finishing at around 240) had an FFR of 0.3. The second (finishing after 480) had an FFR of 0.36, while the third FFR was 0.396.

The three curves show what can happen as the FFR changes by small amounts when the organization's process has started to become unstable. And, of course, as the organization's process becomes unstable, the fault feedback ratio generally increases by *large* amounts, not small amounts, so the effect is even worse.

The ratio is a sensitive indicator of the fault resolution process, since it summarizes a number of tangible and intangible attitudes and actions. This means that the manager who wishes to control the fault resolution process can use the FFR as a control point. For example, CompuBreakfast was suffering from an inability to clear away a large number of faults in its Integrated Menu System. There was a general impression that the system was like Hydra, the monster that grew two new heads when one was hacked off.

As the first step in attacking this problem, the managers did a bit of archaeological work on the source control system. The first figure they extracted was
the average FFR, 0.36, which seemed rather high. But most organizations are
able to improve such a figure very easily with a few simple measures. For instance, they can conduct a brief technical review of each fix before putting it
into the system.

When I returned for a second consulting visit six weeks later, Compu-
Breakfast had not done anything about the review idea. I asked the Information
Systems Manager what had happened, and he told me that after discussing the
idea, his managers had rejected it because "reviewing such small changes was a
waste of time."

I encouraged the managers to return to their archaeological work and
plot the FFR against the size of each change in lines of source code modified.
This research produced the graph of Figure 15-5, which surprised them. They
had predicted something quite different, as indicated by the straight line in
the figure. The difference between the predicted and actual graphs convinced
the managers that reviewing even a one-line change was not at all a waste
of time.

The managers' prediction was linear: Each line of code added proportion-
ately to the difficulty of making a correct change. Thus, large changes would

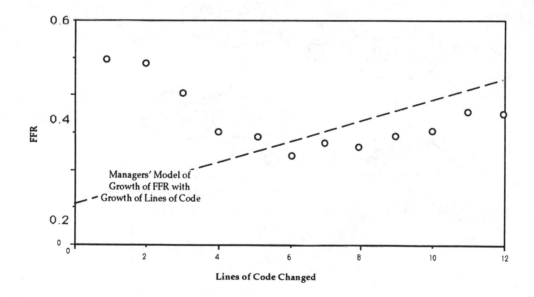

Figure 15–5.   The CompuBreakfast organization predicted the FFR would increase linearly with
the number of lines of code changed. In practice, very small fixes had larger
feedback ratios.

be difficult, they predicted, but small changes would be "trivial." The actual behavior was nonlinear: The difficulty of making a correct change was also influenced by the *care taken by the programmers*. That care, in turn, was affected by the *perceived difficulty of the change,* which in turn was influenced by the managers' own linear model—which said that small changes ought to be easier.

15.2.3   A self-invalidating model

Figure 15-6 shows the dynamic of how in practice this is a *self-invalidating model:*

> **The belief that a change will be easy to do correctly makes it less likely that the change will be done correctly.**

Changing their belief system allowed the managers to mandate that *all* changes would be reviewed, even one liners. This removed the programmers' model from the dynamic; and eventually produced an FFR curve that was much more linear with lines of code, and had a mean of 0.16, which was a noticeable improvement in the project's performance.

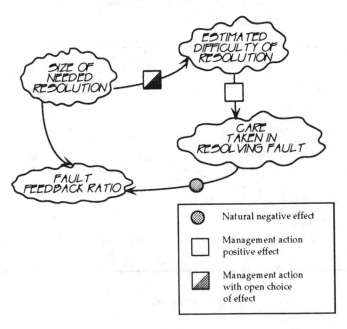

Figure 15–6.   The organization's model that the FFR will increase linearly with the number of lines of code changed creates a nonlinear dynamic that invalidates the model.

15.3 Deterioration Dynamics

Side effects lead to software of lower quality, for the increased faults decrease the value to customers. The code may do the wrong thing. The code may do the right thing, but inefficiently. Even worse, it's not just the *delivered quality* that suffers, but the *internal quality* as well—the value of the code to the developers. Over the life of a software system, this internal quality is more important than the external quality in determining its controllability.

15.3.1 Maintainability must be maintained

In time, existing code may even come to have *negative quality,* meaning that it would be cheaper to develop new code than attempt to keep repairing the old. Many Pattern 1 and Pattern 2 organizations are holding large inventories of negative quality software, but usually they are unaware of that fact. Or if they are aware, they are so unsure of their ability to develop new code that they continue to limp along patching ever more pitiful and expensive systems.

They know they must patch, of course, because they know that any system must have its functions maintained. What they don't understand, however, is that any system must also have its *maintainability* maintained. Even software that is initially well designed and implemented begins to deteriorate and lose its maintainability in a software culture that doesn't regularly invest in maintainability.

What has to be maintained for maintainability to be preserved? Besides functional faults and loss of efficiency, other side effects include increases (or decreases) in size of the code itself, destruction of code quality, loss of design integrity, and obsolescence of documentation. All of these together constitute the decay of maintainability, as indicated in Figure 15-7. Quite likely, the loss of maintainability is the ultimate cause of death for even the best-designed, -built, and -maintained systems.[1]

15.3.2 Ripple effect

One measure of maintainability is the *ripple effect,* the number of separate code areas that have to be changed to effect a single fault resolution. Some years ago, one hardware manufacturer studied this ripple effect of changes to its operating system and found that each change led to approximately three hundred other changes. The company concluded that the slightest decrease in maintainability would have led to one change creating an *infinite* number of changes.

Mathematically, the operating system was equivalent to a nuclear reactor, one that was on the verge of turning into a nuclear bomb. Before that happened, the company quit the mainframe business and discontinued maintaining its operating system. This was not a client of mine, so I don't know if there was a connection between these events. Perhaps it was a coincidence.

The ripple effect can be measured quite easily with a combination of a software tool used with a configuration control tool, and ought to be monitored by management to give it a glimpse of what is happening inside the code.

15.3.3 Destruction of black box design integrity

Where does this deterioration in maintainability come from? A typical cause is the gradual destruction of design integrity by pathological connections across module boundaries. Black box modules are pieces of code that can only be influenced through a known bounded input interface, and that can only influence other code through a known bounded output interface.

Black box modules are a design technique for slowing the Size/Complexity Dynamic for fault correction. Figure 15-8 shows how this happens through the *Modular Dynamic:* The more modular you make the system, the fewer side effects you need to consider. You trade for this effect by creating *modularity faults,* or faults in the interfaces between modules. You never get something for nothing.

Knowing how the Modular Dynamic works, you can also understand how it breaks down. When fixing some fault, the programmer sees a way to shortcut the solution by bypassing the known bounded interface, as in this example:

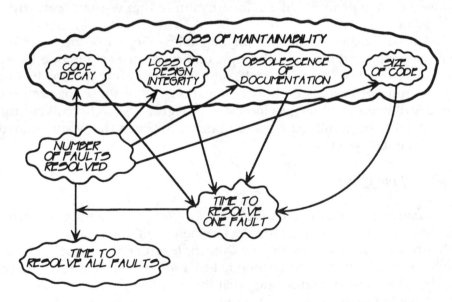

Figure 15–7.   Side effects may show up not only in functional faults and inefficiencies, but also in terms of reduced maintainability, which makes it even harder to resolve future faults.

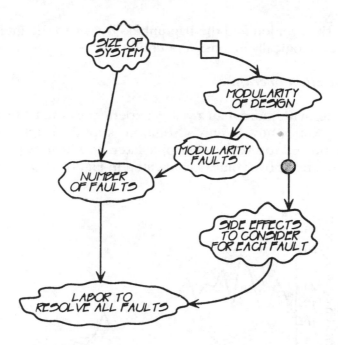

Figure 15–8.   You can slow the Size/Complexity Dynamic on fault resolution by building in black box units of code. If the code units are truly black boxes, the number of side effects to consider when correcting a fault is greatly reduced, but you pay with the possibility of creating modularity faults or interface errors. This is the Modular Dynamic.

Jeremy was fixing an operating system fault in module WYA, deep in the calling tree. The fault involved a failure to consider condition X, known at the highest level, but not known to WYA because it had not been passed through the calling sequences. The proper black box fix would have been to modify all the calling sequences on the way down to WYA, to include the flag for condition X. But this would have required considering and modifying all places that used any of those calling sequences.

Jeremy thought that changing several places would be more dangerous than changing just one. Besides, he was a bit pressed for time. He figured that the fault in WYA could be fixed by reaching directly up several levels to access the flag for X. When necessary, WYA then reached back to the high level and modified the flag. Jeremy made this fix quickly, and it was not reviewed by anyone else. His management praised him for getting the job done with such dispatch.

Actually, "dys-patch" would have been a better description. Seven months later, a series of failures delayed the project for five weeks. It was eventually discovered that one of the intermediate modules in the calling tree had been changed so that it *also* modified the flag for condition X. Under these circumstances, WYA then remodified the flag unbeknownst to the intermediate module, and created a logically inconsistent condition.

15.3.4   Ripple effect over time

Any programmer with more than a year's experience could cite at least a dozen Jeremy stories. Notice how Jeremy's "solution" kept the ripple effect small early in the project, but led to a very large ripple later. In a healthy project, the ripple effect should decrease over time, as indicated in Figure 15-9.

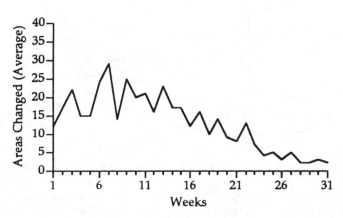

Figure 15–9.   In a healthy project, the ripple effect should decrease over time, because the changes with large scope should have been made early.

Figure 15-10 shows an unhealthy ripple effect curve. The two curves are from two projects within the same organization. Project 15-9 was close to budget and schedule. Project 15-10 was abandoned eleven months beyond its scheduled six-month delivery, after running over budget by a factor of two. Plotting the ripple effect at six months instead of in a postmortem could have led to saving the project. Or if management wasn't competent enough to save the project, it could have killed it at six months and saved a great deal of money and aggravation.

15.3.5   Titanic effect

Figure 15-10 is a typical result of an accumulation of shortcuts that give an early appearance of speed. Perhaps the worst thing about these shortcuts is that they occur in an environment in which management *thinks* that the code is structured—perhaps because it initially was well structured. The managers of Project 15-10 believed they were protected against this sort of aberrant side effect, so they relaxed their guard and thus were hit doubly hard in the fatal moment. I call this the *Titanic effect*.[2]

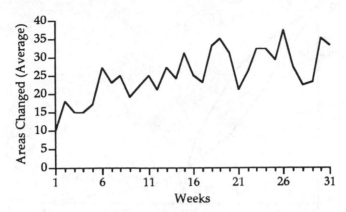

Figure 15–10.   In an unhealthy project, the ripple effect can increase over time, showing that the scope of changes is increasing rather than decreasing as the project nears its supposed completion date. This increase, or even lack of decrease, should serve as a warning to alert management.

The thought that disaster is impossible often leads to an unthinkable disaster.

The rule in poker is that you don't lose your shirt on bad hands, but on hands that "can't lose." The owners of the *Titanic* "knew" that their ship was unsinkable. They weren't going to waste time steering around icebergs, or waste money having needless lifeboats.[3]

Let there be no mistake. Left to itself, structure deteriorates. No matter how great your personal charm or your luck, you're not going to get Nature to set aside the Second Law of Thermodynamics. Unless design integrity is explicitly controlled, such shortcuts cause the design integrity to deteriorate. If events are left to chance, the same phenomenon occurs with code quality and with documentation in all forms.

15.3.6   Maintaining maintainability

If maintainability is not explicitly maintained, a system becomes increasingly difficult to maintain as time goes on—another positive feedback loop. Figure 15-11 shows what this can lead to.

The figure shows the resolution of faults in two similar projects, one of which feeds back a certain number of faults (small FFR), but maintains maintainability. The other feeds back no faults (FFR = 0), but doesn't maintain maintainability. The result of the second project is a faster start, paid for with a long, drawn out tail as removing faults gets slower and slower. Of course, any real project will show a combination of the two effects, with their magnitude depending on the management control processes.

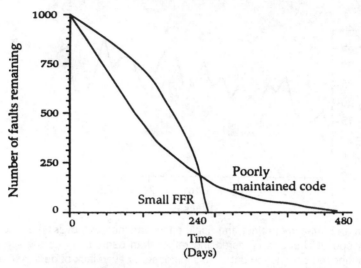

Figure 15–11.   This is the result of a teaching simulation in which there are no faults created by fixing other faults, but the fixes are done in such a way as to reduce maintainability so that later faults are harder to fix. As a result, the last faults seem to stay around longer than anticipated.

15.4   Helpful Hints and Suggestions

1.   As systems grow bigger and as time delays grow longer, it becomes likely that a project will be simultaneously maintaining multiple versions of the same system. Multiple versions are tricky to handle even with the best tools, and organizations in crisis seldom have adequate tools for maintaining their multiple versions. For an outsider, a quick look at the way versions are controlled will give a reliable prediction of the organization's pattern of software culture.

   Multiple versions, of course, double and triple the burden of faults to be resolved, thus magnifying the basic resolution time. They also compound the difficulty of resolving each fault, because programmers may make changes without considering other changes that are being made simultaneously. Consequently, multiple versions cause the feedback ratio on side effects to be even greater, and increase the chance of a "nuclear explosion."

2.   As a project proceeds, you will not usually know how many faults there are to be removed, so it will be impossible to plot graphs such as Figure 15-11. The rate of fault removal and STI resolution can be plotted, but these may give a false sense of what is happening. The FFR and the ripple effect, however, give a better idea of the state of the system. In addition, technical reviews can be used to give estimates of code quality and documentation currency.

3. There is another essential component to maintainability: the competence of the crew, which is affected by turnover, training, and management attitude toward maintenance. Because people are naturally learners, the competence of the crew to maintain a particular system will tend to grow over time, possibly masking the deterioration of the code itself. But the crew's competence must also be maintained, largely by providing them with tools, training, and resources for the job. If there should be a sudden exodus from the maintenance crew, management will quickly discover how ugly a situation has been allowed to fester in the code, masked by the growing competence of the people.

15.5 Summary

√ Basic fault resolution dynamics are another case of Size/Complexity Dynamics, with more faults and more complexity per fault leading to a nonlinear increase in fault resolution time as systems grow larger.

√ Side effects add more nonlinearity to fault resolution. Either you take more time to consider side effects, or you create side effects as one change inadvertently results in another one as well.

√ The most obvious type of side effect is fault feedback, which can be measured by the fault feedback ratio (FFR). Fault feedback is the creation of faults while resolving other faults. Faults can be either functional or performance faults.

√ The FFR is a sensitive measure of project control breakdown. In a well-controlled project, the FFR should decline as the project approaches its scheduled end.

√ One way to keep the FFR under control is to institute careful review of fault resolutions, even if they are for only one line of code. The assumption that small changes can't cause trouble leads to small changes causing more trouble than bigger changes.

√ There are other ways in which a system deteriorates besides the addition of faults and performance inefficiencies, and these ways do not show up in ordinary project measurements. For instance, design integrity breaks down, documentation is not kept current, and coding style becomes patchy. All of these lead to a decrease in the system's maintainability.

√ When the integrity of a modular, or black box, design breaks down, the system shows a growing ripple effect from each change. That is, one change ripples through to cause many other changes.

√ If we are to avoid deterioration of systems, they must not only be maintained, but their maintainability must also be maintained.

√   Managers and developers often show overconfidence in the initial design as protection against maintenance difficulties. This kind of overconfidence can easily lead to a Titanic effect, because the thought that nothing can go wrong with the code exposes the code to all sorts of ways of going wrong.

15.6 Practice

1.   Draw a diagram of effects incorporating the evolution of the maintenance crew into the maintainability dynamic.

2.   Consultant and author Tom DeMarco considers stories of people losing jobs and businesses going bankrupt because of the ripple effect to be "fear tactics," and feels that people should be convinced of the proper software engineering practices without resorting to such stories. Discuss the trade-off between telling the true outcome of such stories to make them harder to ignore and softening the stories to make them more palatable. If possible, draw a diagram of effects incorporating other factors in getting people to accept or reject new ideas.

3.   Have you ever experienced a Titanic-like project? If so, discuss what might have been done to prevent a disaster. If not, why do you think you have not?

4.   Estimate the degree of ripple effect on a system with which you are involved. Do you think it is too high? What could be done to reduce it in one day? In a week? In a month? In a year?

5.   What's the most bizarre side effect you can recall in your career in software? What's the most *costly* side effect? Get together a group of colleagues and share these side effect stories. See if you can extract any common elements found in bizarre and costly side effects.

Part V
Pressure Patterns

The great contribution of Pattern 2 cultures to software engineering is the routinization of software development. As long as things go according to plan, Pattern 2 cultures can turn out valuable software at a reasonable price. But this great strength can become a weakness when things don't go according to plan. Pattern 2 managers may then behave in ways that turn a modest deviation into a full-fledged breakdown.

To readers who have worked in projects that have broken down, this part of the volume may be the culmination of all our work to understand software thinking patterns. They have experienced managers who manage by telling, and they have experienced managers who manage a crisis by telling **louder**. They've always suspected there was a better way, but perhaps never had the good fortune to experience it. Once they have, I believe, they won't easily settle for management by telling.

I would like to dedicate this part to the memory of Bruce Oldfield, for something he said more than thirty years ago. Bruce was one of the most competent software managers of his time, but like all of us, he had limits to how much pressure he could handle congruently. Here's the story: The date of the first test flight for Project Mercury was rapidly approaching, and there were still three serious failures unaccounted for in the tracking system. It was our goal in the project never to go into a flight with any serious failures unresolved, but the regular fault resolution procedures were getting nowhere with these three. At the weekly problem resolution meeting, I suggested that we form a special team of our best programmers to concentrate on these problems off-site. "A little clear thinking," I said, "is what we need."

The idea seemed to have considerable support from the other managers until Bruce stood up and looked me straight in the eye. I can still see him glowering at me, the THINK sign just over his head like a halo. "Listen," he said, *"thinking is a luxury we can no longer afford!"*

Over the years, I've heard the equivalent of that immortal phrase—so characteristic of Pattern 2 managers under pressure—dozens of times. Each time it

245

makes me shudder, but also brings me back to the good old days in Project Mercury. There's something dramatic about working in a Routine organization that's falling apart under pressure, something you remember all your life. Still, there's enough drama of different kinds in Steering organizations, and we know we can produce quality software without abusing people. No, I won't have regrets if these chapters help managers improve their abilities, and ultimately eliminate the drama of the broken employee.

16

Power, Pressure, and Performance

If you can keep your head when all about you
Are losing theirs and blaming it on you;
If you can trust your self when all men doubt you,
But make allowance for their doubting too; . . .
—Rudyard Kipling
"If"

Systems with nonlinear dynamics are easily tipped into collapse. That's why we're so anxious about controlling them. Sometimes, however, the intended control mechanism actually contributes to the collapse. A crisis will rapidly occur in a controlled system when

1. the control actions are irrelevant, because they are at best linear attempts to counter a nonlinear dynamic

2. the control actions are backward, in the sense that they actually contribute to making the dynamic nonlinear, or more strongly nonlinear

In this chapter, we'll look at how Pattern 2 managers often respond to a potential crisis by increasing their pressure on workers, and how this pressure may indeed create the dynamic that triggers a breakdown. We'll also see some alternative

247

management styles, such as those used by Pattern 3 managers, that might offer a better way to stabilize performance.

16.1   The Pressure/Performance Relationship

In general, when human beings work in low-pressure situations, their performance may be quite low. As most managers know, increasing the pressure may increase their performance—for a while. Thus, increasing pressure on the workers can be an effective control mechanism if used correctly. This *Pressure/Performance Relationship* is best described through several models.

16.1.1   The linear model

Figure 16-1 shows the worst managers' understanding of the natural human dynamic in response to pressure. As one manager told me, "If you want performance, you look 'em in the eye and stare them down until you get *commitment*." Another expressed it this way, "More push, more production!"

This is the dynamic model in management that corresponds to Newton's model in physics:

$$\text{Force} = \text{Mass} \times \text{Acceleration}$$

or

$$\text{Acceleration} = \frac{\text{Force}}{\text{Mass}} \qquad \text{Production} = \frac{\text{Push}}{\text{Resistance}}$$

As in physics, this Newtonian model is a good approximate linear model for many situations. When there is a fire in the theater or a mortar shell whistling toward the foxhole, there's no time for reasoned, fully participative discussions of every alternative course of action. I wonder, though, if software development ever needs *that* extreme an emergency.

16.1.2   The burnout nonlinear model

In physics, the Newtonian model fails in relativistic situations—that is, situations in which the assumption of slow speed and small change is no longer valid. The same is true in human relationships. Figure 16-2 shows the more widely applicable understanding of the more astute manager. This manager recognizes that pressure *can* increase performance, but that the reaction of performance to pressure soon becomes nonlinear. After a certain point, the curve slows its climb and then flattens out completely. This manager knows how to push people, but also knows how to take notice of signs that pushing is no longer leading to the same increment of performance.

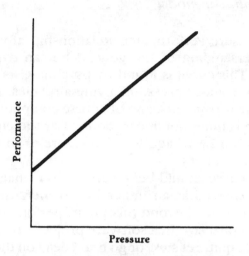

Figure 16–1.   A poor manager's view of the natural human dynamic of pressure and performance is completely linear. The more you push, the more you get.

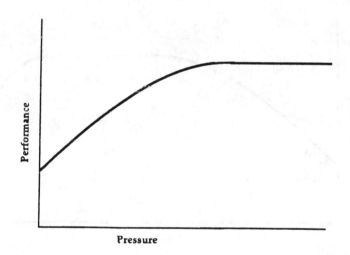

Figure 16–2.   Increased pressure initially results in increased performance. Eventually, however, performance levels off as pressure continues to increase.

Managers call this flat part of the curve "burnout." People can recover from burnout, given rest, recreation, and time. Some managers actually recognize the burnout phenomenon, but simply view people as interchangeable parts. When one person-part burns out, replace it with another one. This is what Curtis calls the "commodity view" of people.[1] Perhaps the commodity view works in carrying sandbags or in operating sausage factories; but in a software engineering project, when you lose a person, you lose a large part of the project.

16.1.3   The collapsed nonlinear model

There is more to the Pressure/Performance Relationship after burnout. Figure 16-3 shows our understanding of the general human dynamic over the whole range of pressure. This curve is found by psychologists in studies of all sorts of skilled performance under pressure: flying airplanes, taking examinations, assembling precision instruments, and of course computer programming. Evidently, the relationship is quite nonlinear. Soon after the curve flattens out completely, the further response to additional pressure is an irreversible collapse, not a recoverable burnout.

The flattening of the curve should be a warning to management to lower the pressure, but it is often read as an indication to *increase* pressure even further. As the pressure increases beyond this point, performance starts to decrease, and then suddenly collapses. In a software project, you see the collapse in a variety of forms: People quit, get sick, or go brain dead on the job. Whatever the symptom, these people no longer contribute to progress on the project, so their performance goes to zero.

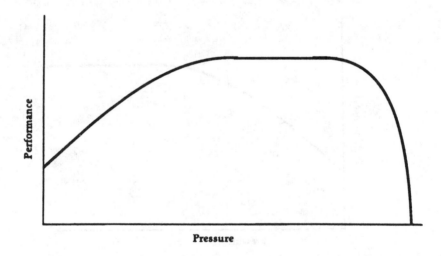

Figure 16–3.   This Pressure/Performance Curve is the general human response to pressure found in all sorts of skilled performance, including programming. Increased pressure initially results in increased performance. Eventually performance levels off, then declines, then collapses as pressure continues to increase.

Actually, the worst situation occurs when they stay on the job and keep writing code. Pattern 2 managers may believe that processes are so routinized that it doesn't matter if individual performance varies, and to a certain extent that is true. No matter how routine your software process, it can't be done with zombies. They keep on writing code, all right—code with huge numbers of faults. In that case, we could justifiably say that performance has gone below zero. The longer these "living dead" are on the job, the worse the project's performance, no matter how routine the process.

16.2 Pressure to Find the Last Fault

Let's look in some detail at the consequences of the Pressure/Performance Relationship in a common software engineering situation. Sometimes, when we get down to the job of locating the faults behind the last few STIs (as happens just before a release date) the location time dynamic is distorted by the application of management pressure (Figure 16-4).

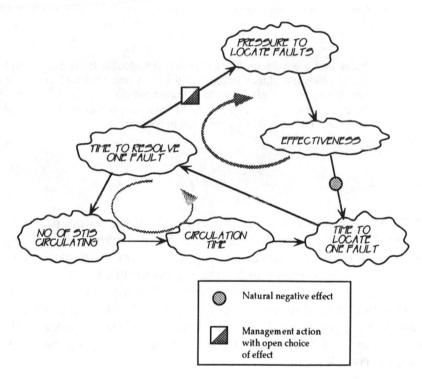

Figure 16–4.   Increased pressure may result from desperation to resolve the last batch of STIs, especially as the time to find each fault gets longer and longer. Here we see this pressure added to a circulation dynamic to produce two potentially positive feedback loops indicated by the shaded arrows. Whether or not the top loop is positive depends on management's use of pressure in response to observed performance in locating and resolving faults.

As time goes by and significant STIs are still unresolved, the pressure mounts. Sure enough, performance improves for a while. Then, without anyone realizing what's going on, performance tapers off. The time to pin down the source

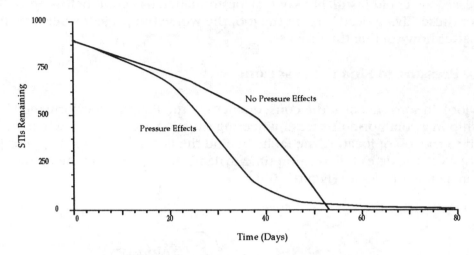

Figure 16–5.   Increased pressure on those attempting to locate faults behind STIs leads to a faster initial rate of fault location. If the pressure continues, however, the ultimate result may be a much longer time to remove the final few STIs. In this model, for example, one STI remained after 80 days with pressure, whereas without added pressure, the last STI was resolved in 53 days.

of the STIs becomes even longer, as illustrated by the model in Figure 16-5. To understand this model, imagine that an enlightened manager, knowing the problems of size, selection, and circulation, decides to meet the planned release date by working the programmers under a small amount of extra pressure. A typical way to do this is to schedule paid overtime. For a while, this increased motivation does indeed lead to more rapid location of STIs. Up until about day 40, things are looking very good indeed, with the Pressure curve well under the No Pressure curve. The manager can report excellent progress, and may even promise an early release.

But if the pressure is maintained too long, the effect of the Pressure/Performance Relationship begins to take its toll. People become tired, they get sick, rates of fault location slow down so people become discouraged, and the manager starts railing at people because the promised delivery date rapidly approaches . . . and then passes.

In the end, the entire fault location operation may collapse, and this is one reason management often ships products with many known faults. In view of all the nonlinear dynamics, this collapse should not surprise anyone, but it usually does.

16.3   Stress/Control Dynamic

Every individual has a unique Pressure/Performance Curve, though all the curves have the same general shape. Moreover, it's not the *applied* pressure that leads to the Pressure/Performance Relationship, but the *perceived* pressure. What motivates me to work a hundred hours a week may simply provoke you to yawn.

Physicists make this distinction by calling the applied pressure "stress" and the reaction of the system "strain." Unfortunately, the medical and psychological literature doesn't make this distinction, and neither do many managers. They use the term "stress" for both applied and perceived pressure, which tends to confuse their understanding of the dynamics involving pressure. When you say, "I'm under a lot of stress," do you mean that a lot of pressure is being applied, or that you are reacting poorly to the pressure?

Once we make the distinction between the situation and the *reaction* to the situation, we can begin to investigate some details of different reactions to applied pressure. One set of psychological experiments demonstrates that the *feeling* of stress is tied to the feeling of *control,* by the dynamics illustrated in Figure 16-6 and Figure 16-7.

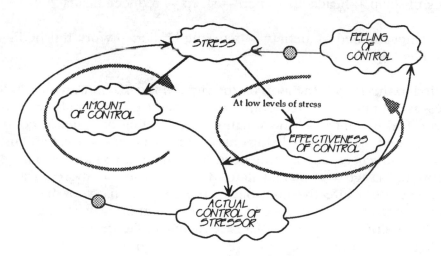

Figure 16–6.   There are two major feedback loops involving stress and performance, because the relationship between stress and the ability to control is itself nonlinear. Under low levels of perceived stress, both feedback loops are stabilizing.

Figure 16-6 shows how low levels of stress are normally handled. The stress you experience is used as *information*—a signal that things are getting a little out of control. Based on this signal, you take some actions to get things back in control. If you are a competent controller, your actions are effective; so the more you

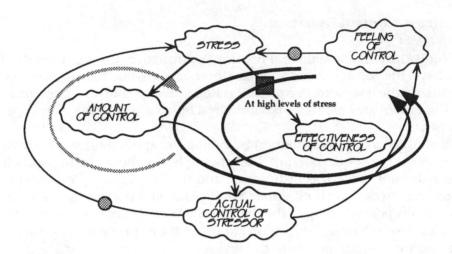

Figure 16–7.   Under high levels of perceived stress, the right-hand feedback loops become destabilizing, which explains the breakdown of performance.

act, the more you get the stressor under control. Your success is signaled by the reduction in perceived stress. Examples include:

Lack of sleep → headache → nap → sleep → reduced headache

Work not finished → anxiety → working harder → work finished → good feeling

Added to this loop is the loop on the right of the diagram, which indicates that stress is not only generated from the external stressor, but also by whether or not you feel in control of the situation. The feeling of being in control reduces stress, and the feeling of being out of control increases stress.[2] Thus, your mental state influences, and is influenced by, your ability as a controller. If you know how to master your mental state, this gives you one more advantage in the struggle to be an effective controller. To the extent that your mental state is out of your control, your presence in a stressful situation may be the very factor that sends the situation into the collapse dynamic of Figure 16-7.

In Figure 16-7, the only change we see from Figure 16-6 is the influence of the arrow from stress to effectiveness of control. This represents the downward portion of the Stress/Performance Curve. Once this has happened, you—the supposed controller—begin to act ineffectively. At the same time, the number of control actions increases, so you are being ineffective more often. This contributes to the worsening of the situation, and also makes you feel even more out of control, both of which increase your felt stress. These two cooperating cycles create a sure-fire recipe for breakdown. The only question is who will break down first, you or the system you're trying to control.

16.4   Forms of Breakdown Under Pressure

Organizations and individuals also differ in the details of *how* they break down under pressure. Our particular interest is in the breakdown in controllers. Let's look at a few of the more common breakdown dynamics seen in the Pattern 2 mechanisms that are supposed to control software projects.

16.4.1   Pressure/Judgment Dynamic

One of the common ways to lose your effectiveness as a controller is to lose your ability to observe accurately. For instance, you may succumb to the social pressures from others in the project who want you to see things through their rose-colored glasses.[3]

When your judgment starts to go, you lock yourself into this version of a pressure/performance breakdown, which I call the *Pressure/Judgment Dynamic*:

pressure → conformity → misestimating → lack of control → more pressure

Once this cycle starts, managers will find it impossible to get the kind of information they need to exercise control over a project. The typical interaction goes like this:

Manager: "How's it going?"
Worker: "Nothing I can't handle."
Manager: "Great. Keep up the good work."

Understanding this dynamic allows the Steering (Pattern 3) manager to beat the effect by decoupling the flow of information from the pressure cycle. One way is by having measurements that are taken automatically, without human intervention. Another way is to take secret surveys, so that nobody knows who said that the project had zero probability of finishing on time.

16.4.2   Lost Labor Dynamic

Another way Pattern 2 controllers often break down is by losing the ability to act, or at least to act quickly and effectively. Brooks's Law tells us how adding workers late in a project slows down the project. One wag suggested that if Brooks's Law is true, the way to get projects done on time is to *subtract* workers at a late date. Unfortunately, subtraction doesn't work that way and is in fact even worse than adding.

Figure 16-8 shows one part of the dynamic of losing experienced workers late in a project. Each time a worker is lost, the amount of raw labor is obviously reduced. At the same time, there is additional coordination work required to sort out the lost person's tasks. These two effects, however, don't create a feedback loop; but since they slow down the project, management may step up the pressure on the remaining workers. Or, it may step up the pressure on itself. In either case, the increased pressure may lead to more people leaving (either physically or mentally), and now the loop is complete.

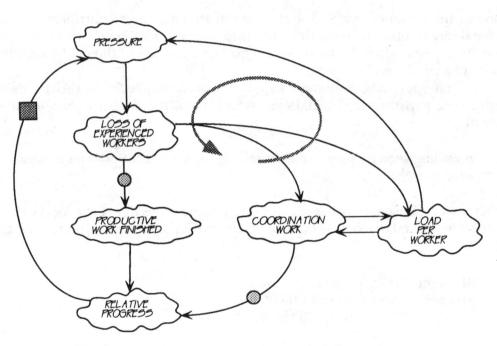

Figure 16–8.   Losing workers late in a project increases the pressure on the remaining workers, which makes it likely that they, too, will be lost to the project.

16.4.3   Pile-On Dynamic

Losing workers is one thing. A worse thing is when the controllers start acting in destructive ways in response to stress. A curious feedback loop can be set in motion by management at any time the software work load is increased, as indicated in Figure 16-9. When managers have more work to be assigned, the first place they tend to look is to the people who have the most knowledge of the system. The people who get all the assignments, of course, are the people who get the most chance to acquire more knowledge of the system, so they are the ones who are most likely to be chosen the next time there is additional work to do.

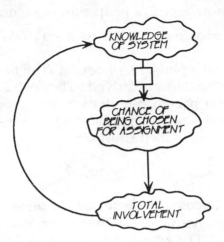

Figure 16–9.   It's only natural to pile work on your best people, which also naturally leads to overload, burnout, and breakdown.

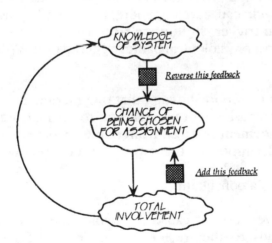

Figure 16–10.   Piling on can be stopped by reversing natural unconscious tendencies.

This loop creates a lock-on of knowledge, because whoever gets the first few assignments becomes the expert to the exclusion of the others. The other side of this lock-on of knowledge is the pile-on of work to be done, which often leads to burnout or collapse of the most critical people in a project.

Steering managers who want to avoid the loss of their most critical people learn to recognize their own involvement in this *Pile-On Dynamic,* and take control of their own actions, as shown in Figure 16-10. Managers have two control points in this diagram:

1.   They can choose less knowledgeable people for the training value.

2.   They can choose those people with the *least* work to do.

Each of these interventions has a problem, of course. The first must be started early, not when the crunch has already arrived. The second may be seen as rewarding the least competent people. But perhaps the people with the least work to do are those who truly know the most about the system, for they are the ones who are most in control of their situation.

16.4.4   Panic reaction

Another way that controllers become ineffective under pressure is by going into a *panic,* when their actions are not simply ineffective or countereffective. They either freeze and can't act at all or go into a frenzy of irrelevant action. Once management panics, the project is doomed unless the panic is immediately arrested or the managers are removed—which may trigger another panic in someone else.

Panic is a well-defined physiological state, whose dynamic is illustrated in Figure 16-11.[4] The cycle can start anywhere, but often begins with an external physical or emotional trigger. In Routine (Pattern 2) software cultures, I have seen managers go into a physiological panic triggered by any of these nonroutine events:

- the arrival of a report showing that one module has slipped a week
- a programmer asking for two days off to get married
- the announcement of a visit from upper management
- a team leader reporting that two team members would be going to a class
- the arrival of a consultant

Such triggers, however, do not cause the panic; the cause is how your personal system responds to the trigger. For example, if you start to hyperventilate, this instantaneous reaction can't be avoided because it's built into your body. If hyperventilation continues for a few moments, it leads to a carbon dioxide deficit in the blood, which causes some of the following symptoms:

- uncomfortable awareness of the heart (palpitations)
- racing heart (tachycardia)
- heartburn, chest pain
- dizziness and light-headedness, poor concentration
- blurred vision
- numbness or tingling of the mouth, hands, and feet

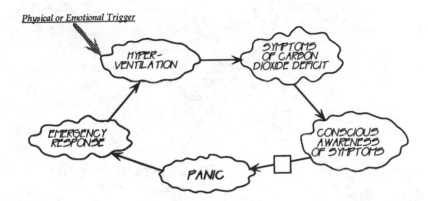

Figure 16–11.   Panic is a positive feedback phenomenon, based on a cycle of physical and mental reactions to some external trigger.

- shortness of breath, asthma, choking sensation
- lump in the throat, difficulty in swallowing, stomach pain, nausea
- muscle pains, shaking, muscle spasms
- tension, anxiety, fatigue, weakness, sweating
- poor sleep, nightmares

As you become aware of one or more of these symptoms, you start giving yourself messages *interpreting* the symptoms; because again it's not the event that counts, but your reaction to the event. Normally, you might interpret these symptoms in a relatively benign way, such as "Oh, I'm really overtired and stressed out." But in a panic-prone individual, the interpretation becomes "Oh, my God! Something awful is going to happen!" In that case, the feeling of emergency leads to further hyperventilation, and the cycle goes around once more.

We all go into a panic some of the time, but normal people quickly recover when they become aware that their life is not threatened if someone takes off two days to get married. People who cannot easily recover from their instant panic reactions should not be in project work, let alone project management. Unfortunately, they may be attracted to Pattern 2 project management because of its promise to eliminate all surprises through the total routinization of work. Instead of trying to control everyone else as a way of dealing with their inability to control themselves, they should be getting professional help—which has a good chance of being successful.

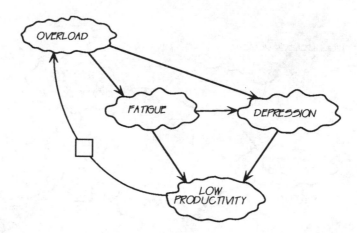

Figure 16–12.   Chronic overload is self-perpetuating. Conversely, reducing the load early in a project can have a positive snowballing effect.

16.5   Management of Pressure

Some managers don't just overload people in response to *stress*. Acting as if they are in continual panic, they overload their projects as a matter of principle. Figure 16-12 shows the basic dynamic of the chronically overloaded project.

16.5.1   *The self-regulating worker*

The manager's idea in chronically overloading a project is to take advantage of the linear part of the Pressure/Performance Curve to keep everyone operating at peak efficiency. This is the direct effect from overload to low productivity. At the same time, chronic overload risks wearing people out and turning their morale toward depression, both of which tend to reduce productivity.

Figure 16-13 shows the dynamic of an organization that responds well to this kind of overload strategy. The organization is characterized by self-regulated workers, individuals who carry the best of Pattern 1 culture. When they become fatigued, they recognize their fatigue and take whatever steps are necessary to reduce their fatigue. When their morale droops, they recognize it and do whatever they need to raise their morale.

16.5.2   *The disempowering manager*

For chronic overload to work as a tactic, however, it's not sufficient for the workers to be self-regulating. In addition, their managers must be empowering. That is, they must trust the workers enough to let them regulate themselves as

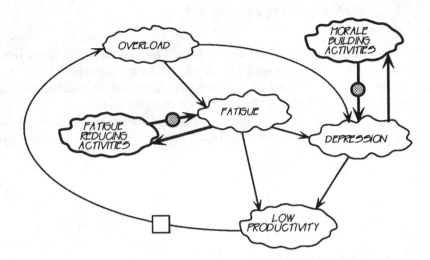

Figure 16–13.   This is the overload dynamic of an organization characterized by self-regulated workers, who know how to take care of themselves when overloaded.

they see fit. Unfortunately, I've encountered very few Routine (Pattern 2) managers of the overload persuasion who also believe in empowerment. Instead, their reaction to workers' attempts to self-regulate are to block all possible avenues of stress reduction.

Whether the overall result of continuous management pressure is positive is a matter of balance among these effects. Pattern 2 projects often stay in balance until they come close to some scheduled delivery date, at which point overload reactions cut in and destroy the balance. At that point, the typical management response is to

- cancel all vacations for the duration
- mandate scheduled overtime
- prohibit compensatory time off for overtime worked
- void all travel plans
- cancel all course enrollments
- put all applications for sick leave under microscopic scrutiny
- eliminate all "frivolity," such as office parties and sporting events
- monitor the cafeterias for "excessive" lunch breaks
- break up all hallway conversations

In short, managers do their utmost to get rid of any activity that might reduce fatigue or raise morale. To compensate, they may begin to issue memos urging the workers to greater efforts in service of the Great Cause. Anyone with any project experience at all knows how effective these memos are. Pattern 3 managers know that they *are* effective: as indications of impending breakdown.

16.5.3   Law of Diminishing Response

The Pressure/Performance Curve of Figure 16-3 sometimes goes up and sometimes goes down. To represent this U-shape in a diagram of effects, we need to put in extra boxes or extra lines, which can make the diagram hard to read. However, instead of plotting the height of the performance curve, we can plot its slope, as in Figure 16-14.[5] That is, instead of measuring *performance* versus pressure, we measure how *responsive* performance is to added pressure at various levels.

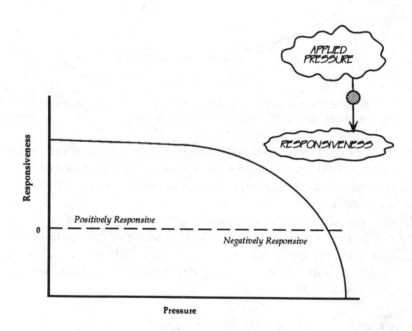

Figure 16-14.   Although performance actually moves in different directions in response to pressure, the slope of the performance always moves in the same direction—downward. We can reasonably call this slope "responsiveness." Responsiveness always decreases as management pressure increases, although for a while it will be relatively flat before it starts to plunge.

Responsiveness, defined this way, is *always a decreasing function of increased pressure*. This allows us to represent the relationship between responsiveness and pressure with the simple diagram of effects shown alongside the graph. The diagram says succinctly that the greater the applied pressure, the less people respond to it. In effect, it is a Law of Diminishing Response:

The more pressure you add, the less you get for it.

16.5.4   The responsive manager

Putting all of these dynamics together, we begin to see how a Steering (Pattern 3) manager thinks. Unlike the Routine (Pattern 2) manager, the Steering manager *can* successfully apply management pressure as a control intervention. To get maximum productivity out of workers, such a manager must do two things:

1.   Allow—and encourage—workers to regulate their own response to management pressure.

2.   Use responsiveness, rather than performance, as the clue to applying management pressure.

Figure 16-15 shows how a Steering manager uses the Law of Diminishing Response as a guide to successful control interventions. When you consider adding some pressure, the key variable to monitor is not people's performance, but their *responsiveness*. How are they responding to the existing pressures? When they hear a new "challenge," do they drop their head a quarter of an inch and mumble an acceptance under their breath? Do they become annoyed and give a hundred reasons why it can't be done? Do they show external signs of panic? These are all signs that they've reached the point where responsiveness has gone negative, yet they are unable to control their own response.

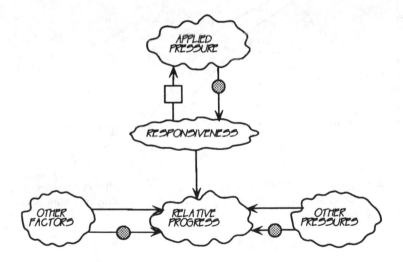

Figure 16-15.   The competent manager recognizes that there are other pressures on a person and other factors influencing performance, and so regulates management pressure based on observed responsiveness, not on performance.

On the other hand, are people alert and genuinely enthusiastic, able to ask penetrating questions that need answering before accepting the extra work?

Can they consciously trade off less important work for high-priority assignments? These are signs that their responsiveness is still above zero, so it's okay to pile a little more fuel on the fire; but don't make any assumptions about next time.

Once you're able to be responsive to other people's responsiveness, then you can turn the same approach on yourself. What is *your* reaction when you get added pressure from your own manager, or from your customers? Do you drop your head and mumble? Do you give a hundred reasons why not? Do you panic? If so, what are you doing to regulate your own morale and fatigue?

Figure 16-16 shows a modification of the model in Figure 16-5, with the pressure applied by management in relation to responsiveness, rather than performance. Time to clear all STIs has been reduced from 53 days with no pressure to 48 days with intelligently added pressure. It shows that at least in theory, responsive management can actually speed up an "unmanageable" process such as testing. Just think what it could do with more manageable processes!

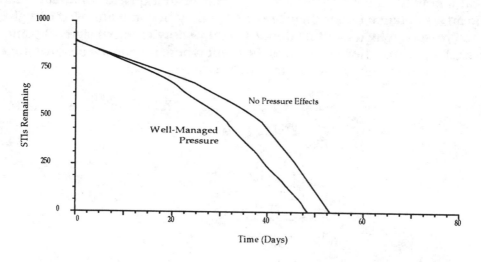

Figure 16–16.   A revision of the model in Figure 16-5 shows that the responsive manager may be able to speed up the testing process by adjusting pressure according to responsiveness.

16.6   Helpful Hints and Suggestions

1.   It's hard to see in yourself the external signs of being overpressured. One way to monitor yourself is to note that pressure works through the Size/Complexity Dynamic. Pressure adds one or more new factors for you to control, which makes your job of exercising control just that much more

complex. You can tell whether you're under too much pressure by noticing how many messages you're giving yourself in an attempt to reduce the complexity of the situation—especially if they are "magical" solutions that take care of everything at once. Examples include

- "I'm trying to keep my manager from firing me."
- "I'm looking for another job."
- "I'm preparing my resumé."
- "If only I had time to find someone to wash my clothes."

2.   People respond to pressure differently, though we don't completely understand why. We do know one reason for the difference is age. Older workers are more skilled, so they generally know better how to handle additional pressure. They've experienced it before. On the other hand, older workers tend to have more outside pressures, such as family concerns and issues about their own health.

One inevitable dynamic is that every day, everyone gets a day older. Often, start-up organizations experience a "growing older" dynamic. In the beginning, their typical programmer is 22 years old, lean and hungry, unmarried, with no previous job experience, and in good health. After ten years of success, their average programmer is 32 years old, 15 pounds heavier, married (and possibly divorced) with 1.7 children, 25 years of job experience (crammed into ten years of real time), and rather tired out. Most important, these older workers must be managed differently, because they don't respond to pressure in the same way they did ten years ago.

3.   Even when managers themselves don't add to the pressure, it tends to mount as schedule dates grow near. Managers often try to relieve the pressure, but they rarely succeed, and often add to it. Examples of this kind of intervention include

- applying Brooks's Law: adding people late in the project to help relieve the work load
- making small slips in the schedule, which often backfires
- unconsciously communicating a feeling of disappointment and disgrace
- adding interesting functions at the last minute to "motivate" workers
- holding official pep rallies to build morale

The best intervention is to start the project right, manage it right, and then let it proceed, approaching its scheduled dates in a natural manner—

for better or worse. If you haven't done it right for two years, what makes you think you can do the right thing now and correct it all in two weeks?

16.7   Summary

√   The Pressure/Performance Relationship says that added pressure boosts performance for a while, then starts to get no response, then leads to collapse.

√   Pressure to find the last fault can easily prolong the time to find the last fault, perhaps indefinitely.

√   The Stress/Control Dynamic explains that we not only respond to external pressures, but also to our own internal pressures when we think we are losing control. This dynamic makes the Pressure/Performance Relationship even more nonlinear.

√   Breakdown under pressure comes in many forms. Judgment may be the first thing to go, especially in response to peer pressure to see things a certain way.

√   As people leave a project, either physically or mentally, it adds pressure to the remaining people, who are then more likely to leave themselves.

√   Managers may create a Pile-On Dynamic by choosing to give new assignments only to those people who are already the reigning experts. This adds to their load as well as to their expertise, which increases the odds they'll get the next assignment.

√   Some people respond to stress with panic, even though the actual situation is not anything like life-threatening. Such people must not be in high-stress projects, or they will only add to the stress.

√   Pressure can be managed. It helps if the workers are self-regulating; if the managers are empowering; and if responsiveness, rather than performance, is used to measure readiness for more pressure.

16.8   Practice

1.   Draw a diagram of effects for the relationship between applied pressure and professional development by the technical staff. Include effects of explicit training, implicit training through group work, and the effects of turnover on average experience level. What are the implications of your diagram for the improvement of a development organization over time?

2.   Draw a diagram of effects for the relationship between the age structure of a population of developers and their performance on projects.

3.   Remember a time when you panicked. Were you aware that you were talk-
      ing to yourself? What messages did you give yourself? Write down these
      messages and get a group of colleagues to share their messages. For each
      message, what countermessage could you use? If you don't know, one
      of your colleagues has probably solved the problem already. Why do you
      think this is so?

4.   Have you ever been a victim of the Pile-On Dynamic? What did you do
      to extricate yourself? What would you do next time to prevent it from
      happening in the first place?

5.   Have you ever stood on the sidelines while someone else got all the good
      assignments piled on? What would you do the next time to ensure that you
      got your share?

6.   What's your characteristic reaction to burnout? What would you like your
      manager to do when this symptom becomes evident? What prevents you
      from telling your manager that before you burn out the next time? What
      prevents you from asking your own employees what you should watch for
      in them, and what they'd like you to do?

17

Handling Breakdown Pressures

Time wounds all heels.
—Anonymous

Poorly managed pressure can lead to collapse, but it's not always clear how the system will actually break down. In software projects, time pressure is almost universal, and time does wound all heels. Time pressure finds the Achilles Heel of any culture. In Pattern 2 cultures, what usually collapses first under time pressure is the manager's ability to make meaningful control interventions.

17.1 Shuffling Work

One characteristic behavior of an overpressured manager is to shuffle work around in ritualistic ways, hoping that rearrangement will accomplish something for nothing. This behavior is a caricature of a management behavior that could sometimes be meaningful, if exercised when things had not already begun to collapse.

17.1.1   Task splitting

During a time crisis, most people are juggling many tasks at one time. In fact, one symptom of overload is the number of people assigned one-half time to project A, one-seventh time to project B, one-twenty-third time to project C, and so forth. Tasks keep coming up, and management simply adds tasks to existing staff, perhaps because it has heard of Brooks's Law and doesn't want to add staff late in the project.

Task splitting, however, has a dynamic very much like Brooks's Law (see Figure 17-1). As with Brooks's Law, the new tasks add learning time to the already overloaded staff. Deciding among these tasks adds coordination time, and additional time is lost each time there is a switch from one task to another. People assigned to more than three tasks will lose at least half their time to switching. Pattern 2 management seems to forget this fundamental rule when the crisis starts to push. Instead, it starts to see not human beings, but boxes on process charts. With automated tools, it's easy to put one name in two boxes, so what's the problem?

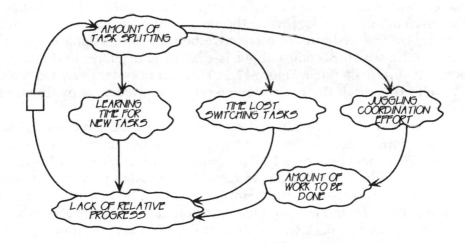

Figure 17–1.   One way to attempt to beat Brooks's Law is to avoid adding people by giving new tasks to experienced people. Task splitting, however, has its own dynamic, which actually leads to the same effect as Brooks's Law—slowing down the project.

About the only factor that prevents this tactic from having worse results is that most overloaded people assigned a new task simply ignore it. Or ignore the old one. Or both. The only ones who get an extra load are the managers, who spend time shuffling assignments around on their project management software.

17.1.2   Everything is number one priority

Ignoring new tasks is a way of assigning priority, because any time there are
many tasks to perform, they must be done in some kind of order. Often during
a crisis, the only directive from management is *"Everything* is number one priority." Here's an illustration of what happens in that situation: After struggling
for three months at Select Southern Software, I finally convinced the General
Manager that slow response time was the major factor in delaying a key project.
At some additional cost, I arranged a priority shipment of a new CPU in only
two weeks. I thought this would relieve the overload, but when I returned two
months later, the CPU had not been installed. "Why not?" I asked.

"We're waiting for a cable," was the General Manager's reply.

"But don't you have your own cable shop downstairs?"

"Yes, but they told us they had higher-priority work to do."

"But this is your *highest* priority."

"Yes, we told them, but they didn't do it."

I walked with the General Manager down to the cable shop. We found that
they were holding up the CPU cable because of another order that the office
manager had told them was "number one priority." I introduced the General
Manager, whom nobody in the cable shop had ever met. Then we all stood
there for 25 minutes chatting while the shop workers made the CPU cable.

Many priority systems are ineffective because "everything is number one
priority." The way this comes about is easy to understand by looking at the
Priority Dynamic shown in Figure 17-2. This sort of system may work if there's
not much pressure. If there's not much pressure, though, why do you have a
priority system?

If a priority system is to work at all, there must be some sort of negative
feedback control to spread out the priority assignments among the different
rankings. This should be the job of a manager who receives information about
competing priorities and who sits at a level high enough to resolve conflicts for
the greater good. Of course, this manager must also be able to act congruently
under time pressure and not just hide in the office and shuffle assignments.

Money is an excellent way to keep the "commons" from being overused,
but any limited resource can be used in the same way. You tie the limited resource to the priority system so that each person has a fixed amount of priority
to use. If the resource is truly limited, this breaks their feedback loop, or at least
stabilizes it short of "everything is first priority."

17.1.3   Choosing your own priority

"Everything is number one priority" is actually equivalent to setting no priority,
another common management practice in Pattern 2. In the absence of clear di-
rectives on what must be done first, people are free to make their own choices.

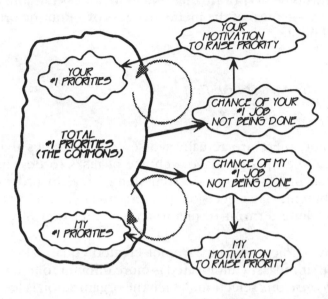

Figure 17–2.   If there is no restraint on the allocation of priority, all priorities tend to move to the highest level, each driven by a positive feedback loop. This is a phenomenon well known in ecology as the Tragedy of the Commons, which explains why common lands tend to be overgrazed or deforested.

Since they are generally unaware of the overall goals of the organization, they tend to suboptimize, choosing whatever looks good to them at the moment.

In one organization, I interviewed a number of programmers who were handling STIs. When asked why she had chosen a particular task, one programmer explained, "This customer is an SOB. If I solve this problem, he'll stop calling me."

Another programmer in the same organization said, "I'm solving this problem because the customer is so nice to me. The ones who get abusive on the phone go to the bottom of my stack. Besides, he has to call long distance."

A third programmer explained, "I do the customer work last. The jobs I have to do for the development staff come first, partly because it's more important work, but mostly because they're right across the hall."

In three interviews, I had identified the following "priority" rules:

- SOBs get highest priority.
- SOBs get lowest priority.
- Whoever's farthest gets highest priority.
- Whoever's closest gets highest priority.
- Whichever work I decide is most important gets highest priority.

The result of this type of "prioritizing" is a more or less random order to the way the jobs get done—typical of the ineffectiveness of a Routine organization trying to handle exceptions.

17.1.4   Doing the easiest task first

Believe it or not, there are actually worse control tactics than a random priority scheme. When people have a choice of tasks to do, they often choose the *easiest* task first, so as to "do something," and in order to get a feeling of accomplishment. This decision process gives a short-term feeling of relief; but in the long term, it results in an accumulation of harder and harder problems.

As we saw earlier, all faults are not created equal. The Failure Detection Curve shows that the last fault located is more difficult to find than the first, and that's only *unconscious* selection. When the organization is feeling the pressure of a crisis, we can add to this effect the *conscious* selection processes whereby people set aside or avoid any problem they think will be difficult.

When we simulate the time to clean up all faults in a system, we must add a component that takes this distortion into account. Figure 17-3 shows the results of a teaching simulation illustrating how this selection effect could increase the time to locate the source of the last STI in our 90,000 line system. One curve shows how fast the STIs are located if all STIs are treated equally. The other shows what happens with a selection effect added—easy STIs being handled before hard ones are tackled. And of course, the effect will be even worse if we add the time to *resolve* the faults to the simulation.

Notice how the time is extended from 53 to 72 working days, though even at the 25-day mark, the difference between the two curves is essentially undetectable. Thus management has no warning—unless it understands the "worst-last" selection process.

Sometimes management installs a system of rewarding developers for the *number* of customer problems solved. Clearly, this encourages programmers to tackle the easiest ones first; and under crisis conditions, management is unaware of what it has induced. Thus, estimates of progress are always optimistic.

We find a similar tendency toward optimism in the test department. Some tests are harder to administer than others. Some tests cannot be administered until the blocking faults detected by other tests are cleared away. Tackling the easiest tests first leaves all the hardest tests for the last. If test "progress" is being reported to management by "number of tests completed," then although eighty percent of the tests have been done, perhaps ninety-five percent of the testing *effort* is still ahead.

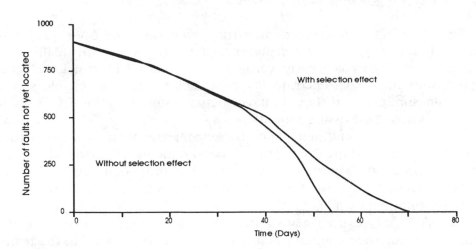

Figure 17–3.   We first locate those problems that are easiest to locate, thus leaving the more difficult ones for the end. This selection effect lengthens the time to locate the final failure. Early estimates based on the rate of location cannot distinguish between these two curves.

17.1.5   Circulating hot potatoes

Another way an individual can relieve overload is by passing problems to other people. As a result, in a quality crisis, problems don't get solved, they merely circulate. We've already seen this problem with the handling of STIs.

For one client, the average time STIs circulated was 7.5 months. I found one that had been circulating for almost three years. Some of this circulation was simply poor administration, but most circulation was caused by the practice of moving STIs to another desk in order to show "progress" on management reports.

Problem circulation is usually the result of a spasmodic management style that punishes people who happen to be holding a problem when a manager's interest reawakens. This dynamic is exactly equivalent to the children's game of hot potato, so I don't need to simulate it. Under hot-potato management, of course, it's not only STIs that circulate. Any problem that doesn't have an immediate, obvious solution will show this same dynamic if management punishes whoever happens to be holding it when the bell rings.

17.2   Ways of Doing Nothing

Passing problems around quickly is an effective way of doing nothing, but there are many more effective ways of doing nothing. Observing how many people are in fact doing nothing is a good way to assess the load on a project. Let's look at a few of the most common techniques.

17.2.1   Accepting poor quality products

The first clear fact available to demonstrate overload is the poor quality of the products being developed. When measurements are made of the quality of work in progress, managers have early warnings of the crisis. Unfortunately, Pattern 2 organizations that experience quality crises seldom have a reliable system of quality measurements. If they do have such a system, it's the first thing to be sacrificed when the pressure mounts.

The lack of measurement defends poor management. It's easier to deny the existence of poor quality when no measurements are made of the quality of work in progress. Eventually, however, products are delivered to customers. Once the product is in customer hands, it becomes more difficult to deny poor quality—but not impossible.

Pattern 2 cultures are usually rather adept at denying the existence of poor quality. One hardware company actually gave a $50,000 award to the team that developed a compiler because there was only one STI in the first year after shipment. When I investigated that STI, I found it was a fault that made it impossible to install the compiler in the operating system. Thus, the reason there were no STIs was that the compiler was of such poor quality that nobody was using it!

The only truly reliable way to find out about the quality of your shipped products is to speak directly to the people who are using them—not their purchasing department, nor their managers, but the actual users. Even there, it is possible for people trapped in a crisis mentality to deny poor quality.

After a devastating user group meeting, for instance, one manager told me, "Look, only the chronic complainers show up at these user meetings. The satisfied users are home using our system." In a few months, he was home, too, drawing unemployment compensation.

17.2.2   Not accepting schedule slippage

When there is no reliable direct measurement of product quality, it's still possible for the dedicated investigator to read some less direct signs. One thing to look for is schedule slippage, which is always a euphemism for poor quality.

In a well-managed project, schedule slippage on some component of the system may mean only moderately poor quality. When acceptance tests are not all satisfied, the component is held back. In this case it's a good idea for the manager to find out exactly which tests were not passed, and perhaps get an independent appraisal of how serious they are. The testers and developers themselves are always a bit too optimistic for a reliable picture.

In poorly managed projects, there may not even be any explicit, predetermined acceptance tests for components. In that case, you can predict that quality will always be poor, but schedule slippage indicates *outrageously* poor quality. Why? Because without explicit tests, component functionality testing is simply run forward into system testing. Developers will pass the component on to the next stage where it merely compiles clean and runs to the end of a job without crashing something. Therefore, if they can't even get *that* far, you can be ninety-nine percent sure that the overall component quality stinks.

In poorly managed projects, of course, "making the schedule" doesn't imply good quality. There won't even be meaningful component delivery schedules, so the only time you become aware of slippage is when the entire product is due to be shipped. When somebody points out to management that the system doesn't work, management says, "We'll ship it to the customer and call it maintenance." A manager who *cannot* slip a schedule has no standard of quality, and thus is actually doing nothing.

17.2.3   Accepting resource overruns

Of course, there's always *some* standard of quality, if only in the hearts and minds of the developers. Any programmer, no matter how inept, has some reservations about releasing total junk. Thus, if the developers feel that their component isn't ready, they will try to hold it back.

Some managers, however, don't understand Brooks's Law. They will meet any request for schedule slippage with promises of extra resources because "the schedule is not negotiable." With such a management style, extra resources become a reliable sign of poor quality, and you can be sure that the organization will feel the full nonlinear dynamic of Brooks's Law.

Terrible managers, of course, will meet a request for schedule slippage not with promises, but with threats. In that case, resources will not increase, and the schedule "will be met." Consequently, if management is terrible enough, we can't make any inferences about quality from being on time and under budget. This is Weinberg's Zeroth Law of Software:

> **If the software doesn't have to work, you can always meet any other requirement.**

17.2.4   Managers not available

One kind of resource consumption can always be used as a reliable indicator of an impending quality crisis. When managers are overloaded, we know that the control system is overloaded. Why does a control system overload? As Figure 17-4 shows, the amount of controller activity is itself controlled by the amount of uncontrolled system behavior. When the system shows signs of going out of bounds, the controller swings into action. If that action is effective, the system's uncontrolled behavior will diminish, and therefore the controller's activities will also diminish.

In other words, we are not speaking of short-term overloads. A crunch lasting a week or two will occur in any normal project. Longer crunches will not

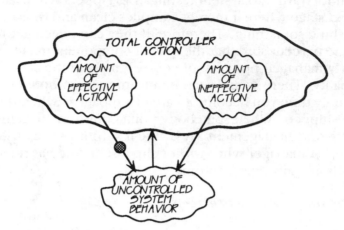

Figure 17–4.   An effective controller will be busy from time to time, but a controller that is always busy is by definition ineffective.

occur, however, because an effective control system will bring them quickly to an end. Therefore, when managers are out of touch for longer than a week or two, it must be that their attempted control interventions either aren't working, or are working backward.

Managers often say that it's not their fault they're so busy, and they are often right. Outside factors may indeed be too disturbing to be regulated, but that's usually because managers at a higher level are not doing an effective job of regulating the outside factors. When upper levels of management pass the pressure down, the project is subject to the dynamic shown in Figure 17-5. In household terms, this dynamic is equivalent to holding a blowtorch on a thermostat in an attempt to warm the room.

This kind of higher-level ineptness does tend to make it impossible for a lower-level controller to be effective. Whatever the originating level, however, the conclusion is the same: At some level the managers are not acting effectively, or

Busy managers mean bad management.

Managers who lack self-confidence, of course, will always *say* they are busy. It isn't befitting a Pattern 2 manager to admit to slack time. You can test the quality of management by interviewing employees and finding out how long they had to wait to see their manager for an unscheduled contact. Also notice how many employees tell you they no longer bother trying to see their manager without a long-standing appointment.

Some of these employees use electronic mail. With some electronic mail systems you can tabulate the time needed for a brief response. If the drop-in

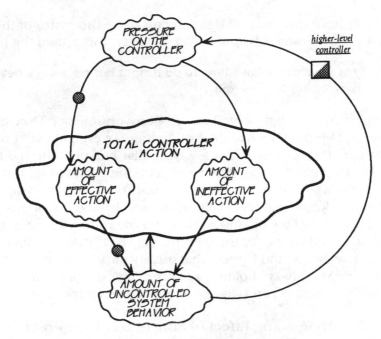

Figure 17–5.   Higher levels of control can interfere with lower levels by putting pressure on the lower controllers past the point of improved performance. The lower controller's ineffective action then amplifies the amount of uncontrolled behavior.

time or electronic mail response time remains greater than twenty-four hours for a couple of weeks, a crisis is well on its way.

These tests for management slack do not mean I advocate "management by reaction." On the contrary, I advocate "management by proaction." To be proactive, however, a manager must have time to

- gather information outside of normal channels
- digest information from the normal channels
- consider a variety of alternatives
- sell a plan of action
- adjust plans in the face of day-to-day realities

Thus, if managers don't have a reserve of time, they *cannot* be managing effectively. In a well-run project, nowhere near a crisis, the managers may put in a full day, but they have lots of time to damp out crises before they get off the ground.

17.2.5   No time to do it right

"We don't have time to do it right" seems to be the motto of the organization in crisis. In one start-up software company, I saw this sign in the president's office:

> **Why is it we never have time to do it right but we always have time to do it over?**

Unfortunately, his sign proved to be overly optimistic. They kept doing things wrong, and before they had time to do them over, they went bankrupt.

In effect, this president was saying that he knew the right way to develop software and that the way they were working was wrong, but that he couldn't do anything about it. It's bad enough not to know what you're doing, but it's far worse to know and then take shortcuts. It's even worse if you're supposed to be the leader of the organization, to whom everyone looks for guidance. The president sets the tone for the culture, but usually does it unconsciously. That's why Crosby insists, and I agree, that quality improvement must begin at the top. The president is always holding a control like that of Figure 17-5—a control that can undermine all controls lower down in the organization.

17.3   The Boomerang Effect of Short-Circuiting Procedures

When schedule is all-important and people are overloaded, everybody desperately seeks relief. If the crisis is short term, one useful tactic is *short-circuiting* standard procedures. An organization may not have many procedures, but people may be able to save time by short-circuiting those procedures that do exist. In a Routine (Pattern 2) organization, the voluminous procedures themselves are likely to take the blame for the overload; so short-circuiting them will occur to everyone as a source of relief.

In a long-term crisis, however, the short-circuiting tactic is used for so long that it becomes standard operating procedure. People routinely sign off that they have completed tasks they haven't even started. Checkmarks go in boxes on the project schedule, which everyone knows is a fantasy anyway—everyone, that is, except the Routine project manager.

In the early stages of a long crisis, you'll hear a lot of complaining about procedures. Later, the complaining stops, and the managers feel better. But the complaining has stopped because people have learned to avoid many of the procedures. By not complaining, they don't draw attention to what they're doing—or, rather, not doing.

17.3.1   The boomerang effect

The pressure of the exponential increase in the number of quality problems leads to a second-order type of increase. The incessant pressure tempts people at all levels of the organization to take shortcuts, hoping that quality will "somehow come out all right." It won't. The end result of the shortcuts is a *boomerang effect:* Things take longer, not shorter.

Attempts to shortcut quality always make the problem worse.

Why is this boomerang inevitable? Figure 17-6 illustrates one common cycle of effects. The cycle can start anywhere, so there is no sense trying to determine which action comes "first." Perhaps increased problem demand or customer demand resulted in a product shipment that was not well accepted by the customers, so that the organization was flooded with STIs. Perhaps a manager made a poor schedule estimate and then insisted on saving face by pushing the product out.

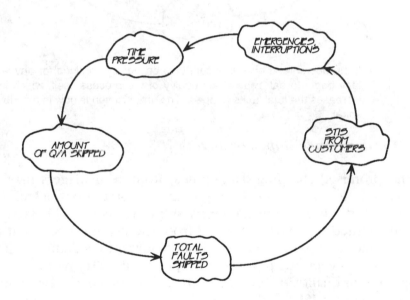

Figure 17–6.   Boomerang effects of shortcuts on quality can easily become self-perpetuating.

Figure 17-6 doesn't tell the whole awful story. The cycle of Figure 17-6 will not go away by itself. If it is not arrested quickly by effective management action, the cycle starts to become established as part of the culture of the organization. Soon, the development process itself begins to deteriorate in irreversible ways, as suggested in Figure 17-7. Let's look at some of the effects wrapped up in this diagram, most of which we've already studied as separate dynamics in their own right.

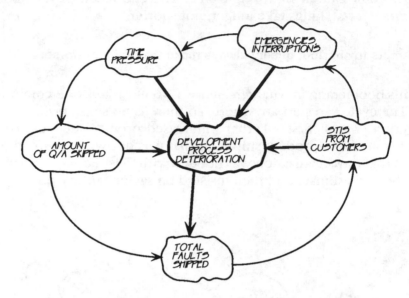

Figure 17-7.   If the boomerang effects of shortcuts on quality continue for any length of time, they begin to eat away at the quality of the process itself, which in turn further increases the total faults shipped. The organization is now in a serious downward spiral.

17.3.2   The decision to ship poor quality

When the promised shipping date comes, Routine managers may be embarrassed to admit that they can neither predict outcomes nor control them. They can cope with the immediate clamor by shipping "as is." This tactic does buy them some immediate short-term relief from the clamor, because it takes time for the pipeline to fill with feedback about failures (thus completing the return cycle). Soon, however, the pipeline fills. As a result of trying to meet schedules by shipping poor quality, the eventual schedule performance becomes worse—a perfect boomerang. If the original managers are lucky, however, they will be promoted before that happens for "successfully" shipping the product, and the boomerang hits their successors.

17.3.3   Bypassing quality assurance

One of the ways to save time in shipping is to bypass quality assurance or at least skimp on quality assurance effort. Not only does this save steps in the process, but the less quality assurance work you do, the fewer failures you see. The fewer failures you see, the easier it is to believe that the quality is okay, and thus make the decision to ship the product.

In such a situation, Routine managers may confidently say, "We will ship no product before its time." But by skimping on quality assurance, they have cut off the information that would let them know if it's time to ship the product.

This self-induced illusion that there aren't so many faults results in more faults being shipped to the field. These faults come back later as failures, in a less disciplined environment, resulting in even more faults—another perfect boomerang.

17.3.4 Emergencies and interruptions

When failures return, there is a corresponding increase in the number of interruptions and emergency situations coming from the system's users. The result is a miserable work environment, which increases time pressure and disrupts the development process for items in process. These new projects will be full of faults and behind schedule, just like previous projects. These then lead to more emergencies and interruptions, and the boomerang returns again.

17.3.5 Morale effects

Perhaps the most striking effect of shipping a product before its time is that the technical staff sees this decision as a betrayal by management. Management may be judged by upper management on cost and schedule, but the technical staff judge themselves on the quality of their work. And they are harsh judges, and the thought that they are shipping garbage puts them into a deep depression. In this state, they have no motivation to maintain the process, let alone to improve it (Figure 17-8).

A decision to ship poor quality is interpreted in various ways by the technical staff:

1. Managers are stupid; they don't know enough to recognize quality.

2. Managers are dishonest; they know the quality is poor, and they're trying to fool the customers.

3. Managers are spineless; they know they can't fool the customers, but they are too afraid of their own managers to stand up for what's right.

4. Managers are greedy; they could stand up to their managers, but they want to get promoted and get away with personal gain.

You can take your pick of interpretations, since none of them leads to a well-motivated technical staff; and development quality as a result begins to suffer noticeably.

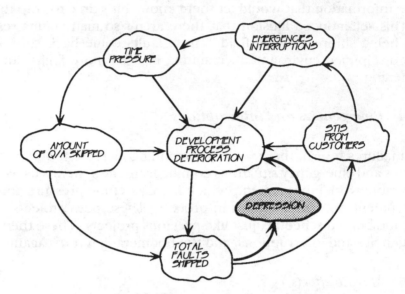

Figure 17–8.   The decision to ship a product known to be of poor quality sends the development
                 staff into a deep depression, which has destructive effects on future process
                 quality.

17.3.6 Managers are human

Technical staff members always interpret a management decision to ship a poor-quality product as a betrayal of trust. Once this happens, they feel they can never count on their managers again. It's unfortunate that the technical staff hardly ever makes a fifth interpretation:

5.   Managers are trying to be helpful; but managers are human, just like the technical staff.

If this kind of trust has been established *before* the organization goes into a boomerang cycle, there's a much better chance of it getting out before the situation degenerates into a downward spiral. Once the boomerang starts, however, managers cannot build trust by telling the staff "Trust me!"

17.4 How Customers Affect the Boomerang

The boomerang cycle may have started because of customer demand, especially in an organization that sells software to many customers. The more people who use the system after it is released, the worse the effect. Let's see why.

17.4.1 More failure reports

The difficulty may start with yielding to customer pressure to ship a product, but as soon as the customers start using the product, they begin generating STIs. The more customers there are, of course, the more STIs come in, so the more emergencies and interruptions there are to disrupt the development process.

17.4.2 Multiplying costs after release

Because each system goes out in multiple copies, shipping an error means multiplying the costs of finding that error and correcting it. Some of these costs may be hidden from the people in software development because they are incurred in the field environment, but many of them come back as STIs and interruptions. We know the effect that interruptions and a heavy work load of fixes has on the development process. The work load increases, and the mistakes increase—two more boomerangs.

17.4.3 Increased temptation

Paradoxically, the "ship anyway" tactic seems most tempting for software products with many customers. The pressure to ship may be much greater, coming as it does from so many customers, with a large multiplier on income from the product. This pressure may be particularly strong on new "error correcting" versions of the software, which may decrease the time of the release cycle, thus further increasing the pressure on the development organization.

On the other hand, first releases generate pressure because of the fear of "losing market share" if the product is late to market. Once the customers buy a copy, it will be easy to sell them a "fix release." It will even generate extra income.

Individual software systems with a single customer generally don't have a series of long delays in the cycle from developer to customer to developer. They've learned that shipping faults to the customer will buy them little, if any, time, even in the short run. Also, their customer may have learned the folly of pressing for delivery of a system that doesn't work right.

17.4.4 The final solution

There is, of course, one stabilizing dynamic, but it's not very cheerful. If the releases are bad enough, the number of customers will start to decrease, thus relieving some of the pressures. Customers tell other customers, and somebody tells the press.

How strong is this effect? In a classic study of word-of-mouth effects, the Coca-Cola Company analyzed complaints from consumers in 1980.

Customers who complained and weren't satisfied with the response typically told 8 to 10 friends or associates about their experience, and, in 12% of the cases, told more than 20 people. And complainers did more than gripe: 30% said they stopped buying Coca-Cola products altogether and another 45% said they'd buy less in the future. If the complaint was resolved satisfactorily—as 85% were—the average consumer told 4 or 5 people about it and, in 10% of the cases, also bought more of the company's products.[1]

If you attend user group meetings, you can confirm that software users are at least as unforgiving as Coke drinkers. And many experiences with failed personal computer software products show that once the first flush of novelty has worn off, buyers know what's good and what's bad, and won't buy anything that has the scent of poor quality.

In other words, it may not be fair, but the arithmetic of word-of-mouth is very strongly biased against shippers of poor quality. Work out the dynamics of this biased reporting, and you'll see why poor quality hurts you much more than good quality helps. Pretty soon, the number of new customers decreases, and if things get bad enough, faithful customers stop using the product.

However, once the organization actually starts losing customers, other pressures mount to more than compensate for this effect. The eventual result of shipping poor quality is loss of revenue through installation delays, poor reputation, and canceled orders. In many organizations, the final result is lawsuits for nonperformance of contracts or simply going out of business. Failure of management to control this poor-quality cycle is undoubtedly the major cause of failure among software organizations today.

17.5   Helpful Hints and Suggestions

1.   A rule of thumb can help when estimating the effects of splitting tasks. The following table is what I use:

Number of Tasks	% of Time on Each
1	100
2	40
3	20
4	10
5	5
more than 5	random

Sometimes you do better than this for certain people for short periods of time, but if you plan on doing better, your plan will fail.

2.   The Priority Dynamic, when tied to money, produces the Law of Supply and Demand, because more priority (higher prices) will lead to more ca-

pacity (greater supply). If you don't want prices to rise, you may want to use some artificial limited resource to regulate the priority system. In that case, however, the one who limits the resource needs to be able to resist the seduction of "just once" granting an exemption.

17.6 Summary

√ Software projects commonly break down when the reality of time finally forces them to realize where they actually are. When this happens, however, the symptoms displayed are unique to each project and individual.

√ Many symptoms are equivalent to shuffling work around, accomplishing nothing or, even worse, actually sending the project backward. One such backward dynamic is the attempt to beat Brooks's Law through splitting tasks among existing workers.

√ Ineffective priority schemes are common ways of doing nothing. They include setting everything to number one priority, choosing your own priority independent of the project's priority, or simply doing the easiest task first.

√ A final way of doing nothing is to circulate hot potatoes, which are tasks that management counts against you if they are on your desk when measurement time comes.

√ There are ways to observe that managers are actually doing nothing. They may, for example,

- accept poor-quality products
- not accept schedule slippage
- accept resource overruns
- be unavailable to their workers
- assert that they have no time to do the project right

√ A sure sign that a project is breaking down under time pressure is when managers and workers start short-circuiting procedures. This invariably creates a boomerang effect in which the very quality the manager intended to improve is made worse by the short-circuiting action.

√ The decision to ship poor quality to save time and resources always creates a boomerang effect. Bypassing quality assurance is similar. Both of these tactics lead, among other things, to destruction of the development process, more emergencies and interruptions, and to devastation of morale.

√ When morale deteriorates into project depression, process quality will not be maintained, let alone improved. Trust built before the crisis will help an organization recover more quickly, but attempts to build trust during the crisis will probably backfire—especially if they are in the form of telling "Trust me!"

√   Multiple customers increase the pressure on the boomerang cycle, up to the point that the resultant poor quality drives away customers, thus stabilizing the organization—or killing it.

17.7 Practice

1. Draw a diagram of effects showing how money or some other rationed quantity can stabilize a priority system. Give three examples of actions that can disrupt such a system, and show how they would affect your diagram.

2. What management activities will build a cushion of trust that can help an organization pull itself out of a boomerang cycle? What activities tend to destroy trust?

3. Work out a diagram of effects of the number of customers on the boomerang effect. Include the effects of biased reporting of failures, and show why poor quality hurts much more than good quality helps.

18

What We've Managed to Accomplish

Truth emerges more readily from error than from confusion.
—Sir Francis Bacon

If we look back through this volume, what seems to emerge is a sad story of error and confusion in the software industry. To reach such a conclusion would be to commit a selection fallacy, for although it's a story of error and confusion, it's not a sad story at all. Although there has been no shortage of sad events, the software industry as a whole has accomplished remarkable things in the past forty years. So that we don't end on a fallacious note, it's time to take stock of where we've been—and where we're going—both in this book and in the software industry.

18.1 Why Systems Thinking?

One of the most frightening events of my life was to wake up one morning and find that I had been transformed from a competent programmer to an incom-

287

petent manager of programmers. The stroke of a pen was all it took to change my title, but I didn't know how long it would take to make me as competent a manager as I was a programmer. It certainly didn't happen overnight.

Over the years, I've learned that being a programmer is rather poor preparation for becoming a manager of programming for several reasons:

1. An effective manager requires excellent observation skills. Working alone as a programmer, staring at a screen all day, is poor training for observation skills.

2. An effective manager must be able to act congruently in difficult interpersonal situations. Interacting with an unemotional machine is no training at all for handling human emotions.

On the other hand, programming is at least partial preparation for one aspect of managing programming:

3. An effective controller needs models of the system being controlled. Working as a programmer supplies some raw data that can be food for dynamic models of the software process. Moreover, the thought processes in programming are logical, and they train us in the kind of thinking that we need to make usable models.

Programmers with any skill at all appreciate the value of planning. Good programmers start a project with a clear idea of what they intend to do. They also have a clear idea of what isn't clear yet—what needs to be clear before they're finished. This is exactly what good managers need to do. When I woke up a manager, I would have been lost without my systems thinking abilities. Using these abilities, I was often able to work out

- what things to observe
- what meaning to make of my observations
- what actions to take to achieve my goals

In other words, for me, the study of systems thinking comes naturally *before* the study of observation and action. In my struggle to become an effective manager, my thinking ability often pulled me through error and confusion, which is why I believe improved thinking will help other people trying to make the same transition.

18.2 Why Manage?

After reading some of the horror stories in this volume, why would anyone want to manage software? It can't be the money. If you're interested in money, you'd probably do better investing your time in becoming a top developer, rather than taking a chance on becoming a mediocre manager. It can't be the admiration of your peers, because they'll probably despise you for "selling out" to management.

Over the years, I've found very few programmers who went into management for money or prestige. Instead, I've met thousands of them who went into management for the same reason so many abused children become therapists. It's called the "wounded healer" syndrome: You take up healing because of the experience with your own wounds. Programmers go into management because they have a cause: They think they can make the software business better than it is.

It was that way for me. When I was a programmer, I had such insufferable experiences with managers that I knew I would be able to do a better job. I was wrong. Like many programmers, I was exactly the wrong type of person to take up management. I was afraid of people. I didn't even like people unless they were techies like me. I couldn't look people straight in the eye when I talked to them unless I was shouting blame at them. I hadn't the foggiest idea of how to get people to understand me, and no idea at all of how to understand them even if I had wanted to. I had no social skills; I didn't know how to dress, to eat in public, or to carry on polite conversation. In short, I was a consummate nerd.

I still don't know how to dress, to eat in public, or to carry on polite conversation; but in forty years, I've learned a few of the other things, mostly the hard way, but also by some dedicated study. I think that today I can be a pretty good manager, but how many of our software managers have had forty years to learn their trade? Like me, most of them had to learn in their sleep the night they got "promoted" from programmer to manager.

Our business is still too young and growing too fast. We haven't had the luxury of developing competent managers the way they are ripened in construction, manufacturing, finance, or any other sensible trade. We have neither the centuries of experience nor the luxury of slow apprenticeship.

What we do have is *dedication to a cause*, and that keeps us going even when we know we are managing poorly, or being managed poorly. We *know* in our deepest way of knowing that computers can make a difference in the world—a difference for the good. That's why we exchange the fun and acclaim of programming for the agony and ridicule of managing; *helping others use their programming talents to make a difference in the world*.

That's why I became an ex-programmer to try my hand at managing. That's why I've spent the past twenty years or so training other ex-programmers to be better managers. That's why I've written this book, and I certainly hope that's why you're reading it.

18.3   Estimating Our Accomplishments

So, have we made a difference in the world, or have we sold our birthright for a mess of pottage? If you read the newspapers, you might believe it's all pottage, because they're full of stories of how horrible we are. Reviewing my forty years in the software business, however, I'd have to say that we've made enormous progress.

18.3.1   Productivity increases

A few years ago, I made an estimate of Pattern 1 progress using my own experience:

> In 1956...I had a chance to write my first real application program. Working with a young civil engineer, Lyle Hoag, I wrote a program to analyze hydraulic networks—the systems that serve the water needs of a city....
>
> [In 1979,] using my [IBM] 5110 and programming in APL, I reproduced that application from the past in order to see if my productivity as a programmer had increased. In 1956, two of us worked more than four weeks, full-time plus lots of overtime to write and test our system. In 1979, I produced a version 2 of the program in about two-and-a-half-hours' work, an increase in productivity of over 200 times. That amounts to over 25 percent per year.[1]

This level of productivity increase is an astonishing accomplishment for our industry, and not at all consonant with the lamentations of the press. According to the perceived wisdom, programming productivity has increased less than three percent per year, though I've never seen anyone justify this oft-repeated figure. Moreover, I now hear that productivity increases are declining in recent years, but that's what I've heard every year for at least thirty years. Curiously enough, I always hear these figures from someone who is selling a new productivity tool.

Figure 18-1 reproduces a graph I've seen several times at software engineering conferences. No source is given; the graph is presented as if everyone knows it is "the truth." Although "productivity" is never defined and the Y-axis is never scaled, the message it presents could be expressed this way:

√   "For the past twenty-five to thirty years, we've seen new technologies appearing approximately every four years. They promise great increases in productivity, but you can see from the chart that productivity is really going to take off if you use object-oriented programming. This time, unlike all the other times, the promise of the technology will be realized. Why? Because I say so."

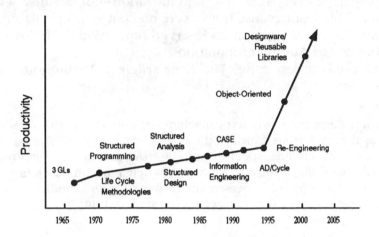

Figure 18–1.   The accepted wisdom about software productivity, given at many conferences, without proof or evidence, over the past twenty-five years. Only the labels change.

If the perspective of forty years in the software business is worth anything, it saves me the time wasted looking at these graphs and saying, "Gee whiz!"

Sometimes, the graph is supported by another slide that gives "real numbers" on "assimilation of new technologies." Here's a typical example:

- Only ten percent of software organizations have a life cycle methodology that is accepted and consistently used.
- Only fifteen percent use structured programming.
- Only twelve percent do structured analysis.
- Only fifteen percent have some form of CASE tool in use.

The repeated word "only" suggests that the anonymous author feels the usage of these tools should be greater. The message continues,

√   "Although most organizations never used these previous tools (which is why they didn't help productivity that much), *my* new tool will be different. *Everyone* will use it, and so productivity will shoot up into the sky like an arrow." (Applause!)

18.3.2   Why we're suckers for magic bullets

Why for more than thirty years have we continued to be suckers for the continuing promise of magic bullets that will suddenly increase productivity? Perhaps it has to do with the reasons we chose to go into this business in the first place. Each of us wants to be recognized for a great innovation that helps the world, and in the early days, everything *was* an innovation—not because we pioneers were so brilliant, but just because there were no computers available to anyone before we came along. We got an undeserved reputation for being innovative, and we got hooked by our own reputation.

We also biased the reporting. The *Time* article of 1950 quoted in the Preface went on to say,

> Will the time come at last when the machines rule—perhaps without seeming to rule—as the mysterious "spirit of the colony" rules individual ants?
>
> To all such chilling speculation, the young engineers in Professor Aiken's laboratory have a breezy answer: "When a machine is acting badly, we consider it a responsible person and blame it for its stupidity. When it's doing fine, we say it is a tool that we clever humans built."[2]

Even forty years ago, we blamed the machine for the failures, while taking personal credit for the successes. Nowadays, there are more systems to fail and fewer easy innovations. Everyone still wants to be the first to do something, but most of the "innovations" are clones, or clones with small variations, as in natural selection. When seen through its cumulative effects over decades, this kind of evolutionary progress is astounding: twenty-five percent increase in individual productivity per year. But we don't consider it astounding, because it doesn't get us the applause we crave.

18.3.3   Pattern 1 productivity; Pattern 2 ambition

Another reason we don't consider this twenty-five percent annual increase astounding is that it's merely Pattern 1 productivity. As our productivity grew, so did our ambition. Soon, we were attempting systems that one person could not implement, and so we tried to put together the software cultures of Pattern 2.

In this process of routinizing programming, we lost some of that twenty-five percent per year we might have had. We lost productivity for all the systems reasons given in this volume, and for others besides. For example, there has been a continuous removal of our most experienced programmers to become managers. So our accomplishments are not living up to our ambitions, but for many of our customers, it's still been worth it.

18.4   What Each Pattern Has Contributed

How can we keep a proper perspective on our own accomplishments? Perhaps we should stop struggling from time to time and take a quick review of what each pattern has accomplished, without any ulterior motive such as selling software tools. Let's try it now.

18.4.1   Pattern 0: Oblivious

Even a cursory review reveals the accomplishments of Pattern 0. Today, literally millions of people can solve many of their own problems without the intervention of computer specialists. To a great extent, we have democratized the software business and weakened the caste system of "young engineers." I believe we can take credit for this transformation. Cheap hardware takes some of the credit, of course; but without good personal software, cheap hardware would have fallen under the control of the existing software hierarchy.

A few years ago I heard something on the radio news that marked our Pattern 0 progress better than any productivity measure. A space shuttle launch had been delayed because of a "computer malfunction," and the newscaster said, "Isn't it amazing that an entire mission can be delayed by the failure of something so common and ordinary as a computer!"

The accomplishment of Pattern 0 is precisely in "making computers ordinary"—making them something about which we can indeed be *oblivious*.

18.4.2   Pattern 1: Variable

I've already indicated my own measure of Pattern 1 accomplishments—perhaps twenty-five percent per year increase in individual programmer productivity. Pattern 1 is where most of the big innovations have come from, but we still haven't learned how to innovate on demand. You don't command someone to go out and invent something as revolutionary as a spreadsheet, yet I don't think that's a criticism of what we've done to improve Pattern 1.

Of course, Pattern 1 suffers a bit because all the programmers are trying to make revolutionary innovations. I recently read a summary of more than two hundred CASE tools on the market for the IBM PC. Did each "inventor" think that this was the real thing? Given the twenty-five percent increase in productivity, I suppose we can absorb a small overhead in Pattern 1 to feed the vanity expressed in that famous MIT graffito:

> "I'd rather write programs that write programs than write programs."

18.4.3   Pattern 2: Routine

The accomplishments of Pattern 2 are difficult to detect, because the job of Pattern 2 is making software work routine. Moreover, the positive accomplishments tend to be erased in our minds by a few spectacular failures. For these reasons, I always recommend to Pattern 2 organizations that they take an inventory of their accomplishments, to counteract their tendency to dwell on failures.

Another reason we tend to underestimate Pattern 2 accomplishments is the software industry's tendency to focus on tools rather than on people. For instance, Phil Crosby's first emphasis in any quality program is "management understanding and attitude."[3] Isn't it curious, then, that in the original IBM articles[4] tying the software industry to Crosby's work, the authors simply dropped all of Crosby's remarks about managers?

If you knew Crosby only through these IBM articles, you would never imagine that he considers management the number one factor in improving quality. You would get the impression that quality improvement comes primarily through "adherence to process and methodologies, tools, change control, data gathering, communication and use of data, goal setting, quality focus, customer focus, and technical awareness"—the items in IBM's Process Grid.

All of these items are important to software management, but the omission of management thinking, observing, and acting is a typical Pattern 2 blind spot. To Pattern 2 managers, these items *are* management, the things they had to struggle with to become Pattern 2 managers. But they're not all there is to management. This omission of management is not just an IBM bias. It's typical of the software industry over the past forty years.

Make no mistake, the major contribution of Pattern 2 is a contribution to management. Pattern 2 managers may not handle the extraordinary very well, but they have succeeded in making ordinary things ordinary. That may not seem very dramatic, but I think we wouldn't need so much drama if we were secure in our solid contributions to the world.

18.4.4   Patterns 3, 4, and 5

Up until now, Patterns 3, 4, and 5 haven't made many great contributions to the welfare of the world because until now, very few software cultures have arrived at Patterns 3, 4, or 5. We do have examples to show that Pattern 3, through steering, knows how to make *extraordinary things ordinary,* thus correcting some of the deficiencies of Pattern 2. Perhaps this book will make an incremental contribution to the realization of that Pattern 3 promise.

We also know enough of the promise of Pattern 4 to believe that it will help in making things more *efficient.* Though Pattern 5 remains largely a vision, we believe it will help by making good cultural practices *transferable,* and propagating them through the generations.

18.5   Meta-Patterns

All in all, we have every reason to expect that the productivity curve, regardless of how it is measured, will continue to rise for the next forty years. For one thing, this has been the experience in other engineering disciplines. For another, we have not only done better, but signs show we're *getting better at getting better*. These signs are what I call the *meta-patterns.*

Meta-patterns are patterns not just for one organization, but for the whole software industry. Meta-patterns are not just the incremental improvements from month to month or year to year, but are those accumulated small steps that are improving quality over generations.

Even though our industry is still young, we can already see what each pattern has contributed to the meta-pattern. Pattern 0 has been removing the fear of computers. Pattern 1 has been developing individual prowess. Pattern 2 has been bringing order to disorder, automating what it can, but leaving the hardest problems to be solved by effective management. Pattern 3 is bringing better management to software, eliminating disasters, which may bring us better press (though I doubt whether journalists will ever lose their ability to capitalize on the sensational).

The successes of all these patterns are allowing our aspirations to rise, creating new problems but also new opportunities to make the world a better place. Pattern 4 promises to improve the orderliness of our business, automating many of the routines arising from Pattern 2, and making them efficient enough for general use. Pattern 5, we hope, will create the global environment for software progress, setting the next iteration of hope, struggle, and improvement for everyone.

It is this vision that permits us to carry on through some of our stupid failures. And carry on we must, because

> One begins to recognise that falling into trouble, encountering some unexpected difficulty however harassing at the time, is in fact an opportunity for making a fresh advance and most advances in engineering have in fact been made by turning failure into success.[5]

In other words, it's not the events that count, but the reaction to those events. We can't always be a winner, and we won't always be a loser. But we can always be a *learner*. That's why we've managed to accomplish so much, and that's why we'll continue to accomplish even more.

18.6 Helpful Hints and Suggestions

1. Software engineering is not alone among the engineering disciplines, but it is the youngster. We can learn a great deal by studying the history of other engineering disciplines. Perhaps we cannot avoid their mistakes, but at least we can learn faster from our own.

2. We can also learn from our own experiences, but these are not as well documented yet as the experiences of other disciplines. Still, we have each other as valuable sources of living history, which is in some ways better than a book. Take the time to share your experiences with others.

18.7 Summary

√   In spite of the impression we might get from studying our failures, we've managed to accomplish a great deal in the past four decades of the software industry.

√   One of the reasons we've accomplished a great deal is the quality of our thinking, which is the strongest asset many of us have, when we use it.

√   Our industry has probably suffered because of the process by which we select our managers. People who choose programming work probably are not the best "naturals" for management jobs. Nevertheless, they could learn to do a good job of managing, if they were given the training. As long as we don't honor management, however, managers are not likely to receive one-tenth the training they need.

√   The accomplishments of the software industry are much greater than we would believe if we listened to the purveyors of software and hardware tools. It is in their interest to make us believe that we're not doing very well, but that their tool will be the magic bullet we need.

√   We tend to be suckers for magic bullets because we want to accomplish great things, but great things are usually accomplished through a series of small steps, contrary to the popular image.

√   We may fail to recognize how much our productivity has increased because we are so ambitious. Once we succeed in doing something well, we immediately attempt something more grand, without stopping to take stock of our accomplishments.

√   Each pattern has contributed to the development of our industry. Pattern 0 has made computers less frightening to the general public. Pattern 1 has made many innovations that have contributed to our productivity. Pattern 2 has strung these innovations together into methodologies that make it possible to complete many larger projects in routine ways. Pattern 3 has taught us what is needed to keep even larger projects under control. The contributions of Patterns 4 and 5 are still more in terms of visions of possibilities, but that's as important to progress as actual accomplishments.

√   Meta-patterns are the development patterns of the culture of the industry as a whole. Each pattern has contributed to the development of meta-patterns, and we are not only learning to handle software, but are learning how to learn to handle software.

18.8 Practice

1. If you work in a Pattern 2 organization, take an inventory of the positive accomplishments made in the past year. How many times did people get off track and start to talk about failures? What insights did you get in making this inventory?

2. If you are a programmer, make a serious estimate of how much your personal productivity has improved over the course of your career. Make a list of the things that have contributed to your improvement. What will make the next increment of improvement?

3. Why did you become a programmer? Why did you become a manager? Which of your reasons for becoming a programmer qualify you to become a manager? Which ones tend to disqualify you?

4. Recall some failure in which you played a part. What did you lose? What did you learn? Was it worth it? What could you have done to increase your learning?

5. Share your experiences of failure with some colleagues. What can you conclude from the commonality of your experiences of failure? Of your reactions to failure? Then share an experience of success and ask the same questions. Did you learn more from failures or successes? Why?

Notes

Preface

1 B.W. Boehm, *Software Engineering Economics* (Englewood Cliffs, N.J.: Prentice-Hall, 1981), p. 486.
2 Anonymous, "The Thinking Machine," *Time*, January 23, 1950, pp. 54-60.
3 Ibid., p. 55.

Chapter 1

1 T. Ziporyn, *Disease in the Popular American Press, Contributions in Medical Studies*, No. 24 (New York: Greenwood Press, 1988).
2 P.B. Crosby, *Quality Is Free* (New York: McGraw-Hill, 1979), p. 15.
3 For an example of such a process, see D.C. Gause and G.M. Weinberg, *Exploring Requirements: Quality Before Design* (New York: Dorset House Publishing, 1989).
4 For the cribbage players among you, here's a hint at a proof: A hand scoring exactly 19 points is impossible. (Indeed, "19" is cribbage slang for a count of zero.) Thus, if Precision Cribbage's scoring algorithm could produce a score of 19 for even one hand, it must be incorrect. A proof consists of constructing such a hand.
5 Crosby, op. cit., p. 15.

Chapter 2

1 P.B. Crosby, *Quality Is Free* (New York: McGraw-Hill, 1979), p. 43. Reprinted by permission of the publisher.
2 Ibid., p. 15.
3 D.C. Gause and G.M. Weinberg, *Exploring Requirements: Quality Before Design* (New York: Dorset House Publishing, 1989).
4 See, for example, H.D. Mills, M. Dyer, and R.C. Linger, "Cleanroom Software Engineering," *IEEE Software*, Vol. 4, No. 5 (September 1987), pp. 19–25.
5 Crosby, op. cit., p. 16.
6 G. Orwell, *Animal Farm* (London: Secker & Warburg, 1945).
7 Crosby, op. cit., p. 34.

8   G.M. Weinberg, *The Secrets of Consulting* (New York: Dorset House Publishing, 1986), p. 58.

9   R.A. Radice, P.E. Harding, and R.W. Phillips, "A Programming Process Study," *IBM Systems Journal,* Vol. 24, No. 2 (1985), pp. 91–101.

10 W.S. Humphrey, *Managing the Software Process* (Reading, Mass.: Addison-Wesley, 1989). See also Humphrey's "Characterizing the Software Process: A Maturity Framework," *IEEE Software,* Vol. 5, No. 2 (March 1988), pp. 73–79. Reprinted in T. DeMarco and T. Lister, eds., *Software State-of-the-Art: Selected Papers* (New York: Dorset House Publishing, 1990), pp. 62–74.

11 B. Curtis, "The Human Element in Software Quality," *Proceedings of the Monterey Conference on Software Quality* (Cambridge, Mass.: Software Productivity Research, 1990).

12 J.P. Spradley, *Participant Observation* (New York: Holt, Reinhart and Winston, 1980).

13 H.D. Mills, *Software Productivity* (New York: Dorset House Publishing, 1988).

14 T. Kidder, *The Soul of a New Machine* (Boston: Little, Brown, 1981).

15 B. Curtis, op. cit.

16 G. James, *The Tao of Programming* (Santa Monica, Calif.: Infobooks, 1987), p. 93. Reprinted by permission of the publisher.

17 F.P. Brooks, Jr. "No Silver Bullet: Essence and Accidents of Software Engineering," *Computer,* Vol. 20, No. 4 (April 1987), pp. 10–19. Reprinted in T. DeMarco and T. Lister, eds., *Software State-of-the-Art: Selected Papers* (New York: Dorset House Publishing, 1990), pp. 14–29.

18 Anonymous, "State of the Practice," *Bridge* (1989), p. 6.

19 Anonymous, *Annual Report* (New York: American Express, 1989).

Chapter 3

1   G. James, *The Zen of Programming* (Santa Monica, Calif.: Infobooks, 1988), pp. 59–60. Reprinted by permission of the publisher.

2   I'm embarrassed to admit this because it reveals that I no longer read journals as they appear. Instead, I wait for someone's work to rise above the academic noise level of most journals. In this case, I'm grateful to Tom DeMarco for extracting the Abdel-Hamid signal from the noise for me, and for strongly recommending I listen to his presentation.

3   T. Abdel-Hamid and S.E. Madnick, *Software Project Dynamics: An Integrated Approach* (Englewood Cliffs, N.J.: Prentice-Hall, 1991). It should provide a vision for you if you want to see where all this modeling is leading your organization in the far future. For a shorter introduction to their outstanding work, see, for example, T. Abdel-Hamid and S.E. Madnick, "Lessons Learned from Modeling the Dynamics of Software Development," *Communications of the ACM,* Vol. 32, No. 12 (December 1989), pp. 273–85.

4   E.B. Daly, "Organizing for Successful Software Development" (December 1979), pp. 107–16. This article was reprinted in D.J. Reifer, ed., *Tutorial: Software Management* (Piscataway, N.J.: IEEE Computer Society Press, 1986).

5   B.W. Boehm, *Software Engineering Economics* (Englewood Cliffs, N.J.: Prentice-Hall, 1981), p. 487.

Chapter 4

1   E. Kübler-Ross, *On Death and Dying* (New York: Macmillan, 1969).
2   G.M. Weinberg and D. Weinberg, *General Principles of Systems Design* (New York: Dorset House Publishing, 1988).
3   See, for example, M.M. Lehman and L.A. Belady, *Program Evolution: Processes of Software Change* (Orlando, Fla.: Academic Press, 1985).
4   O. Mayr, *The Origins of Feedback Control* (Cambridge, Mass.: MIT Press, 1970).
5   N. Wiener, *Cybernetics, or Control and Communication in the Animal and the Machine,* 2nd ed. (Cambridge, Mass.: MIT Press, 1948, 1961).
6   W.R. Ashby, *An Introduction to Cybernetics* (London: Chapman and Hall, 1964).
7   D.C. Gause and G.M. Weinberg, *Exploring Requirements: Quality Before Design* (New York: Dorset House Publishing, 1989).
8   G.M. Weinberg, *The Psychology of Computer Programming* (New York: Van Nostrand-Reinhold, 1971).
9   B. Shneiderman, *Software Psychology* (Boston: Little-Brown, 1980).
10   D.P. Freedman and G.M. Weinberg, *Handbook of Walkthroughs, Inspections, and Technical Reviews,* 3rd ed. (New York: Dorset House Publishing, 1990).
11   For instance, consult G.M. Weinberg's *Becoming a Technical Leader* (New York: Dorset House Publishing, 1986) for more ideas and a bibliography on self-development as a technical leader, including leading product development work.

Chapter 5

1   F.P. Brooks, Jr., *The Mythical Man-Month* (Reading, Mass.: Addison-Wesley, 1982), p. 14. Reprinted by permission of the publisher.
2   For a more detailed description, with a somewhat less elaborate notation, see G.M. Weinberg and D. Weinberg, *General Principles of Systems Design* (New York: Dorset House Publishing, 1988). There you will find, for example, the connection between the diagram of effects and differential equations, which is one way of translating system models into computable models using actual measurements, as done by T. Abdel-Hamid and S.E. Madnick in *Software Project Dynamics: An Integrated Approach* (Englewood Cliffs, N.J.: Prentice-Hall, 1991).
3   B.W. Boehm, *Software Engineering Economics* (Englewood Cliffs, N.J.: Prentice-Hall, 1981). This book provides historical results in the form of raw numbers and various suggested metrics. The data have been collected from a large number of completed software projects.

Chapter 6

1   Lewis Carroll, "Through the Looking Glass," ed. M. Gardner, *The Annotated Alice* (New York: Clarkson N. Potter, Inc., 1960). This was the first text I ever used for

Software Engineering classes at the IBM Systems Research Institute in New York, starting in 1961. It still repays dividends for those who would understand—Lewis Carroll did—the role of models of reality in shaping reality.

2 Mathematically trained readers can augment their knowledge of the solutions by translating these verbal descriptions into differential equations in various forms.

3 Unfortunately, some of the social sciences have given the term "negative feedback" a different meaning. Roughly, the term "negative" is equated with "not nice," so "negative feedback" means "something you tell somebody about themselves that isn't nice." If you want to eliminate this confusion in your speech, you can use the clumsier form, "deviation reducing feedback." Sometimes this kind of feedback is nice, and sometimes it's not so nice.

Chapter 7

1 W.S. Humphrey, "Behind the SEI Process-Maturity Assessment," *IEEE Software,* Vol. 6, No. 5 (September 1989), p. 92.

2 W.S. Humphrey, *Managing the Software Process* (Reading, Mass.: Addison-Wesley, 1989), p. 8.

3 Ibid., p. 257. Reprinted by permission of the publisher.

4 T. Gilb, *Principles of Software Engineering Management* (Reading, Mass.: Addison-Wesley, 1988), p. 88. Reprinted by permission of the publisher.

5 W.E. Deming, *Out of the Crisis* (Cambridge, Mass.: MIT Center for Advanced Engineering Study, 1986).

6 This diagram is adapted from R.B. Grady and D.L. Caswell, *Software Metrics: Establishing a Company-Wide Program* (Englewood Cliffs, N.J.: Prentice-Hall, 1987), p. 9. Copyright © 1987. Reprinted by permission of the publisher.

7 G.M. Weinberg, *The Secrets of Consulting* (New York: Dorset House Publishing, 1986).

Chapter 9

1 R.D. Gilbreath, *Winning at Project Management: What Works, What Fails, and Why* (New York: John Wiley & Sons, 1986).

Chapter 10

1 This relationship was understood to apply to software engineering even before the term "software engineering" was coined. Early reporters of this effect included B. Nanus and L. Farr, "Some Cost Contributors to Large-Scale Programs," *AFIPS Proceedings,* SJCC, Vol. 25 (1964), pp. 239–48; and G.F. Weinwurm, *Research in the Management of Computer Programming* (Santa Monica, Calif.: System Development Corp., 1964).

2 E. Harel and E.R. McLean, "The Effects of Using a Nonprocedural Language on Programmer Productivity," UCLA Graduate School of Management, 1982.

Chapter 11

1   T. DeMarco and T. Lister, *Peopleware: Productive Projects and Teams* (New York: Dorset House Publishing, 1987), p. 66. Reprinted by permission of the publisher.
2   Ibid., p. 63. Reprinted by permission of the publisher.
3   G. McCue, "IBM's Santa Teresa Laboratory—Architectural Design for Program Development," *IBM Systems Journal,* Vol. 17, No. 1 (1978), pp. 4–25. Reprinted in T. DeMarco and T. Lister, eds., *Software State-of-the-Art: Selected Papers* (New York: Dorset House Publishing, 1990), pp. 389–406.
4   F.P. Brooks, Jr., *The Mythical Man-Month* (Reading, Mass.: Addison-Wesley, 1982).

Part IV

1   S. Freud, *A General Introduction to Psychoanalysis* (Garden City, N.Y.: Doubleday, 1953).
2   J.D. Watson, *The Double Helix* (New York: W.W. Norton, 1980).
3   J. von Neumann, *Collected Works,* ed. A.H. Taub, Vol. V (New York: Macmillan, 1961–1963).

Chapter 12

1   J.D. Musa, A. Iannino, and K. Okumoto, *Software Reliability: Measurement, Prediction, Application* (New York: McGraw-Hill, 1987).
2   For applications of the Bolden Rule, see G.M. Weinberg, *The Secrets of Consulting* (New York: Dorset House Publishing, 1986).
3   Cleanrooms are one method proposed for very low fault density programming. See, for example, H.D. Mills, M. Dyer, and R.C. Linger, "Cleanroom Software Engineering," *IEEE Software,* Vol. 4, No. 5 (September 1987), pp. 19–25.
4   W.R. Ashby, *An Introduction to Cybernetics* (London: Chapman and Hall, 1964).

Chapter 13

1   D.H. Root and L.J. Drew, "The Pattern of Petroleum Discovery Rates," *American Scientist,* Vol. 67 (November–December 1979), pp. 648–52.
2   You may wish to check your detection order against the "official" order in the Appendix at the end of this chapter.
3   J.D. Musa, A. Iannino, and K. Okumoto, *Software Reliability: Measurement, Prediction, Application* (New York: McGraw-Hill, 1987) .
4   W. Hetzel, *The Complete Guide to Software Testing* (Wellesley, Mass.: QED Information Sciences, 1984).

Chapter 14

1   H.A. Simon, *The Sciences of the Artificial* (Cambridge, Mass.: MIT Press, 1969).
2   For a well-reasoned and well-written argument on this topic, see Simon, op. cit.

3   This simulation and others in this book were developed and run on the STELLA
     simulation modeling program: B. Richmond, S. Peterson, and P. Vescuso, STELLA,
     2.1 ed. (Lyme, N.H.: High Performance Systems, 1987).

Chapter 15

1   See, for example, G.M. Weinberg, "Natural Selection as Applied to Computer and
     Programs" reprinted in the definitive work on how programs evolve over time:
     M.M. Lehman and L.A. Belady, *Program Evolution: Processes of Software Change*
     (Orlando, Fla.: Academic Press, 1985).
2   G.M. Weinberg, *The Secrets of Consulting* (New York: Dorset House Publishing,
     1986), p. 94.
3   Ibid., p. 94. Reprinted by permission of the publisher.

Chapter 16

1   B. Curtis, "The Human Element in Software Quality," *Proceedings of the Mon-
     terey Conference on Software Quality* (Cambridge, Mass.: Software Productivity
     Research, 1990).
2   S. Miller, "Why Having Control Reduces Stress," *Human Helplessness,* eds. J. Gar-
     ber and E. Seligman (New York: Academic Press, 1980).
3   This effect was first demonstrated by S.E. Asch. See, for example, S.E. Asch, *So-
     cial Psychology* (Englewood Cliffs, N.J.: Prentice-Hall, 1952). For more detailed
     discussion of this effect in software development, see G.M. Weinberg, *The Psy-
     chology of Computer Programming* (New York: Van Nostrand-Reinhold, 1971).
4   R.R. Wilson, *Don't Panic: Taking Control of Anxiety Attacks* (New York: Harper
     and Row, 1986).
5   Students of calculus will recognize this as the derivative curve.

Chapter 17

1   *Wall Street Journal,* October 22, 1981, p. 29.

Chapter 18

1   G.M. Weinberg, *Understanding the Professional Programmer* (New York:
     Dorset House Publishing, 1988), p. 68. Reprinted by permission of the publisher.
2   Anonymous, "The Thinking Machine," *Time,* January 23, 1950, p. 60.
3   P.B. Crosby, *Quality Is Free* (New York: McGraw-Hill, 1979).
4   R.A. Radice et al., "A Programming Process Architecture," *IBM Systems Journal,*
     Vol. 24, No. 2 (1985), pp. 79–90. R.A. Radice, P.E. Harding, and R.W. Phillips, "A
     Programming Process Study," *IBM Systems Journal,* Vol. 24, No. 2 (1985), pp. 91–
     101.
5   R.R. Whyte, ed., *Engineering Progress Through Trouble* (London: Institution of
     Mechanical Engineers, 1975), introduction.

Listing of Laws, Rules, and Principles

Crosby's Definition of Quality: Quality is "conformance to requirements." (p. 5)

The Quality Statement: Every statement about quality is a statement about some person(s). (p. 5)

The Political Dilemma: More quality for one person may mean less quality for another. (p. 6)

The Quality Decision: Whose opinion of quality is to count when making decisions? (p. 7)

The Political/Emotional Dimension of Quality: Quality is value to some person. (p. 7)

The Inadequate Definition of Quality: Quality is the absence of error. (p. 9)

Crosby's Economics of Quality: "It is always cheaper to do the job right the first time." (p. 19)

The Quest for Perfection: The quest for unjustified perfection is not mature, but infantile. (p. 21)

Boulding's Backward Basis: Things are the way they are because they got that way. (p. 22)

The Superprogrammer Image: There is no knowledge of management as a development tool. (p. 25)

Using Models to Change Thinking Patterns: When the thinking changes, the organization changes, and vice versa. (p. 35)

The Formula for a System's Behavior: Behavior depends on both state and input. (p. 59)

The First Law of Bad Management: When something isn't working, do more of it. (p. 62)

Brooks's Model (Rephrased): Lack of calendar time has forced more failing software projects to face the reality of their failure than all other reasons combined. (p. 74)

Brooks's Rephrased Model (Rephrased): Lack of calendar time has forced more failing software projects to face the incorrectness of their models than all other reasons combined. (p. 74)

Why Software Projects Go Wrong: More software projects have gone awry for lack of quality, which is part of many destructive dynamics, than for all other causes combined. (p. 76)

Why Software Projects Go Wrong (Part 2): More software projects have gone awry from management's taking action based on incorrect system models than for all other causes combined. (p. 76)

The Scaling Fallacy: Large systems are like small systems, just bigger. (p. 77)

The Reversible Fallacy: What is done can always be undone. (p. 89)

The Causation Fallacy: Every effect has a cause...and we can tell which is which. (p. 90)

Decisions by People: Whenever there's a human decision point in the system, it's not the event that determines the next event, but someone's reaction to that event. (p. 111)

The Square Law of Computation: Unless some simplification can be made, the amount of computation to solve a set of equations increases at least as fast as the square of the number of equations. (p. 130)

The Natural Software Dynamic: Human brain capacity is more or less fixed, but software complexity grows at least as fast as the square of the size of the program. (p. 135)

The Size/Complexity Dynamic: Ambitious requirements can easily outstrip even the brightest developer's mental capacity. (p. 144)

The Log-Log Law: Any set of data points forms a straight line if plotted on log-log paper. (p. 146)

The Helpful Model: No matter how it looks, everyone is trying to be helpful. (p. 154)

The Principle of Addition: The best way to reduce ineffective behavior is by adding more effective behavior. (p. 155)

An Additional Model: The way people behave is not based on reality, but on their models of reality. (p. 156)

The First Principle of Programming: The best way to deal with errors is not to make them in the first place. (p. 184)

The Absence of Errors Fallacy: Though copious errors guarantees worthlessness, having zero errors guarantees nothing at all about the value of software. (p. 185)

The Controller Dilemma: The controller of a well-regulated system may not seem to be working hard. (p. 197)

The Controller Fallacy: If the controller isn't busy, it's not doing a good job. If the controller is very busy, it must be a good controller. (p. 197)

The Difference Detection Dynamic: First, the smallest amount of the test time is spent on a few easy problems; and second, most of the easy problems are found early in the test cycle. (p. 202)

The Failure Detection Curve (the Bad News): There is no testing technology that detects failures in a linear manner. (p. 205)

The Failure Detection Curve (the Good News): Combining different detection technologies creates an improved technology. (p. 205)

The Army Principle: There arc no bad soldiers; there are only bad officers. (p. 212)

The Army Principle (Modified): There are no bad programmers; there are only bad managers who don't understand the dynamics of failure. (p. 213)

The Self-Invalidating Model: The belief that a change will be easy to do correctly makes it less likely that the change will be done correctly. (p. 236)

The Ripple Effect: This effect involves the number of separate code areas that have to be changed to effect a single fault resolution. (p. 237)

The Modular Dynamic: The more modular you make the system, the fewer side effects you need to consider. (p. 238)

The Titanic Effect: The thought that disaster is impossible often leads to an unthinkable disaster. (p. 241)

The Pressure/Judgment Dynamic: Pressure leads to conformity leads to misestimating leads to lack of control leads to more pressure. (p. 255)

The Law of Diminishing Response: The more pressure you add, the less you get for it. (p. 262)

Weinberg's Zeroth Law of Software: If the software doesn't have to work, you can always meet any other requirement. (p. 275)

Managers Not Available: Busy managers mean bad management. (p. 276)

No Time to Do It Right: Why is it we never have time to do it right but we always have time to do it over? (p. 278)

The Boomerang Effect: Attempts to shortcut quality always make the problem worse. (p. 279)

Author Index

Subject Index